Biographies

IN AMERICAN FOREIGN POLICY

Joseph A. Fry, University of Nevada, Las Vegas
Series Editor

The Biographies in American Foreign Policy Series employs the enduring medium of biography to examine the major episodes and themes in the history of U.S. foreign relations. By viewing policy formation and implementation from the perspective of influential participants, the series seeks to humanize and make more accessible those decisions and events that sometimes appear abstract or distant. Particular attention is devoted to those aspects of the subject's background, personality, and intellect that most influenced his or her approach to U.S. foreign policy, and each individual's role is placed in a context that takes into account domestic affairs, national interests and policies, and international and strategic considerations.

The series is directed primarily at undergraduate and graduate courses in U.S. foreign relations, but it is hoped that the genre and format may also prove attractive to the interested general reader. With these objectives in mind, the length of the volumes has been kept manageable, the documentation has been restricted to direct quotes and particularly controversial assertions, and the bibliographic essays have been tailored to provide historiographical assessment without tedium.

Producing books of high scholarly merit to appeal to a wide range of readers is an ambitious undertaking, and an excellent group of authors has agreed to participate. Some have compiled extensive scholarly records while others are just beginning promising careers, but all are distinguished by their comprehensive knowledge of U.S. foreign relations, their cooperative spirit, and their enthusiasm for the project. It has been a distinct pleasure to have been given the opportunity to work with these scholars as well as with Richard Hopper and his staff at Scholarly Resources.

Volumes Published

Lawrence S. Kaplan, *Thomas Jefferson: Westward the Course of Empire* (1999). Cloth ISBN 0-8420-2629-0   Paper ISBN 0-8420-2630-4

Richard H. Immerman, *John Foster Dulles: Piety, Pragmatism, and Power in U.S. Foreign Policy* (1999). Cloth ISBN 0-8420-2600-2 Paper ISBN 0-8420-2601-0

Thomas W. Zeiler, *Dean Rusk: Defending the American Mission Abroad* (2000). Cloth ISBN 0-8420-2685-1   Paper ISBN 0-8420-2686-X

Edward P. Crapol, *James G. Blaine: Architect of Empire* (2000). Cloth ISBN 0-8420-2604-5   Paper ISBN 0-8420-2605-3

David F. Schmitz, *Henry L. Stimson: The First Wise Man* (2001). Cloth ISBN 0-8420-2631-2   Paper ISBN 0-8420-2632-0

Thomas M. Leonard, *James K. Polk: A Clear and Unquestionable Destiny* (2001). Cloth ISBN 0-8420-2646-0   Paper ISBN 0-8420-2647-9

HENRY L.
STIMSON

HENRY L. STIMSON

The First Wise Man

DAVID F. SCHMITZ

Biographies

IN AMERICAN FOREIGN POLICY

Number 5

SR BOOKS

A Scholarly Resources Inc. Imprint
Wilmington, Delaware

Scholarly Resources Inc.
104 Greenhill Avenue
Wilmington, DE 19805-1897
www.scholarly.com

Library of Congress Cataloging-in-Publication Data

Schmitz, David F.
    Henry L. Stimson : the first wise man / David F. Schmitz.
        p.cm—(Biographies in American foreign policy ; no. 5)
    Includes bibliographical references (p.) and index.
    ISBN 0-8420-2631-2 (alk. paper)—ISBN 0-8420-2632-0 (pbk. :
alk. paper)
        1. Stimson, Henry Lewis, 1867–1950. 2. Statesmen—United
States—Biography. 3. United States—Foreign relations—20th
century. 4. United States—Politics and government—1901–1953.
I. Title. II. Series.

E748.S883 S35 2000
973.91'092—dc21
[B]   00-032190

♾ The paper used in this publication meets the minimum requirements of the American National Standard for permanence of paper
for printed library materials, Z39.48, 1984.

To my children,

Nicole and Kincaid

About the Author

David F. Schmitz holds the Robert Allen Skotheim Chair of History at Whitman College, Walla Walla, Washington. He is the author of *Thank God They're on Our Side: The United States and Right-Wing Dictatorships, 1921–1965* (1999); *The United States and Fascist Italy, 1922–1940* (1988); coeditor with Richard D. Challener, *Appeasement in Europe: A Reassessment of U.S. Policies* (1990); and with T. Christopher Jespersen, *Architects of the American Century: Individuals and Institutions in Twentieth-Century U.S. Foreign Policymaking* (2000).

Contents

Acknowledgments

First, I thank Joseph A. Fry, the series editor, and Richard Hopper, Vice President and Editorial Director at Scholarly Resources, for including my book in this series. It is an honor to be associated with so many fine historians. Andy was an ideal editor, providing support, probing questions, incisive critiques, and close editing at all stages. His input has made this a much better work. It has been a pleasure to work with him.

Whitman College provided generous support that allowed me to travel to various archives to conduct research, and to purchase microfilm copies of the Stimson Papers and Diaries. Through the Louis B. Perry Summer Research Scholarship program I was able to employ two students, Alex Rolfe and Kristin Relyea, who each served as excellent research assistants. In addition, Eugene Hansen helped locate writings by Stimson during the 1930s, and he and Laura Krantz assisted with the chronology. Laura and Amy Portwood read the entire manuscript and made numerous valuable suggestions.

My colleague Fred Breit read chapter 6 and generously shared with me his ideas. I have greatly benefitted over the years from his extensive knowledge of twentieth-century history and international affairs, and his thinking has particularly influenced my understanding of World War II. Lloyd Gardner suggested the title. I am grateful for that, for the many conversations on Stimson, and for all that he has done for me since I first arrived to study with him at Rutgers University twenty years ago. Richard and Carla Scudellari offered me a place to stay on research trips at the beginning of this project and remained supportive throughout.

The archivists at Yale University provided professional assistance during numerous trips to the Stimson papers. The late Mitzi Caputo went out of her way to assist me each time I visited the Huntington Historical Society. Her extensive knowledge of the town's history and records were invaluable as she directed me to numerous works and made available the Society's copy of Stimson's

My Vacations. I am deeply saddened that she did not live to see the publication of this work. I also want to thank both Yale and the Huntington Historical Society for permission to reproduce photographs from their collections. Kathy Guizar at Tallman's in Walla Walla gave me expert assistance in preparing the photographs for publication.

It was from my late father, David A. J. Schmitz, that I first learned about and became interested in Stimson. Growing up in Stimson's adopted hometown of Huntington, New York, I played many baseball and football games at Henry L. Stimson Junior High. In response to my question of who Stimson was, my father told me about his service in World War II and as secretary of state. I was later to find a copy of Stimson's memoir, *On Active Service in Peace and War*, in his library. All of my family supported me throughout the years with their questions on Stimson and patience as I verbally worked out many of my ideas. I especially thank my mother, Mary O. Schmitz, for all she has done to assist my work, and my sister Terry Sheerin and her husband Kevin who provide a room and generous hospitality whenever I return to Huntington for research or visits. In addition, I want to thank Terry for taking the photograph of the portrait of Stimson for the cover.

Finally, I dedicate this book to my wonderful children, Nicole and Kincaid, for enriching my life in so many ways.

Introduction

The First Wise Man

On September 21, 1947, Secretary of State George C. Marshall, Secretary of Defense James Forrestal, General of the Army Dwight D. Eisenhower, and sixteen other top-ranking current or former administration and military officials traveled to Henry L. Stimson's Highhold estate in Huntington, New York, to honor him on his eightieth birthday.[1] Except for President Harry S. Truman, they were the most powerful and influential figures in Washington, D.C. Who was Stimson and what had he accomplished that he should be honored by having such a remarkable group of guests leave Washington at the same time to honor him? The obvious answer is that he was their colleague or boss as secretary of war during World War II.[2] But that raises the question of why Franklin D. Roosevelt called upon Stimson, at the age of seventy-two, to serve in his wartime cabinet. How had he come to command such respect, prestige, and influence that the Democrat Roosevelt called upon a lifelong Republican who had first served the government under the Republican Theodore Roosevelt?

Stimson's life (1867–1950), and his remarkable career as one of the foremost makers of American foreign policy during the first half of the twentieth century, provides a unique perspective and framework for analyzing the development of American foreign policy from the imperialism of the 1890s to the emergence of the United States as the world's leading power after World War II and the origins of the Cold War. The Colonel, as Stimson liked to be called after service in World War I, established a reputation for loyalty, a first-rate mind, thoroughness, and probity that would last his whole life and that led no fewer than six presidents to enlist his service. In many ways, Stimson's career was a history of American foreign policy during this period. A Wall Street lawyer, Stimson served every president from Theodore Roosevelt to Truman except Warren Harding. Most notably, he was secretary of war under

William H. Taft (1911–1913), secretary of state under Herbert Hoover (1929–1933), and secretary of war under Franklin D. Roosevelt and Harry S. Truman (1940–1945). In addition, he was a United States Attorney in New York (1906–1909), an early proponent of preparedness who fought in World War I, head of a special electoral mission to Nicaragua in 1927, governor general of the Philippines (1928–1929), and an active public commentator and informal advisor on foreign affairs during the international crises of the 1930s and after World War II.

Henry L. Stimson's 80th birthday at Highhold. (*seated from left to right*), Air Force Chief of Staff Carl Spaatz; General Dwight D. Eisenhower; Secretary of the Army Kenneth Royall; Secretary of State George C. Marshall; Henry L. Stimson; Secretary of Defense James Forrestal; Former Secretary of War Robert Patterson; Undersecretary of State Robert Lovett; Lieut. General Courtney Hodges; (*standing*) Major General Alexander Surles; Harvey Bundy; William Kyle; Major General Norman Kirk; Lieut. General Brehon Somervell; George Harrison; Major General Frank McCoy; Arthur Page; Goldthwaite Dorr; Allen Klots; McGeorge Bundy. *Henry Lewis Stimson Papers, Manuscripts and Archives, Yale University Library*

No matter how one interprets United States foreign policy during the first half of the twentieth century, the central fact of an ever-increasing American involvement in the world must be explained. Heir to the conservative internationalist diplomacy of William McKinley, Theodore Roosevelt, and Elihu Root, Stimson came to exemplify this tradition. He, along with other similarly minded Republicans and Democrats, sought to provide consistency to American policymaking in a rapidly changing international environment and to buffer the conduct of diplomacy from the turbulence and interference of domestic politics. With Roosevelt and Root, Stimson believed that the United States was destined to lead the world. The sense of noblesse oblige that attracted him to Theodore Roosevelt and led to his first public service also reflected his view of the United States' obligation to the rest of the world. As he once told President Hoover, he thought that "it would be better for the world and better for us" if the United States took up the burden of global leadership.[3] American involvement in world affairs, trade, and investment, and at times intervention in other nations' affairs, were necessary in order to provide stability, guidance, and a proper world order, and to combat those who threatened U.S. interests. In order for the United States to carry out its mission to the world effectively, Stimson believed in a bipartisan approach to foreign policy, greater executive authority, and the promotion of American investments, trade, and leadership abroad. Throughout his career, Stimson held to these beliefs and rarely showed any doubts about his judgments.

Stimson's accomplishments were many and all of them reflected these concerns. He played a central role in the reorganization of the War Department prior to World War I that allowed the nation's military to mobilize effectively in 1917–18, shaped Latin American policy at the critical juncture of the beginning of the Good Neighbor policy, and established the Stimson Doctrine during the Manchurian crisis that served as a clarion call for the United States to act against aggression during the 1930s and became an important precedent for later policies; and, during his pivotal tenure as secretary of war in World War II, he directed the mobilization for war, guided the development of the atomic bomb, and influenced, albeit not always in the manner he wanted, postwar policy. Stimson was a complex man who rarely sought credit for his achievements. He was most effective when he could focus on a single issue at a time. This led to his ability and willingness to delegate authority and to depend upon the talents of a hand-picked staff. Although Stimson was known for his quick temper, he nevertheless earned the unwavering loyalty of all who served under him. Stimson's long involvement in the development of American foreign policy allows for an analysis of both the changes and, most important, the continuities in the internationalist position, and an examination of the strengths and weaknesses of that outlook.

Helping to move the nation beyond isolationism and traditional imperialism toward the embrace of internationalism was not without its problems and failures. These, too, were manifested in Stimson's career. In particular, Stimson exhibited the narrow worldview and shared biases of his class and generation. He believed in the inferiority of nonwhite people and all non-European cultures, held to a firm conviction of American superiority and mission, and exhibited an unconcealed paternalism toward the

Third World. Stimson's failures, such as in Nicaragua and in carrying out the internment of Japanese Americans, stemmed directly from these ideas. Overall, his qualities and accomplishments outweigh his flaws and failures, particularly when one remembers that his shortcomings were shared so widely at the time. Nonetheless, his strengths, character, and complete assurance that he was right led to setbacks and crises, both during his lifetime and later for American foreign policy.

While his primary significance lies in his own actions, Stimson passed along his worldview and sense of obligation to serve the nation to the next generation of American policymakers who, after World War II, set the outlook and internationalist perspective of the American foreign policy "establishment." His conclusion in 1947 that "foreign affairs are now our most intimate domestic concern" was central to postwar policymaking.[4] Containment and postwar internationalism appeared to embody all of the most important tenets Stimson worked to establish over his long career: the United States as the world leader with its power and influence extended to all corners of the globe; a strong president in control of a bipartisan policy; international organizations designed to implement American ideas for the world; and a willingness to intervene when necessary to protect America's interests and carry out its goals. As Walter Isaacson and Evan Thomas note in their generational study of the architects of American foreign policy after World War II, *The Wise Men*, Stimson was seen by these men as the "consummate American statesman."[5] Kai Bird, in his study of the careers of McGeorge and William Bundy, opines that "no man cast a longer shadow over the American Century than Henry Lewis Stimson." He "personified the bipartisanship and pragmatic idealism" held to by those who made American foreign policy after World War II.[6]

Having, however, spent so much effort trumpeting the benefits and correctness of American world leadership, Stimson was unable to convey also his own sense of the limits to that role and of American power. Stimson bequeathed to those who served under him during World War II a worldview that, while tested and triumphant in that crisis and apparently universal in its understanding, lacked a capacity for self-criticism and a notion of limits that was to haunt American diplomacy when the successful postwar policies designed for Europe were globalized. As Isaacson and Thomas's title indicates, the term "Wise Men" came to be used during the Cold War interchangeably with the American establishment to describe senior foreign policy officials who moved between the world of business and government in nonelective posts. During the Vietnam War, President Lyndon B. Johnson's meetings, in fall 1967 and again in spring 1968, with many of these men were dubbed the Wise Men meetings. Stimson was mentor to many in this group and the exemplar of the concept that they had a duty to serve the nation, and he set out for them compelling arguments for American commitments to the world and an activist foreign policy in pursuit of American hegemony. He was, indeed, the First Wise Man.

Notes

1. The others who attended were General Carl Spaatz, Commanding General of the Army Air Forces; Secretary of the Army Kenneth Royall; former Secretary of War Robert Patterson; Assistant Secretary of State Robert Lovett; General Courtney Hodges, Commanding General of the First Army; Major General Alexander Surles; former Stimson assistant Harvey Bundy; Colonel W. H. Kyle, Stimson's military aide, 1944–45; Major General Norman Kirk; Lieutenant General Brehon Somervell; George Harrison, Stimson's representative on the Interim Committee for the development and use of the atomic bomb; Major General Frank McCoy; Arthur Page, special consultant to the secretary of war; Goldthwaite Dorr, special assistant to the secretary of war; Allen T. Klots, law partner; and McGeorge Bundy, coauthor of Stimson's memoirs and future national security advisor to Presidents John F. Kennedy and Lyndon B. Johnson.

2. The 1947 National Security Act combined the positions of secretary of war and secretary of the navy as the secretary of defense.

3. Richard Current, *Secretary Stimson: A Study in Statecraft* (New Brunswick: Rutgers University Press, 1954), 120.

4. Henry L. Stimson and McGeorge Bundy, *On Active Service in Peace and War* (New York: Harper & Brothers, 1947), 157.

5. Walter Isaacson and Evan Thomas, *The Wise Men* (New York: Simon & Schuster, 1986), 28.

6. Kai Bird, *The Color of Truth* (New York: Simon & Schuster, 1998), 23.

Chronology

1867

September 21   Henry Lewis Stimson is born in New York City.

1893

January 1   Stimson is made a partner at Root & Clarke.

July 6   Stimson marries Mabel Wellington White of New Haven.

July 12   Frederick Jackson Turner presents his "frontier thesis" at the Chicago World's Columbian Exposition.

1898

April 20   The United States declares war on Spain.

December 10   The United States and Spain sign the Treaty of Paris.

1899

September 6   Secretary of State John Hay sends the first Open Door note requesting all powers to respect the principle of equal trade opportunity in China.

1900

July 3   Secretary of State Hay issues the second Open Door note calling for the preservation of China's independence.

1903

November 18   The Hay-Bunau-Varilla Treaty is signed, authorizing the United States to build the Panama Canal.

1904

December 6   The Roosevelt Corollary is added to the Monroe Doctrine.

1906

January 11   Stimson is named the United States Attorney for the Southern District of New York.

1911

May 13   Stimson is named secretary of war.

1917

April 6   The United States declares war on Germany.
November 15   The Bolsheviks seize power in Russia.

1918

January 8   President Woodrow Wilson announces his Fourteen Points.
November 11   Germany agrees to an armistice.

1919

January 12   The Paris Peace Conference convenes.
June 28   The Treaty of Versailles is signed.

1920

March 19   For the final time the U.S. Senate refuses to ratify the Treaty of Versailles.

1921

November 12   The Washington Naval Conference convenes.

1922

October 28   The Fascists march on Rome, and Mussolini takes power in Italy.

1924

April 24   The Dawes Plan is published.

1927

May 4   The Peace of Tipitapa is negotiated by Stimson.

1928

March 2   Stimson becomes governor general of the Philippines.

1929

January 15   The U.S. Senate ratifies the Kellogg-Briand Pact signed by the United States and France on August 7, 1928, outlawing war.
January 30   Stimson is named secretary of state.

1930

April 22	The London Naval Treaty is signed.
June 17	President Herbert Hoover signs the Hawley-Smoot Tariff Act.

1931

June 20	Hoover announces a debt moratorium on all intergovernmental debts.
September 18	The Japanese destroy part of the South Manchurian railroad at Mukden.
December 2	General Maximiliano Hernández Martínez overthrows Salvadorean President Arturo Araujo.

1932

January 2	The Japanese Army takes Chinchow in Manchuria.
January 7	The Stimson Doctrine of nonrecognition of Japan's conquest of Manchuria is announced.

1933

January 30	Adolf Hitler is appointed chancellor of Germany.
March 4	Franklin D. Roosevelt is inaugurated as President.

1935

August 31	President Roosevelt signs the first Neutrality Act.
October 3	Italy invades Ethiopia.

1936

March 7	German forces enter the demilitarized Rhineland.
July 17	The Spanish Civil War begins.

1937

October 5	President Roosevelt delivers his "Quarantine Speech" in Chicago.

1938

March 13	Austria is absorbed into the Third Reich.
September 30	The Munich agreement cedes Czechoslovakia's Sudetenland to Germany.

1939

September 1	Germany invades Poland.

September 3	Great Britain and France declare war on Germany.

1940

June 19	Stimson is named secretary of war.
June 22	France surrenders.
September 3	The Destroyers for Bases deal is announced.
September 16	The Selective Service Act is signed.

1941

March 11	The Lend-Lease Act is signed.
June 22	Germany invades the Soviet Union.
July 24	Japan occupies southern Indo-China.
July 26	The United States announces a complete embargo of trade with Japan.
August 12	President Roosevelt and British Prime Minister Winston Churchill agree to the Atlantic Charter.
December 7	Japan attacks Pearl Harbor.

1942

February 19	Orders are issued for the internment of Japanese Americans.
November 8	Operation TORCH, the Allied invasion of North Africa, begins.

1943

July 10	The Allied invasion of Sicily begins.
September 3	The Allied invasion of Italy begins.
November 28	The first meeting of the Big Three, Roosevelt, Churchill, and Soviet Premier Joseph Stalin, convenes in Teheran.

1944

June 6	The D-Day invasion of France, Operation OVERLORD, begins.

1945

February 4	The Big Three meet again at Yalta.
April 12	President Roosevelt dies, and Harry S. Truman succeeds to the presidency.
May 8	Germany surrenders.
July 16	The atomic bomb is tested successfully at Los Alamos, New Mexico.

July 17   The Potsdam Conference begins.
August 6   The atomic bomb is dropped on Hiroshima.
August 8   Russia declares war on Japan.
August 9   An atomic bomb is dropped on Nagasaki.
August 14   Japan accepts the Allied terms of surrender.
September 21   Stimson retires as secretary of war on his
                 seventy-eighth birthday.

1950

October 20   Henry Lewis Stimson dies at his Highhold
                 estate on Long Island.

1

Preparation of a Policymaker

In January 1902, while in Washington with Gifford Pinchot, the conservationist, to attend the annual dinner of the Boone & Crockett Club, Henry L. Stimson went riding in Rock Creek Park. From across the creek Stimson was hailed by name by one of the four men who were walking along the other bank. He soon recognized the voice calling him as that of President Theodore Roosevelt. Roosevelt was laughing and asking him to swim across and join his group. When Stimson hesitated, Secretary of War Elihu Root, Stimson's former law partner, called out: "The President of the United States directs Sergeant Stimson of Squadron A to cross the creek and come to his assistance by order of the Secretary of War." Stimson immediately saluted, shouted, "Very good, sir," and pointed his horse at the creek. Due to recent rains the water was high, and it was difficult to tell its depth as the creek was walled on both sides. The horse immediately lost its footing in the rapid current and plunged downstream, with both rider and horse often completely under water. Roosevelt was shouting for Stimson to go back, which was impossible due to the high wall and the rapid current. Finally, Stimson and his horse landed on the branches of a fallen tree.

Stimson dismounted and led the horse downstream to a break in the wall where they climbed the bank. He remounted, rode down to a bridge, crossed, rode up to Roosevelt and Root, and reported he was "ready for duty." The president and Root, Stimson recalled, "looked like two small boys who had been caught stealing apples."

Roosevelt said he did not think the order would be obeyed: "I thought you could see that the bank on the other side was impossible." Stimson replied, "Mr. President, when a soldier hears an order like that, it isn't his business to see that it is impossible." The president laughed and said it "was very nice of you to do it, now hurry home & drink all the whiskey you can." Root simply added to this that he and the president "didn't care a dam [sic] about Harry; but we were a good deal concerned about the horse!" That night at the Boone & Crockett Club dinner, Roosevelt, in his retelling of that day's events, hailed Stimson as "young Lochinvar."[1]

This incident captures much that is important for understanding Stimson and his role in the making of American foreign policy. At the age of thirty-four, Stimson was already a well-established Wall Street lawyer with connections to the most powerful men in the nation. Roosevelt and Root, along with his father, were the greatest influences on his life and understanding of the world. Stimson's reply to the president was not after-the-fact bravado or hyperbole. He acted in the manner he believed was required of him and anyone else in that situation. Stimson held honor, duty, service, honesty, obedience to authority, and physical challenge as the highest of values. He had a patrician's sense of the obligation of service by those who, as he saw it, were best able. This led him to accept the importance of public service by right-minded conservatives to reform the social order, protect property, and maintain progress. Stimson's sense of the importance of duty and service is underscored by the fact that, when he began to keep a diary in 1909, this was the first event of his life that he recorded.

As a lawyer, Stimson had very clear views of right and wrong that he held to throughout his life, believing in certain absolutes and correct ways of conduct, guided by tradition, morality, and, most important, the law. As a Progressive Republican, or a "progressive conservative," as he called himself,[2] he saw a need for federal intervention in the domestic economy to regulate corporations and their behavior, and for United States intervention abroad to maintain order, protect business, and ensure the proper conduct of nations. Holding to the Social Darwinist and the essentialist racial attitudes that were common to people of his class and background in the early twentieth century, he believed in a hierarchy of peoples in terms of abilities and the superiority of whites and Western nations over the rest of the world. Stimson, therefore, distrusted mass politics, had concerns about too much democracy, and believed in a greater concentration of power in the executive branch of the government. He was comfortable only with those of his own class and attitudes, and those who accepted authority and followed clear lines of power.

Stimson never questioned the need for a greater United States involvement in the world. He was a nationalist who accepted the notion of the "White Man's Burden." His understanding of the U.S. role in the world was shaped by his relationships with Roosevelt and Root and their positive views of expansion and war as the paths to national greatness. He was, as his membership in the Boone & Crockett Club attests, an avid outdoorsman and member of numerous elite clubs. These formed his circle of friends, confirmed his attitudes, and represented the people he thought should be in charge of the nation. Like Theodore Roosevelt, Stimson believed in the virtue of struggle and war and the positive influence of expansion. Just as the nation had been shaped by the frontier and the conquest of the continent, it needed to challenge itself in the international arena. This, Stimson concluded, would serve both the interests of the United States and the rest of the world. A dominant role for the United States in the world would bring stability and a more peaceful international system that would, in turn, be more receptive to American ideas and economic interests. Stimson placed a good deal of faith in treaties and the great powers' cooperation to maintain international law. Social order abroad, not reform, was the primary goal. To succeed, the United States had to build up its economic and military strength and expand American "national interests."

Thus, service to the nation, military preparedness, and United States leadership in the world became central components of Stimson's worldview and guided him in all of his various positions. Stimson believed in the universal application of American values, laws, and institutions. If led by the right group of men, the future of the nation and the world would assuredly be better. Never questioning these precepts, or seeing his ideas as those of a particular class and those endorsing the status quo, Stimson was convinced that other people needed exposure to Americans and their ways, and to follow American training and leadership. Those wise enough to understand this would develop and advance, while those who resisted would have to be controlled. The challenge was to make sure that the right men, and for Stimson the public world was the world of men, were in charge.

Andover, Yale, and the Law

Born on September 21, 1867, in New York City, Stimson was raised in a world of privilege and service. His ancestors arrived in Massachusetts in the seventeenth century. Stimson described them as "sturdy, middle-class people, religious, thrifty, energetic, and long-lived," attributes he would ascribe to himself. After service in the Revolutionary War, a George Stimson moved to upstate New York, where he was the first settler of the town of Windham. George Stimson's grandson moved to New York City, where he bought a seat on the New York Stock Exchange and became the senior partner of Henry C. Stimson & Sons of 8 Wall Street. Stimson's father, Lewis, joined his father's firm after service in the Civil War. He prospered during the rapid postwar expansion of New York's financial power, met Candace Wheeler, and followed her to Europe and married her in the American embassy in Paris in November 1866. Lewis Stimson was well enough off that when his wife's health began to fail he could sell his business and take the family to Europe in 1871.

He began the study of medicine in both Zurich and Paris in order to try to understand his wife's illness. Upon their return to the United States in 1873, he completed his medical degree at Bellevue Hospital Medical College, subsequently becoming a professor of surgery in the New York University Medical College and the Cornell Medical College from its founding, and an attending surgeon at Presbyterian, Bellevue, and New York hospitals. From his father, young Henry obtained his sense of obligation to serve and the idea that there was more to life than the earning of money.

Stimson's mother died in 1875. Lewis Stimson did not believe he could raise his children alone properly and, therefore, sent Henry and his sister Candace to live with their grandparents on East 34th Street in New York, where they would be under the care of their Aunt Minnie. Stimson adored his grandparents and aunt as much as he loved his father and internalized their strict Victorian values and behavior. In 1880, when he was only thirteen, his father sent young Henry off to Phillips Academy in Andover, Massachusetts, where he was the youngest student. His connection with Phillips Andover was to last his whole lifetime. He became a trustee in 1905 and served in that capacity until 1947. Stimson thrived on the strict rules, which were similar to those imposed by his aunt, the classical curriculum, and the sense of duty and obligation that were instilled in the students. He found great companionship and what he saw as a "new world of democracy" with boys from throughout the United States, all drawn, he said, "by the desire to get the teaching given by a school which was known to have represented for over a hundred years the ideals of character and education believed in by the founders of our country."[3]

Stimson graduated from Andover in 1883, but owing to his early start was a year too young to begin at Yale. He spent the interim period being tutored in New York and Andover, and enrolled at Yale in the fall of 1884. Again, at Yale, he claimed to have found a "potent democratic class spirit" that produced what he saw as the superior attributes of so many of its graduates and his colleagues, and that provided them the right to rule. He was tapped for the select senior society Skull and Bones. Upon graduation in 1888, he went on to Harvard Law School where he studied for two years. Stimson returned to New York in 1890 and lived with his father and sister, who had returned to run her father's household, while he established himself as a lawyer. He was admitted to the New York Bar in 1891, the same year he joined the Wall Street firm of Root & Clarke as a clerk. On January 1, 1893, he became a partner in the firm. With his position secure, Stimson was finally ready to move out of his father's house, and, on July 6, 1893, he married Mabel Wellington White of New Haven, whom he had met while a student at Yale. They had waited, in a demonstration of their Victorian values, until Henry had established his career and financial independence before wedding. Theirs was a happy marriage that lasted fifty-three years, and they remained devoted to each other until Stimson's death in 1950. The couple, however, was unable to have children and so gave their energies to Stimson's career. In part to make up for the lack of offspring, Stimson surrounded himself with bright, energetic young protégés throughout his career who became part of the Stimson household.[4]

No matter what firm he joined, Stimson was destined for a distinguished and profitable career as an attorney in New York. He was intelligent, energetic, and easily earned the trust of others. But he might not have been a public figure without the assistance of his law partner, Elihu Root. It was through Root that Stimson first met Theodore Roosevelt and began to become active in public affairs. Their law practice flourished, in large part due to Root's contacts with the leaders of the New York business community and the Republican Party. In 1897, the firm became Root, Howard, Winthrop & Stimson. When Root left to become secretary of war in the McKinley administration in 1899, the firm was renamed

Winthrop & Stimson. Stimson saw Root as an "exemplar of what a high-minded counselor should be," a man whose "rectitude, wisdom, and constructive sagacity" were a constant guide. Moreover, he was "far and away the greatest American statesman" of his day, the one American, in Stimson's opinion, whom the leaders of Europe seek out "in times of crisis." Throughout his career in both law and government he attempted to emulate and meet what he saw as Root's exacting standards for public service and the good that could be done for the nation by those who combined hard work, intelligence, and reason.[5]

After his first year at Yale, Stimson had traveled to the western United States to hunt, explore, and climb mountains for the first time. It was a trip he would repeat after marriage, usually accompanied by his wife, almost annually for over twenty years. The West held a mythical and romantic attraction for Stimson. The frontier, he believed, had shaped the American character, demonstrated the correctness and superiority of American values and government, and foreshadowed the benefits that would be gained for both the nation and others by the expansion of American wealth, power, and influence abroad. He saw the land beyond the Mississippi and Missouri Rivers that he first visited in 1885 as "still a western frontier . . . with untamed Indians and wild animals in great numbers." He always craved, perhaps, he speculated, because it was only three generations since his ancestors had fought for their lives and homes in northern New York, to hunt game and to test himself against nature: "to show that I was able to support my life in that wild country in spite of the difficulties and dangers which might confront me." He regretted that he was not part of what he thought of as the "vast majority of young Americans" who had engaged in the "excitement of conquering a new continent."[6]

His most notable experiences came in 1887 and 1891. On his first solo trip to Colorado in 1887, Stimson found himself caught up in one of the last series of battles of the Plains Indian Wars. A band of Utes had left their reservation and were being chased by the National Guard. One night he discovered four Utes who were unexpectedly and uncomfortably close to his campsite. He brandished his rifle and stood behind his mule, but no shots were exchanged. This "encounter" strengthened his conviction of the necessity of the tutelage of whites over people of color. The natives would have to be controlled, Stimson believed, until they could learn the ways of civilized society and no longer constitute a threat. Four years later, finding Colorado's days as a wilderness gone,

Stimson sought out George Grinnell, a naturalist and student of Indian life, to get his recommendation of some area, "which had not felt so heavy the foot of the white man." Grinnell recommended the area that is now Glacier National Park in northwestern Montana. In 1891, Stimson set out to meet Grinnell there, near the home of the Blackfoots, who, Stimson noted, "had been 'pacified' and persuaded to live on a reservation only a few years before." Travel was by work train as the Northern Pacific line was not yet complete, and "civilization was not even around the corner."[7]

It was during this trip that Stimson had a peak in Montana named after him by Grinnell. Exploring unmapped land north of Upper St. Mary's Lake, Stimson and Grinnell's group came upon a circle of unknown mountains. Grinnell, who on a previous trip had named various other mountains in the region, named one of the glacier peaks for Stimson. While all the other names were adopted and used in later surveys, Stimson's was "accidently lost in the shuffle by the Geodetic Survey," leaving his name attached to a peak farther south that he had never visited and had only seen from a distance. On his return east he spotted Chief Mountain, which he learned had never been climbed. He vowed to return and be the first to accomplish this feat, which he did the next year.[8]

Through his annual trips, Stimson became a good horseman and rifleman and, as he recalled, at home in the wilderness, where he could "pack my own horses, kill my own game, make my own camp, and cook my own meals." He became a lifelong advocate of conservation of wild areas, believing that the land needed preservation and that Indians needed proper tutelage. More important, he believed that these experiences were vital to his work later in life. He not only gained self-confidence, but also found that ethical principles became "simpler by the impact of the wilderness and by contact with the men who live in it. Moral problems are divested of the confusion and complications which civilization throws around them." Stimson compared it to the code of honor learned by soldiers in the field, where courage, truthfulness, and frankness are central. He believed that he had passed all of the tests requisite to high office and power.[9]

Stimson's understanding of the impact of the frontier on American society was similar to that of Frederick Jackson Turner and his famous and influential "frontier thesis." In 1893, Turner argued that the passing of the frontier was the end of an epoch in American history. He maintained that up to 1890 and the end of the existence of the frontier, "American history has been in a large degree the history of the colonization of the Great West. The existence of an area of free land, its continuous recession, and the advance of American settlement westward, explain American development." It had shaped and protected, Turner argued, American individualism and democratic institutions. In Stimson's view, the closing of the frontier "mark[ed] the close of an era," and meant the end of the "great safety valve against discontent."[10] It should not, however, signal the end of American expansion. Rather, the passing of the period of free lands necessitated reforms at home to respond to growing political unrest and continued expansion abroad to extend the benefits that he found for the nation and others in the conquest of the West, while continuing to secure new markets for American production. Together, Stimson believed reform and expansion would serve the same purposes the frontier had in furthering American democracy, maintaining political stability, and promoting economic growth.

As the demands of his career made it more difficult to travel to the West for a month each year, Stimson and his wife began searching for a permanent residence that would allow them to escape from the city and maintain the contact with nature on which they thrived. In 1903, Stimson purchased over a hundred acres of land in the West Hills of Huntington, Long Island, to build his country home. Named Highhold because of its commanding view of the Long Island Sound to the north and the Atlantic Ocean in the distance to the south, the estate allowed the Stimsons to live the life of country squires in the midst of Long Island's Gold Coast. Theodore Roosevelt's home at Sagamore Hill was close by in Oyster Bay, while the Vanderbilts and the banker Otto Kahn also lived in Huntington. The village of Huntington was six miles away, and the only access to it in those early days, prior to the coming of paved roads for the automobile, was by horse and wagon. In order to get to work, Stimson rode his horse to the train station at Cold Spring Harbor for his commute to New York City.

Foxhunting occupied nearly every Saturday from September to March and riding was a year-round love. Farmers' cart paths served as excellent bridle paths, there were few fences, and roads for cars were kept far away. Because they rode, on both the hunts and for pleasure, over other peoples' land, the Stimsons hosted all of their neighbors once a year for the annual "Highhold Games." Originally held on Thanksgiving, and later on Columbus Day, the games consisted of a variety of competitions in riding, shooting, and running for young and old alike. A large tent would be set up

Stimson's Highhold estate, Huntington, New York. *Collection of the Huntington Historical Society, Long Island, New York*

Stimson begins the Highhold Games. *Henry Lewis Stimson Papers, Manuscripts and Archives, Yale University Library*

in front of the house to serve food and beverages, and championship cups were awarded to the winners. Stimson's sense of service and obligation was clear. "It's a lot of trouble," he remarked concerning the hosting of the games, "but we like to keep it up because it is good for the community." This annual event lasted into the 1920s, when the coming of the motorcar brought an end to the horse age on Long Island's north shore.[11]

The Stimson who had answered the order of his president by plunging into Rock Creek was a man of considerable wealth, partner in one of the most powerful law firms in New York, married to a woman whom he adored and who adored him, and about to purchase his dream estate. Although he had much to be thankful for, he never questioned that all this was deserved due to his character, moral probity, and hard work. In fact, up to that time he had only one regret in his life. As he noted in his memoirs, the 1898 war with Spain in Cuba and the Philippines "caught me napping." His youth had been spent in a time of peace, and the nation was free from strife, "barring occasional small affrays with Indians on our western frontier." The century was ending, he thought, with a "growing extension of democracy, freedom, and peace throughout the world." He had, therefore, not given any thought to possible military service, and found himself with the outbreak of war "entirely untrained and unprepared for military service." Stimson had immediately enlisted in Squadron A of the New York National Guard, but the war ended before he could see combat duty. He remained active in the guard for nine years and emerged from the experience determined that neither he, nor his nation if he could help it, would be found unprepared again. His attention was, for the first time, beginning to turn to affairs beyond the nation's shores, and he observed closely Root's work at home in reorganizing the military establishment through the creation of a General Staff and War College, and abroad in the creation of America's empire.[12]

Stimson came to share the views of Roosevelt, Root, and other advocates of American expansion regarding the positive benefits of the Spanish-American War on American society and the nation's mission in the world. Nations, similar to individuals, needed to test themselves and maintain a martial spirit or be overtaken by others. Although creating wealth and earning money were quite acceptable, and Stimson spent his private life assisting some of New York's wealthiest people, he believed that true honor and achievement came from service to the nation. He worried about the negative impact of material acquisition on people and thought war was

in many ways a "wonderfully good thing for this country" in order to "lift men out of selfish, individual work."[13] Things worthwhile, at times, have to be fought for or protected. Similarly, it took
power to influence other nations in the proper direction. Stimson
was convinced by Roosevelt and Root, and from his own experiences and observations, that the United States was destined to be
the leading nation of the world, and that the world needed its leadership. The government and the people had to recognize these responsibilities and awaken to the opportunities and costs they
created. Stimson made this struggle central to all of his activities
for the next forty-five years.

He, therefore, supported the taking of various territories in the
wake of the war with Spain and the announcement of the Open
Door policy of free trade and low tariffs in 1899 and 1900. In addition, he saw cooperation with Great Britain as essential for the
United States, and he supported American intervention in Latin
America and taking control over the Isthmus of Panama. He did
not want the United States to emulate England's territorial imperialism, but he thought it was necessary for "inferior" populations
to receive guidance. Stimson's was a benevolent imperialism that
called for both order and uplift. For this reason he opposed independence for both Cuba and the Philippines after the Spanish-
American War, while also rejecting any notion that these lands
would be brought into the Union as states.[14] They were not, Stimson
believed, ready for self-rule and needed the guidance of a great
nation. The Platt Amendment for Cuba drafted by Stimson's mentor Elihu Root, which allowed for American intervention in Cuban
affairs, provided for Stimson the right mixture of control and limited self-rule, while holding the Philippines as a colony was, due
to the distance of the archipelago from the mainland, a necessary
burden that had to be accepted as part of the nation's obligation to
the world.

During the next decade, Stimson supported all of Roosevelt's
efforts to increase American influence throughout the Western
Hemisphere and his strengthening of the American Navy. He agreed
with Roosevelt that the Panama Canal was vital to American interests and the advance of civilization and supported American intervention in the region to protect the canal and prevent anarchy. The
Roosevelt Corollary to the Monroe Doctrine, which declared that
the United States had the right to intervene in other nations' affairs
where "flagrant cases of . . . wrongdoing or impotence" threatened
established order or prevented meeting international obligations,

was a policy Stimson deemed necessary to protect American interests and to promote the development of Latin America.[15] It was obvious to Stimson that Latin Americans and Filipinos were inferior to whites and that they needed protection, tutelage, and the benefit of the U.S. example. Indeed, they were fortunate that the United States took so much interest in their affairs.

Stimson's growing interest in foreign affairs was matched by a concern with domestic politics, and his first forays into public life concerned New York City politics and domestic events. He joined other wealthy and high-minded Republicans in New York in their efforts to reform local politics and government. During the mid-1890s, Stimson became actively involved in the Good Government Clubs in Manhattan designed to wrest control of the city's politics from the grip of Tammany Hall, the Democrats, and their ostensible pandering to the lowest elements in society. He believed that "under proper leadership" by the better citizens of the city, these clubs could improve municipal life and "be made the source of great good in the conduct" of the city's affairs.[16] His was the progressivism of efficient and more centralized government led by patrician reformers who saw the need for both change and social control. To Stimson, it was crucial that the Republican Party, consisting of what he saw as the better, more intelligent, and most able citizens of the country, should take the lead in reform and prevent that leadership from falling to "either an independent party," such as the Populists or Socialists, "or a party composed, like the Democrats, largely of foreign elements." If the right citizens did not take the lead and institute the necessary changes, then these changes could not be accomplished "without much excitement and possibly violence."[17] Reform was needed to organize government in accordance with "the structures which have proved effective in business."[18]

He also used his contacts in the West to fight against William Jennings Bryan and the free coinage of silver during the 1896 presidential election. For example, Stimson, who voted for Grover Cleveland in 1892, wrote a friend in Montana that the election of Bryan "would cause a great panic among business circles and more suffering and distress among the wage-earners." The Democratic platform was "in favor of free riot, free silver, and the overthrow of the Supreme Court." Bryan had to be defeated so "no one hereafter will ever try to gain votes at the expense of honor, law and order."[19]

In addition to the unruly masses and the politicians who sought to incite class hatreds, Stimson also feared the trusts and the malefactors of great wealth who ran them. In pursuit of their own limited aims of riches at any cost, they provided those whom Stimson saw as demagogues, such as Bryan, with popular targets and issues for attacking the social order and endangering the well-being of the nation. Stimson knew that monopolistic practices and abuses of power were causing a great deal of legitimate discontent in the nation, and he feared that without any action by responsible leaders these new concentrations of wealth would drive people to radical political solutions. Moderate reforms and enforcement of the Interstate Commerce Law and the Sherman Anti-Trust Act could forestall radical unrest.[20] To Stimson, obedience to law was supreme and had to be upheld at all times if stability was to be maintained and progress continued. This applied to the wealthy as well as the poor. The government, Stimson maintained, had to protect both the basic liberties of citizens while serving as an agent for the positive development of the nation as a whole. In an industrial society, where the power of business could overwhelm the rights of certain citizens, it was the duty of the government, and particularly the executive branch, to protect the general welfare. As Stimson later noted, "I am by nature a Federalist and a Progressive."[21] He was, therefore, an ardent supporter of Theodore Roosevelt's efforts at reform and controlling the trusts, and jumped at his first chance for public service to the nation as United States Attorney for the Southern District of New York, where he could carry out Roosevelt's policies.

United States Attorney

Stimson was called to Washington in December 1905 by President Theodore Roosevelt to discuss the position. Elihu Root, now the secretary of state, was the main promoter of Stimson for the job. He told his former junior partner that his own experience as United States Attorney in New York was the "best training in advocacy" that he had had in his life. Stimson made it clear to the president that he was enthusiastic about the position and the possibilities for reform, and his appointment was quickly announced in January 1906. Stimson now found himself, at the age of thirty-eight, at the center of Roosevelt's campaign against what he termed bad trusts. This would not be the last time Stimson followed Root's path in public office.

Roosevelt had gained the passage of the Elkins Act in 1903, which increased the penalties for illegal rebates by the railroads, that is, the return of an amount given in payment to create an unfair competitive advantage, providing the government with an effective weapon to use against those discriminatory practices and allowing for the prosecution of both the shipper and the railroad. Yet after two years, no significant convictions had been obtained by the government under the statute. The president and Attorney General William Moody did not believe the United States Attorney's office in New York was fulfilling its role in litigating cases under the act or battling the well-financed and experienced attorneys of the trusts. To take advantage of this legislation, Roosevelt needed his own experienced attorney who was willing to take the fight to the trusts. Stimson perfectly fit the role the president had in mind. He was a personal friend whom Roosevelt could trust, had extensive litigation experience in New York, and was familiar with all of the issues. Moreover, he came from one of the top corporate firms in New York and did not have to worry about damaging his career by making powerful enemies.

The two big cases that awaited Stimson were rebate suits against the New York Central Railroad and the sugar trust. Moody told Stimson he wanted a district attorney who "would try the important cases of the office instead of asking for special counsel." That meant Stimson had two tasks to carry out simultaneously, prosecuting corporate violators of federal law while reorganizing the office so that he, with his own assistants, could try the cases rather than retaining private lawyers. Roosevelt and Moody let Stimson know that he would have a free hand in conducting his business, an agreement that both held to. While not related to the rest of his public career in developing the nation's foreign policy, Stimson's tenure as a United States District Attorney was important because much of what he learned in that role about organizing his office and how government worked he applied in later assignments, and because his success there made all his other opportunities possible.[22]

The attorneys in the New York office that Stimson inherited were low paid, unmotivated, and less competent than the private lawyers they faced in court. Stimson knew he needed a much more talented staff if he hoped to have any success against the corporations, yet his limited budget prevented him from recruiting experienced, established lawyers. Stimson's solution was to seek out and recruit the most talented young attorneys just out of law school who were eager for challenges and willing to work long hours and learn on the job in return for the opportunities presented in this new field. Stimson asked deans of the leading law schools for recommendations regarding their best students and recent graduates. Over the next three years, Stimson hired sixteen assistants, all of whom went on to become "leaders in private practice," widely recognized and respected by other attorneys. The two best-known appointees were Thomas D. Thacher, who later served on the New York State Supreme Court, and future U.S. Supreme Court Justice Felix Frankfurter.

While Stimson assembled his staff, he also quickly gained a number of indictments and fines against smaller shippers and offenders. But he learned that prosecuting the big trusts was a difficult, complex, and time-consuming matter. There was an overwhelming amount of evidence that had to be examined as rebates were well hidden inside other documents and financial reports. Stimson and his staff had to master these tricks and then reconstruct the deceptive actions taken in a clear enough manner to present to a jury. To accomplish his tasks, Stimson developed an administrative style that he would employ throughout all his later posts. He delegated much of the work, but always maintained control and final authority. He could pick talent and trusted his staff to follow his guidelines and to bring him well-developed briefs and plans. Stimson, therefore, gave his assistants a great deal of responsibility and leeway in working on the facts and details of the cases, while he oversaw the final drafting of indictments and examined for himself the most important aspects of a case, including the key witnesses. The trust he placed in his subordinates was rewarded by hard work, creativity, and an unquestioning loyalty. Moreover, it played to Stimson's strengths of conceptualizing problems and organizing plans and allowed him to pay attention to the larger policy questions and concerns of his office and pursue a number of high-profile and difficult cases simultaneously. To Stimson, receiving credit was not very important. He was a man with little ego or desire for public praise. What did matter was getting the job done correctly.

Stimson was determined to be better prepared than the defense. Moreover, the cases he prosecuted convinced Stimson that the best means to prevent rebates, and corporate wrongdoing in general, was to keep bringing forth indictments for each separate offense until the railroads and the shippers understood that they would be punished for their transgressions. The American Sugar Refining Corporation gave in after only one trial because of the proof of its guilt in public and all the bad publicity. In the two other major areas he emphasized during his time in office, the misapplication of bank funds and customs fraud, Stimson employed the same strategy of multiple indictments. He successfully prosecuted Charles Morse for the misuse of the funds of the Bank of North America and the sugar trust for the fraudulent weighing of its products to avoid paying customs duties. For Stimson, the fraud in each case was objectionable, but the more important point, and what made the actions worse than just cheating, was the "callous indifference to the law and the interests of the United States." Having used the law to its fullest extent, Stimson, upon his leaving of the office in 1909, recommended to President William Howard Taft that, in cases where the law had not yet caught up to the evasions developed by the corporations and business leaders, it might be necessary to employ the "punishment of publicity." A record of the transgressions should be made public after the indictments and trial to bring forth the "tonic of public indignation" to set things right for the future. "Known wrongdoing must be stamped as wrong by public opinion," and those whose "moral sense had been blunted must be made to understand how their actions looked" to the larger community. In his use of public exposure and popular opposition to control outlaw behavior, Stimson was foreshadowing a strategy that he would use as secretary of state twenty years later under the Stimson Doctrine.

When he resigned as United States Attorney in April 1909, Stimson had effectively ended rebates as a practice and clarified much of the confusion in the law concerning customs and banking. Having never found private practice completely satisfying, because the "life of the ordinary New York lawyer is primarily and essentially devoted to the making of money," Stimson took great pride in his time in office and achievements. His prior experience had taught him that, "wherever the public interest has come into conflict with private interests, private interest was more adequately represented," as the latter "had the ablest and most successful lawyer to defend it." He was glad to have worked to redress the balance. He had reorganized the District Attorney's Office and established new precedents in the law. The work also brought him his first public attention and gained him the respect of the people he most desired it from, the legal and business community and, most important, Roosevelt and Root. From this experience, he would seek and readily accept other opportunities to serve the nation, although they would be in a very different arena from the courtrooms of New York City.[23]

Electoral Defeat

Prior to his next service to the nation, however, Stimson entered into his only election campaign as a candidate for the governorship of New York in 1910. Stimson's decision to run stemmed from his loyalty to Elihu Root and Theodore Roosevelt, the Republican Party, and his sense of duty. By 1910, there was already a growing rift in the Republican Party between the progressives who supported Roosevelt and the regulars who were committed to President William H. Taft. In New York State, this division became a problem when the popular reform governor, Charles Evans Hughes, accepted a position on the United States Supreme Court in April 1910. Hughes had angered party regulars by his promotion of the direct primary, and the party was deeply divided over whom it would nominate for governor. The problem was exacerbated by the prospect, due to its being an off-year election, that 1910 would become a Democratic year at the polls.

Stimson's name was mentioned for the nomination prior to Roosevelt's return to the United States from his hunting trip in Africa and grand tour of Europe. Once back in Oyster Bay, the former president, by now an opponent of President Taft, energetically thrust himself into the middle of the party's fights by being elected as New York's temporary chairman, defeating Vice President James Sherman, the candidate of the Republican machine. While Roosevelt protested that he really sought an upstate man and that he did not want to subject Stimson to a sure defeat, he also informed Stimson that he thought he "would make the best Governor, but not the best candidate." When the party met in September, it was clear that Roosevelt would get his choice for the nomination.[24]

At the beginning of the nominating convention, Stimson met with Root and Roosevelt in the latter's room to discuss the situation. Root asked Roosevelt, "Isn't there some way we can keep Harry out of this? I hate to see him sacrificed." Roosevelt concurred, but thought that defeat in a good fight would not hurt Stimson. Root thought that might be so in most years, but that the Republicans were "in for a terrible licking. . . . I think the country has made up its mind to change parties. It is like a man in bed. He wants to roll over. He doesn't know why he wants to roll over, but he just does; and he'll do it." Roosevelt's mind was set, and Stimson saw it as "my duty to run."[25]

Once committed, Stimson, with Roosevelt's aid, set out to win. Stimson's willingness to run reflected more that just his high sense of personal duty. He believed that the stakes for the Republican Party and the nation were high. He told Roosevelt that he did not want to run if his candidacy would have a negative affect on Roosevelt's prestige. "If I run and am defeated, as looks now almost certain, it will be made a defeat for you." Roosevelt waved off these concerns, and argued that they were "fighting for a big issue."[26] For Stimson, these issues were clear—the regeneration of the Republican Party and the direction of the nation. He believed that the country was reaching a critical crossroad and that it was "vitally important that the Republican party, which contains, generally speaking, the richer and more intelligent citizens of the country, should take the lead in reform and not drift into a reactionary position." If leadership fell into the hands of the Democrats, composed "largely of foreign elements and the classes which will immediately benefit by the reform, and if solid business Republicans should drift into new obstruction, I fear the necessary changes could hardly be accomplished without much excitement and possibly violence."[27]

Stimson and Roosevelt traveled the length of the state for the next six weeks giving campaign speeches, meeting with people, and attempting to rally support. The former president's prediction that Stimson, given his formal manner and distrust of the masses, would not be a good campaigner were borne out. It was trial by error, with Roosevelt being frequently heard imploring Stimson: "Darn it, Harry, a campaign speech is a poster, not an etching!" Roosevelt's commitment to the campaign made it seem at times as if he were the candidate and brought forth charges that Stimson was just a pawn for the former president who would govern through him. Stimson's most effective moments came in addressing this charge. "If they mean when they say that," Stimson would reply, "that I admire the standards of courage and integrity and civic righteousness which Theodore Roosevelt has shown for thirty years, . . . why then I am frank to say that I am Roosevelt's man and I am proud of it." But if they meant that he would govern "according to any other suggestion or any other dictation than my own will, . . . why then I say to you that I am not only not Mr. Roosevelt's man but I am not any man's man and I think you will find that Colonel Roosevelt . . . will be the first one to tell you so."

The Republicans remained divided, and little support was forthcoming from Washington and the Taft administration. In the end, Stimson lost by 66,000 votes, which was much less than the 300,000 pundits had been predicting in September. Stimson gave Roosevelt most of the credit, and had no regrets because he believed in his cause and motives for running.[28] But it was clear that the stump and electoral politics were not Stimson's arena. Ironically, it was his defeat as a Roosevelt man that made him both available for the next stage of his public life and valuable to Taft as well in his effort to try to hold on to the presidency by aligning himself with some of Roosevelt's supporters within the party. In an effort to solidify his hold on the Republican nomination in 1912 against a possible challenge from Roosevelt, Taft asked Stimson to join his cabinet in 1911 as the secretary of war. This new position would bring Stimson his first direct involvement in the nation's foreign policy, place him in charge of America's colonial possessions, and begin a career of service in Washington that would continue over the next four decades.

To these tasks Stimson brought the primary lessons of his training as a lawyer, work as an attorney, and experience in public affairs. Stimson believed in careful preparation, a willingness to serve, and a judicious use of the centralized power of the federal government in support of the law and policies. This meant to Stimson greater executive power at home to regulate the economy and continued involvement of the United States in the affairs of the world. "My experience . . . has tended to bring forcibly to my attention the extent" of the problems in working with Congress, which tends to take "more and more the viewpoint of the locality rather than the viewpoint of the nation. On the other hand the President and his Cabinet by force of their position represent the national viewpoint."[29] Stimson had no doubt that he understood the national viewpoint and was ready to serve. With the right people in charge, there would be greater stability, order, and eventually progress through gradual change. As secretary of war he saw it as his task to oversee the reorganization and the modernization of the nation's military begun by Root, the completion of the Panama Canal, the oversight of America's possessions to make sure they were being properly managed, and the preparation of the nation for the challenges of world leadership.

Notes

1. "Memorandum of interesting (to me) occasions & events in my life during the past few years," 17 January 1909, Henry L. Stimson Diaries, Sterling Library, Yale University (hereafter HLSD).

2. Current, *Secretary Stimson*, 12.

3. Stimson and Bundy, *On Active Service* (New York: Harper & Brothers, 1947), xi–xviii; Godfrey Hodgson, *The Colonel* (New York: Knopf, 1990), 26–34.

4. Ibid.

5. Stimson and Bundy, *On Active Service*, xviii; Stimson to Carter, 11 April 1916, Henry L. Stimson Papers, Sterling Library, Yale University, microfilm edition, reel 44 (hereafter Stimson Papers followed by reel number).

6. Stimson, *My Vacations* (privately printed: Henry L. Stimson, 1949), 1–2, 43–64.

7. Ibid.

8. Ibid.

9. Stimson and Bundy, *On Active Service*, xvi.

10. Stimson to Roosevelt, 2 September 1910, Stimson Papers, reel 19.

11. Stimson, *My Vacations*, 165–80; Current, *Secretary Stimson*, 11.

12. Stimson and Bundy, *On Active Service*, xx–xxi.

13. Elting E. Morison, *Turmoil and Tradition: A Study of the Life and Times of Henry L. Stimson* (Boston: Houghton Mifflin, 1960), 32.

14. Stimson to Pepper, 14 July 1898, Stimson Papers, reel 1; Stimson to Garrison, 4 May 1900, reel 2.

15. Department of State, *Foreign Relations of the United States, 1904*, (Washington, D.C.: Government Printing Office), xli.

16. Stimson to Jarvin, 29 October 1895, Stimson Papers, reel 1.

17. Stimson to Roosevelt, 2 September 1910, ibid., reel 19.

18. Stimson to Kent, 29 December 1910, ibid., reel 6.

19. Stimson to Haggerty, 8 October 1896, ibid., reel 1.

20. See Stimson to Speer, 2 December 1910, ibid., reel 6; Stimson to Sempers, 8 March 1912, ibid., reel 7.

21. Stimson to Templeton, 5 August 1912, ibid., reel 30.

22. Stimson Diary, 17 January 1909 and 15 August 1909, HLSD; see also Stimson to Moody, 5 April 1906 and 10 August 1906; Stimson to Bonaparte, 22 December 1906 and 15 July 1907, Stimson Papers, reel 11.

23. Stimson Diary, 17 January 1909 and 15 August 1909, HLSD; Stimson and Bundy, *On Active Service*, 3–17.

24. "Personal Recollections of the Convention and Campaign of 1910," HLSD.

25. Ibid.

26. Ibid.

27. Stimson to Roosevelt, 2 September 1910, Stimson Papers, reel 19.

28. Stimson and Bundy, *On Active Service*, 22–28.

29. Stimson to Ford, 3 April 1913, Stimson Papers, reel 6.

2

Taft, Roosevelt, and the Progressive Stimson

Stimson saw Taft's invitation to be his secretary of war as an unparalleled opportunity for him to serve the causes of progressive reform at home and national greatness abroad. He hoped he could use his position to continue the changes begun by Roosevelt, forestall the widening rifts within the Republican Party, particularly between Taft and Roosevelt, consolidate and advance the reforms of the military initiated by Root, ensure American possessions were being properly managed, and prepare the nation for the challenges of the modern world. He was confident that he was well prepared for the task of promoting positive change at home while continuing to further the internationalists' cause of the United States assuming the mantle of world leadership. Stimson's first term as secretary of war placed him at the center of the debates concerning the nation's role in the world from 1911 to 1920, and the shaping of American foreign policy during a critical juncture of America's growing involvement in the world.

Similar to other progressive reformers, Stimson believed in gradual change and the overall improvement of society. He was optimistic and excited about the prospect of moving society forward. The proper application of science, reason, order, and efficiency would promote stability, prosperity, and peaceful change. This meant using the power of government wisely to block what Stimson saw as reactionary and obstructionist conservatives on the one hand and wild radicals on the other. He saw 1911–1912 as a critical time for the Republican Party, when it must continue to be the party of progress and "turn its face toward a sane and sound liberalism." With a consistent progressive program, it could be sure of public support, and if wise enough "to avoid the Scylla of a hardened conservatism or the Charybdis of a thoughtless radicalism, it will achieve a lasting success." The present unrest and problems arose, Stimson wrote in 1911, "out of a change in our economic conditions and can be allayed only by a careful study of that change, a recognition of what the line of remedy is, and a brave and frank attempt to apply such remedies." The Taft administration, therefore, had to "take the lead in conservatively solving the problems" through moderate reform.[1] With proper order, study, and control, the material conditions of the society and the lives of its citizens could be consistently improved.

These thoughts guided Stimson in all of his work, providing him with overwhelming confidence, determination, and a high sense of purpose and duty. The need for conservative change applied to the military as much as any other area of American society. As secretary of war, Stimson defended the institution of the General Staff, created a shorter enlistment term and reserve that fit his vision for the proper training of troops, and instituted a tactical reorganization of the army that allowed for the implementation of an overall plan of battle and rapid growth in the time of war. In these critical years for the development of American foreign policy, Stimson took pride in the reforms he initiated, especially when his accomplishments helped the nation successfully mobilize for the Great War. Yet, these years would also be painful ones for Stimson. He suffered personally from Roosevelt's challenge to Taft and the splitting of the Republican Party. More important, he was bitterly disappointed in his party and the nation for rejecting the Treaty of Versailles and the country's failure to join the League of Nations and assume what Stimson saw as the proper responsibilities of the United States in the world.

Secretary of War

Taft had both political and practical reasons for asking Stimson, in May 1911, to become his secretary of war. The president hoped the appointment would help heal the divisions within the party, particularly in New York, by bringing a noted Roosevelt man into the administration. But Stimson, based on his work as a United States Attorney and well-known views on reform, was also selected on his merits. It was Taft's private secretary, Charles D. Hilles, who first approached Stimson about the post. He told Stimson that the

"President thinks that you are in general sympathy with his attitude which is of a 'middle-of-the-road progressive,' not running to extreme radicalism on one side or to conservatism on the other." Stimson concurred with this assessment, noting that he saw no fundamental differences between Taft's policies and Roosevelt's views.[2]

Before accepting his new job in Washington, however, Stimson informed Taft that he had to consult with Roosevelt. With relations between the former president and his hand-picked successor already strained, Stimson wanted to be sure he had Roosevelt's approval before taking a position in Taft's cabinet. Roosevelt "strongly urged" Stimson to accept, and when Mrs. Stimson expressed reluctance about joining the Taft administration, noting how "difficult it would be for her to feel any great loyalty toward that administration," Roosevelt cut her off by declaring that "the question of loyalty is settled 'by Harry's doing his best in the War Department so as to help make Mr. Taft's administration a success.' " He also noted that it would be much better for Stimson "to be spoken of as ex-Secretary of War than merely as the defeated candidate for governor." Stimson left his meeting with Roosevelt "with the feeling that I virtually carried his commission to do my best to make Mr. Taft's administration a success."[3]

The army that Stimson inherited was not, in his estimation, adequately organized or prepared for the responsibilities of a great power. Although the nation had possessions in the Caribbean, Central America, the Pacific Ocean, and Asia, new obligations under the Platt Amendment and the Roosevelt Corollary that led to interventions in Cuba, the Dominican Republic, Haiti, and Nicaragua, and trade that reached all corners of the globe, the army was still organized in the manner used to fight the Plains Wars of the late nineteenth century and thus unable to defend the country's interests from another power. The army's nearly seventy-five thousand troops were scattered throughout the nation in forty-nine different posts. In a maneuver just prior to Stimson's taking office, the army had failed after three months' effort to organize a division-size force of approximately ten thousand troops in Texas. This military unpreparedness stemmed from the general sense that there were no threats to the nation, the desire of many members of Congress to maintain outdated and unnecessary posts in their districts and states, and the lack of military planning and direction. Stimson began with the last problem. Change in one area would provide the direction and education necessary to bring about further reform and awaken the nation to its global duty.

Elihu Root had begun efforts to overcome these problems, most notably by the establishment of the General Staff in 1903. Stimson saw the General Staff as the crucial organization for the modernization of the army and set out to consolidate its position and further strengthen its role. Central to Root's General Staff was the position of the chief of staff who was responsible to the secretary of war and the president. The structure provided clear civilian control over the military, allowed officers the time and freedom to plan, centralized the direction and supervision of the several bureaus that provided the goods and services to the troops, and called for the rotation of officers between the high command in Washington and leading forces in the field. The power of the General Staff was theoretically clear on paper, but there remained sharp divisions and opposition within the army over this reorganization, and its leading opponent, Adjutant General Fred C. Ainsworth, had powerful allies in Congress. Ainsworth sought to protect the power of the bureau chiefs and the traditional ways of the army. It fell to Stimson, in conjunction with Chief of Staff General Leonard Wood, to assert the full authority of the General Staff and force the army to accept these changes. At the time of his appointment, Taft warned Stimson that he "would probably have trouble with General Ainsworth and he was ready to back [him] up" if Stimson needed it. It was a promise the president would keep.[4]

After several months of study, travel, and consultation, Stimson implemented the reforms needed to produce a modern army. His chief sources for ideas were Root, whom he relied upon for his understanding of the fundamental issues of organization, and Wood, whom Stimson saw as "one of the most far-sighted and efficient men in the service." For Stimson, the key was to create an army that contained a committed and highly trained small group of professionals who were ready to fight at once, if necessary, in case of war, and, more important, were prepared to expand indefinitely by enrolling citizen soldiers. This would provide for maximum flexibility and, in the case of an emergency, allow the rapid creation of a large force in a short period of time. To do this Stimson had to tackle three interrelated problems: the question of the lines of authority and the relationship of the General Staff to the bureaus, the organizational structure of the army and, primarily, the location of bases, and the training and length of service of soldiers.

Stimson aired his views in his first annual report of December 1911. In a modern nation, Stimson argued, a large professional army was neither wise nor efficient. Strength mainly came from productive capacity and from an army able to mobilize a trained reserve and expand its ranks. Stimson and Wood believed in short enlistments, followed by time in the reserves, and a large turnover of soldiers to achieve military training diffused throughout the population. Stimson asserted that the "discipline and training which a soldier gets in our army has elements that would be of great advantage to any citizen," and that the army should be "less and less professional and more and more closely connected with the ordinary life of our citizens."[5] The General Staff was the foundation for a sound organization, whereas the tradition of promotion based on seniority had left "much deadwood in the Army." The numerous posts scattered throughout the nation produced mere "groups of local constabulary instead of a national organization," did not follow the principles of "proper and scientific economy," and left the nation unprepared for war against a first-rate power. He likened his proposed changes to the introduction of the Taylor system used in industry for more efficiency and better production.[6]

Stimson's report drew the attention of the Congress and brought the conflict between Stimson and Wood, on the one side, and Ainsworth and his supporters, on the other, to a head. Stimson and Ainsworth had already clashed the past summer over Ainsworth's objections to Wood's assignment of some officers to recruiting stations. Ainsworth had appealed to Stimson to overturn Wood's orders, claiming that such an order was outside the Chief of Staff's jurisdiction and that it created the appearance of punishment, because some of the reassigned officers opposed Wood's ideas for change. In response, Wood wrote Stimson a lengthy memorandum arguing that the issue was the authority of the Chief of Staff over the army. Wood noted that the law established the Chief of Staff's "supervision over the Adjutant General's Department," and that Ainsworth was "a subordinate officer of the War Department" who was expected to perform his assigned duties "conscientiously and loyally in accordance with the policy and wishes of his superiors." Stimson fully backed Wood in this matter and took this opportunity to put Ainsworth on notice that he would not tolerate any more challenges to the authority of the Chief of Staff. He wrote the adjutant general that "I greatly regret and reprobate certain passages of your memorandum" challenging Wood's orders. In all cases, the "President has a right to expect that all of the officers of the Department will act as a unit."[7]

It was, as Stimson noted, "inevitable that an explosion should come" from Ainsworth that would force a final resolution to the matter. Among the reforms Stimson sought was increased efficiency of reporting and record keeping by abolishing the bimonthly muster roll and combining the biographical information it contained with other army records. Ainsworth took this as another attack on his power and the traditions of the army. In February 1912 he protested to Wood about the work of "incompetent amateurs" challenging the "vital bearing" of the muster roll on the public welfare.[8] Wood brought the memorandum to Stimson who, upon reading it and "seeing its character," instructed Wood to turn the matter over to him.

Stimson contacted the Judge Advocate General, General Enoch Crowder, to ascertain what disciplinary measures the law allowed. Crowder suggested that there were two methods, an administrative punishment or a court-martial, and recommended the former be employed. Stimson, determined to "find out whether the army was ready to stand for the kind of language that General Ainsworth had used as proper language for a subordinate to use to a superior," immediately decided to court-martial Ainsworth. He told Crowder that he "preferred to use a big gun rather than a little gun," and that he "believed in striking hard." Stimson next consulted with Root and informed Taft of his plans. Root told Stimson that "when a man pulls your nose there is nothing to be done but to hit him," and advised that he should make his opening blow as swift and complete as possible. Taft told his secretary of war that "it has fallen to you to do a dirty job which your predecessors ought to have done before you." Taft's complete support, and keeping his word at some political cost, was the type of loyalty that Stimson admired and would repay.

As soon as the paper work was prepared, Ainsworth was relieved of his responsibilities and preparations for the trial began. Following Root's advice, Stimson sent Ainsworth a seven-page letter that quoted their earlier correspondence and the actions that Stimson found necessitated a court-martial. Stimson, "knowing Ainsworth's reputation as a fighter" and numerous political allies, expected a battle. Ainsworth, however, quickly gave in. A cabinet meeting the next day was interrupted by word that Ainsworth's good friend, Senator F. E. Warren, wanted to talk with the president. When Taft returned to the room he said, "Ainsworth wants to retire. How is it? Good riddance?" Stimson agreed, as long as it was done immediately. He concurred with Root that this was the "best possible result" and wrote to his father that "I could not have arranged it better if I had had control over his actions myself."

Ainsworth's decision not to fight harmed his reputation in the army, as it demonstrated that he was wrong, and thus made it much easier for Stimson and Wood to assert the ultimate authority of the General Staff. It also, Stimson believed, "enabled the department to work as a harmonious team."[9]

Stimson's victory over Ainsworth did not, however, clear the way for all of his reforms. The secretary spent seven months fighting Ainsworth's allies in Congress who sought to use the Army Appropriations bill as a way to remove General Wood, reestablish the power of the bureaus, and make the army a force for lifetime professionals only. Stimson, with the assistance of Root, defeated all these efforts by persuading Congress to remove these provisions, and having President Taft veto the bill once and threaten to do so again if the same provisions reappeared. When the bill was finally passed and signed in August, Stimson had been able to remove all of the "vicious substantive legislation." The final bill was, to Stimson, "important constructive legislation" that included the consolidation of many of the bureaus for reasons of efficiency, an enlistment provision that met Stimson's desire for a shorter term and provided the "first step towards creating a regular army reserve," and a protection of the right of the president to select his own Chief of Staff.[10]

Although the issues of the authority of the General Staff and the creation of a reserve force had been settled, Stimson was unable to persuade Congress to consolidate the various army posts to effect better organization, efficiency, and training. He concluded "that even in the moderate reforms that we have been working at we have been too radical" for some and have tried to do too much at once. "The only way by which rational military progress can be made . . . is to keep the educational lamp set by the General Staff steadily burning, developing the chart by which we must advance, and then take one step at a time whenever the occasion offers."[11]

In order to continue what he saw as rational progress for the army and to get around the parochial and obstructionist actions of Congress, Stimson took his next step through executive action. He ordered a tactical reorganization of the army that created a divisional structure for the units spread across the country. Stimson's plan to organize the army into four divisions allowed the commanding generals of each unit to begin to coordinate the training and equipping of their forces for their probable use in war. Stimson held a series of conferences with every active officer of the army to persuade them of the value of reorganization. It was not necessary,

Stimson believed, to enlarge the army, but rather to place "its establishment upon a proper system—one fitted for war as well as peace; one which will change our present force from disconnected groups of armed men into a properly balanced and integral body." Even though the army would remain physically scattered until Congress provided the funds to bring the units together, it was a sound plan that, along with the General Staff and the creation of shorter enlistments with a reserve, allowed for the creation of the modern army.[12]

Stimson's reorganization plan quickly proved its effectiveness when first tested by developments in the Mexican Revolution. The fighting in Mexico had already spilled over the border in 1911 and led to the deaths of a half-dozen Americans in El Paso. Stimson strongly believed "that such occurrences should not be allowed again and that our Government ought to have taken more drastic measures . . . to prevent it." He fully supported the arms embargo against Mexico that Taft adopted to prevent American weapons from being used in revolutionary attacks against the new Mexican president, Francisco Madero. He saw the question of protecting American interests would be a difficult one and hoped that Madero could strengthen his grip on power and "hold the forces of law and order together." If not, "and the very worst should happen and it should become necessary for the United States to take action," he was prepared to use force.[13]

Following an attack against Madero in early 1913, the Taft administration decided, in the president's final days in office, that a show of American power was necessary to protect American citizens, property, and territory. Battleships were dispatched to Vera Cruz and a full division of the army was ordered into Texas in case it was needed. Stimson strongly supported these moves even as he hoped there would be no need for direct intervention. "Either Madero or [his opponents] ought to get definitely on top in a day or two, and that will probably mean the total elimination of the other." Moreover, as he wrote his father, "I should hate to have an interesting war break out just as I am going out with all the fun to go to my successor! It has been very dramatic coming just as it did on top of the completion of our new organization."[14] Prior to reorganization, it would have been necessary first to create in Washington the entire force by assigning various units to a new division, and then to send out literally several hundred orders to bring it together. Now, as Stimson informed Taft, "only a single order is necessary; namely to mobilize the First Brigade which has already been created under the new plan of organization" and send it to Texas. The Mexico crisis offered a timely demonstration of the value of Stimson's tactical reorganization plan and ensured its final acceptance by the army.[15]

Colonial Secretary

As Felix Frankfurter noted at the time, the secretary of war was also the nation's colonial secretary, and Stimson was actively concerned about the governance of America's insular empire and the Panama Canal.[16] Here again he sought to build on the work of Theodore Roosevelt and Elihu Root, to implement and oversee their paternalistic vision of empire, and, as he saw it, to demonstrate the benefits the United States could bring to the world. In their views on Latin Americans and Filipinos there was little difference between Roosevelt and Stimson. Both believed in a racial hierarchy that placed whites at the top and all other peoples below in terms of intelligence and ability to govern themselves. By the beginning of the twentieth century, Social Darwinism and other quasi-scientific ideas had become central components of American thinking about the world. American officials likened people in the less-developed countries to children who were unable to care for themselves and needed protection and guidance.

Roosevelt believed that through historical development Anglo-Saxons had reached a more advanced state than any other people, and with this progress came the responsibility of directing the development of others. He declared that "what has taken us thirty generations to achieve," in terms of preparation for democratic rule, "we cannot expect to see another race accomplish out of hand." Referring to Filipinos, Roosevelt stated that they were starting "very far behind the point which our ancestors had reached even thirty generations ago. In dealing with the Philippine people we must show both patience and strength. . . . We hope to do for them what has never before been done for any people of the tropics—to make them fit for self-government after the fashion of the really free nations." He found them "utterly incapable of existing in independence." Stimson fully agreed with Roosevelt's assumptions and assertions. In general, U.S. officials dismissed Latin Americans as "usually lazy, insolent," and "only partially civilized." Due to the "Latin temperament and climate," and the "low racial quality" of the people, new diplomats were instructed that they should not expect modern democracy in any of the nations of Latin America.

These peoples needed to be guided and could be influenced toward proper behavior because they were "very easy people to deal with if properly managed." Latinos allegedly "responded well to patience" and could, therefore, be protected from their own ignorance.[17]

Prior to making his first trip to the Caribbean to inspect the progress of the construction of the Panama Canal and to visit Puerto Rico, the Dominican Republic, Haiti, and Cuba, Stimson sought out Roosevelt's advice and ideas while escorting him home on horseback after a dinner at Highhold. Roosevelt strongly encouraged him to take Mabel Stimson on the trip because he knew "that in the Latin American countries they particularly appreciate having a high visiting official bring his wife. It makes them feel that they are treated as social equals." More important, a visit by the secretary of war to the region was good because "nothing could have a healthier or more steadying influence . . . than the visit of a warship . . . to Havana and San Domingo. Those countries can remain independent always if only they will not be too foolish, will not contract debts they cannot pay, and will not indulge in revolutions; and it is a good thing for them, and tends to promote sobriety, to see the power of the United States tangibly expressed before their eyes."[18]

For Stimson, the main concern was to keep U.S. policy focused on the development of the people under American tutelage, and to keep those under American rule from concerning themselves with political issues. "In such a problem as we have in the Philippines and in our other insular possessions," Stimson wrote in 1911, "it is of great importance that the attention of the people should be directed to material improvement and better business methods," and not to matters of governance and independence. "The temptation of the Latin American people had nearly always been towards over attention to political thought and discussion and under attention to commerce and business." He was particularly concerned with the "crudeness" of their methods of production and the "tremendous room for improvement that there is in that respect." It was "the duty" of the United States to improve these systems and help these areas develop. Stimson was not overly "afraid of paternalism in these respects," and he believed that the United States had "a tremendous amount to learn, for instance from the Germans, and it is in the direction of how much can be accomplished for a nation in trade by paternalism—if intelligent cooperation between the Government and the individual merchants is paternalism."

Concerning the Philippines, he found that the problems the United States faced in helping its people were made more complicated by the "backwardness of the Filipinos" and their "crude and undeveloped land tenure" system. It was, therefore, important that the United States oversee their economic development in order to prepare them for self-rule. "If we do our duty to the Philippine Islands," Stimson believed, "it will be necessary for us to stay there for a long time yet, and it will be necessary that the Americans who go there shall be as good a class as possible and shall retain their virility and character during their long sojourn into the tropics."[19]

In the Caribbean, Stimson saw the Panama Canal as one of the greatest achievements of the nation and proof of its beneficial role for mankind in terms of material and scientific progress. It would be a great commercial waterway that would benefit all nations, while also serving as a vital military installation for the United States. He believed, therefore, that the Canal Zone should remain under the direct rule of the United States with "an executive or administrative government rather than an attempt to form a local republic."[20] He wanted to be sure that once the canal was finished an effective and efficient administration was in place. He was most optimistic about Puerto Rico, where he found the "pleasure loving, volatile and altogether attractive inhabitants" responding well to the direction of American officials. They were devoting their "attention to developing the methods of production, business and commerce" of the island, and the result was "already marked" by the time Stimson visited in 1911. "The people are no longer talking politics as much as they were but are talking business," and he recommended that the United States increase the opportunities for industrial education.[21]

Stimson found Cuba to be full of "intrigue and unrest" and vigorously defended the necessity of the Platt Amendment. He lectured local officials on the Platt Amendment, stating that it represented "a declaration of American policy" and the right of the United States to demand certain policies and to intervene when necessary to maintain order and good government in Cuba. This is what the "American Government intended it should mean and . . . the proposal to treat the relations of the United States and Cuba under it as if they were the relations of wholly independent nations under an ordinary treaty was impossible." Stimson found the most cause for despair in the Dominican Republic and Haiti. He lamented that he never felt "more sorry" for any group of American officials than those trying to accomplish the "very useful work" of the United States "under the most trying circumstances." Blocking all of their efforts "was the pall of the negro despotism of the island. You suddenly realized after a little experience what these men were contending against." The whole island was "weighed down by a far more hopeless population than existed on it when Columbus discovered it four hundred years ago."[22]

On leaving office, Stimson vigorously defended American colonial policy and interventions. In the Philippines, Stimson argued that the United States had "introduced law and order and justice among Moro tribes of a character more bloodthirsty than any of the Indian tribes we had to deal with on this continent." The islands were made up of "savage and uncivilized races." Yet, Stimson proclaimed, "great general progress" was being made in education, medicine, and sanitation "in spite of the conservatism of a backward peoples, opposing in their ignorance and superstitions every effort towards modern" ways. None of this could have been accomplished if the Filipinos had been left to govern themselves. To Stimson, self-rule would ensure a return to the "state of anarchy and turmoil and constant rebellion and fighting" that marked Spanish control; and he had no doubt "that the work of pacification was necessary and in the interest of the race as a whole." Indeed, Stimson believed "that American history presents no nobler page of high ideals and difficult duty worthily performed than does the history of our government in the Philippines."[23]

Similarly, Stimson believed that "notable progress" continued to be made in Puerto Rico in terms of education and commerce, and that the special efforts "for the promotion of vocational and industrial training" were necessary and successful. He hoped that the residents of Puerto Rico would soon be granted American citizenship because it was "amply earned by sustained loyalty on the part of the inhabitants." This should not, however, lead to statehood. Puerto Rico should gain the fullest possible legal and fiscal self-government, with citizenship serving as a bond with the United States, but the island should stay under the rule of the federal government. Stimson thought this would bring the "economic and political benefits of being under the American flag" to Puerto Rico, while continuing the guidance and order provided by colonial rule. Stimson opined that, as was true in the Philippines, "it takes a long time and much experience to ingrain political habits of steadiness and efficiency. Popular self-government ultimately must rest upon common habits of thought and upon a reasonably developed public opinion. No such foundations for self-government, let alone independence," were yet present in America's possessions. It remained the duty of the United States to provide political guidance and stability to allow for the cultivation of orderly political habits, education, and economic development. Finally, the near completion of the Panama Canal provided reason for celebration. Stimson reported to Taft that, "Although the official date of the opening has been set for January 1, 1915, the Canal will, in fact, . . . be opened for shipping during the latter half of 1913." All the necessary "provisions for executive responsibility in the management of the Canal and the government of the Canal Zone" were in place. Stimson believed that the record of American intervention abroad was truly unassailable.[24]

Staying with Taft

Stimson, having been appointed secretary of war in large part due to his relationship with Theodore Roosevelt, found himself caught in the middle of the split in the Republican Party when Roosevelt decided first to challenge Taft for their party's nomination for president and then, in defeat, bolted the party to make an independent run for the presidency. To Stimson, Roosevelt's decision was unnecessary and wrong. He could not see any fundamental differences between the political views of Taft and Roosevelt and he hoped that TR would put party unity and national issues above his personal differences with the president. When that failed, Stimson remained loyal to the president he was serving.

The first indication Stimson had that there were any problems between Roosevelt and Taft came when he visited Roosevelt soon after the latter's return from his trip to Africa and Europe in 1910. Roosevelt clearly felt slighted by what he saw as Taft's ingratitude for his assistance during the 1908 campaign, and he was hurt by the claim, filed in the government's suit against the steel trust, that stated Roosevelt had been deceived in 1907 when he allowed U.S. Steel to absorb the Tennessee Coal and Land Company. Sensing danger in the growing estrangement, Stimson worked hard, before joining the Taft administration and after, to reconcile the positions of the two men and to prevent Roosevelt from breaking with Taft. He urged Roosevelt as early as September 1910 to state his support for Taft in order to avoid any unfounded speculation about his desire to break away from the Republican Party. All he needed to do was "emphasize the continuity" of his and Taft's reform program publicly. Moreover, he reminded Roosevelt that Taft was "now the official head" of the party. Concerning the steel trust case, Stimson assured TR that "Taft had not been consulted in regard to the allegation of the bill . . . and knew nothing about it until the bill was filed."[25]

Once he joined the Taft administration, Stimson remained in close contact with Roosevelt, often seeking his advice and support on various matters. As speculation grew in late 1911 and early 1912 that Roosevelt intended to run for the presidency, Stimson always, based on his contacts and conversations with Roosevelt, denied that his neighbor and friend had any such intent. In order to make sure that Roosevelt knew the reasons many of his friends did not want him to run and in the hope of putting the rumors to rest, Stimson traveled from Washington to Sagamore Hill with Secretary of the Navy George Meyer on January 7, 1912, to press his case. Meyer emphasized that only the Democrats would benefit from a Roosevelt–Taft split and that it would harm the party's efforts at reform. Stimson then spoke frankly to Roosevelt about his concern with both the political situation and Roosevelt's reputation. People, he told Roosevelt, will think you treated Taft unfairly and turned against a friend. The citizenry also could not see any rationale for a third term. Stimson left convinced that "under no circumstances, would he become a candidate for the presidency." He believed Roosevelt agreed with him that it would be a betrayal of the Republican Party and of Roosevelt's own interests and policies. Moreover, he still could not see any issue of principle or policy that divided Roosevelt from Taft and justified a split.[26]

Yet Stimson kept hearing from various sources that Roosevelt was under great pressure to run and that he was wavering in his conviction. Demonstrating a level of self-confidence and stature that indicated he was no longer operating in the shadows of Root and Roosevelt but rather as an equal, Stimson wrote Roosevelt a letter on February 7 to make the case against a split with Taft once more. In his usual honest and straightforward manner, Stimson told Roosevelt that he had no doubt that wild and inflammatory charges would be leveled against him should he decide to run. There is "among the best people in the country a very wide and strong feeling against anything that can be under any pretext labeled a third term." Furthermore, Stimson did not see "any such issue in official policy between you and Mr. Taft as would justify it," or any reason Roosevelt should sacrifice his good name and endure such criticism.[27]

Roosevelt, however, had made up his mind, and he officially declared his candidacy later that month. Stimson was bitterly disappointed and angry with Roosevelt. He knew the fight between the two men would lead to a Republican defeat and the loss of friendships, but Stimson never doubted that his loyalty had to be with Taft. The president had supported him on all issues, was the head of the party, and, in Stimson's estimation, had remained faithful to the reform cause. There was never any doubt in his mind that his proper course was to stay with Taft. As Stimson put it, "In the first place I had not gone in myself with any political commission, but had gone in to make as good a Secretary of War as I could." In addition, "I had gone in with that express commission from Roosevelt. When he now turned against the President I could no more resign than I could openly come out against the President. Either one would have been rank disloyalty."[28]

Stimson, therefore, wasted little time in making his position clear. He wrote his father the day Roosevelt announced his candidacy that he was "going through about as tough a time as I have ever had." He found it strange "to be speaking for Taft as against Roosevelt. But when I sit down to analyze it my course is perfectly clear, and it is not I who have changed." Moreover, he "could not remain silent whether in or out of the cabinet without losing my self respect . . . and as I think Roosevelt's candidacy . . . is a great mistake, I shall say so." He told others that he was "of course, going to support the president. I think his administration had been clean, capable, and progressive, and that to repudiate it would be to give countenance to very unjustified criticisms and slander." He had advised Roosevelt, and those who urged him to run, that his candidacy would damage the progressive cause and the positions Roosevelt believed in by splitting the party. "Such a course is bound to make the pendulum swing back into destructive reaction."

He wrote Roosevelt the week after his announcement to inform him of his position and of a speech he was to make in Chicago. "As you can easily imagine," Stimson began, "the past week or so has not been a very happy one for me. There is no use pretending that I was not surprised or that I don't feel that you have made a mistake; for I do." He told Roosevelt that he thought Taft should be renominated and that he would say that in his speech. In it, he declared that he had entered public life due to Roosevelt's inspiration and policies, and that he thought of him as a dear friend, but that his candidacy was "jeopardizing instead of helping the real cause of progress in the nation" and would weaken the party no matter who gained the nomination. As Stimson noted, he was "a poor hand at keeping quiet or balancing on a fence," but he wanted Roosevelt to know that he was not going "to change his views of or friendship for [him] and I trust you won't of me." Although Roosevelt responded that he was not concerned about Stimson's position and that he had always told Stimson he had to support Taft, he did criticize him as ungrateful in speaking to the press and broke off their friendship.[29]

In the end, for Stimson, Roosevelt was wrong for both political and personal reasons. He concluded that "it was not principle but personality, not purpose but method," that divided Roosevelt from Taft. There was "no real issue of political principle between the two men" that could justify Roosevelt's "sacrificing personal loyalty to a friend and to an administration which was his own child." Roosevelt had violated the highest values, the code of honor that Stimson lived by, and this made his actions unjustifiable no matter what shortcomings, perceived or real, existed in the Taft administration. In Stimson's eyes, however, Roosevelt's greatest sin was his attack on Root, who had also remained loyal to the incumbent administration. Stimson noted that Root, out of loyalty to the party and a sitting president, placed himself at the "storm center in support of a man whose mistakes and shortcomings as President he saw most clearly and against a man whom he had known a great deal longer and for whom he had a warm personal regard." Roosevelt "owed Root politically and personally more than he owed any man on earth." Yet Roosevelt could not see that Root's actions were taken for reasons of principle and publicly attacked him, accusing him of aligning himself with the most reactionary elements of the party for personal gain. As Stimson noted, the "attack on Mr. Root made a worse impression on me than anything" else Roosevelt did.[30]

The bitter campaign and Republican defeat in 1912 made it a difficult year and one of the most unhappy of Stimson's life. But the political battles did not deter him from seeing through the army reforms he sought, and while the break with TR was painful, it did not take away the satisfaction he found from the job and the changes he had brought about. All his achievements, however, could be undone by the change of administrations. Stimson was, therefore, concerned over whom the new president, Woodrow Wilson, would appoint to replace him. He feared that the position might go to a political appointee or a "second-rate man" who would seek to reverse the significant changes Stimson had won and implemented.

He wrote many friends who knew Wilson, supporting the importance of the War Department and maintaining "that the Secretary should be a man who represented the executive rather than the congressional standpoint." Just before Wilson's inauguration, the president-elect sent Hugh Wallace to visit Stimson and query him about the job in order to assist Wilson in his selection. Stimson noted that "the inquiries made showed what I suspected, that Wilson did not have the faintest idea of what the War Department was doing." Wallace returned two days later with more questions. As a result, Wallace told Stimson that "Wilson had completely changed his mind and had decided to appoint a man on the lines which [Stimson] suggested."[31]

Stimson was greatly pleased when Wilson selected Lindley Garrison, a former judge, as his successor. The two men met for several days to go over the various issues of the department, and Garrison indicated his support for the "cardinal matters" of reform instituted by Stimson. Garrison agreed with Stimson concerning the central importance of the General Staff, short-term enlistments, the creation of a reserve, tactical reorganization, the closing of undesirable posts, and the consolidation of bases. He even kept General Wood as his Chief of Staff. As Stimson wrote in June 1913, Garrison had supported him on all the major points, and he accepted the army reorganization plan "as *fate accompli* [sic] and seemed very grateful for it."[32]

Colonel Stimson

The outbreak of the Great War in August 1914 shocked the Western world and had an immediate impact upon the United States. To Stimson, it marked the end of an era and the beginning of a new period in American history by bringing the United States directly into European affairs. It also reconfirmed his internationalism and his conviction that the United States had had to modernize its military, and it reinforced his sense of accomplishment in having tried to prepare the nation for the role of world leader. He would devote the rest of his life to making the nation aware of the changed realities of international events and their impact on the United States and grappling with the problems of this new national status.

From the beginning of the fighting, Stimson's sympathies, like much of the nation's, were clearly with the Allies and their cause. He had learned as a child from his father and the time they spent in Europe to distrust the German Empire, while at the same time he became an admirer of France and Great Britain. He also fully supported Wilson on neutrality in the early years of the war. While he denounced the Germans for their violations of neutral rights, he still agreed with the president that it was important for the United States to stay out of the fighting as long as its rights as a neutral were respected. He was, however, willing to use force if the Germans violated those rights. As he declared in a speech at New York's Carnegie Hall in June 1915, "The progress of our race towards civilization has not been along the smooth pathway of logic. We have not succeeded in abolishing war in the name of its inhumanity and in substituting for it a rule of peace and reason. Instead of that, we have struggled along, gradually narrowing and restricting the area of war as we have grown less and less willing to endure its ravages. . . . Now by far the greatest advance which has been thus slowly made in putting brakes on the savagery of war has been in the development of the rights of the neutral . . . buffers of civilization against the shocks of war." Like Wilson, he believed that, for the time being, the United States had to remain neutral to become the upholder of civilization and allow for the continuation of the gradual progress toward peace.[33]

Stimson retained these views for both the ideological reasons noted in his speech and from practical concerns. Few people were more aware than the ex-secretary of war of how poorly prepared the United States was for a major war. For all his efforts and success at reform, the American Army was still unprepared and ill-equipped for battle against a European power. Stimson, therefore, became an immediate advocate for more military improvements and a leader in the movement for preparedness. He supported General Wood in his efforts at Plattsburgh, New York, to train civilian leaders to become officers, visiting the camp in 1914 and 1915, and enrolling himself for a month in 1916. Moreover, he called for a system of universal military training. Stimson argued that the advances in military weapons and tactics since the Civil War "made it necessary, in order to adequately defend the country, to begin training one's army before the outbreak of war." Stimson performed so well at Plattsburgh that he was pronounced fit for service despite being almost fifty and nearly blind in one eye. His efforts to rally the nation to greater military spending and a universal draft brought about a reconciliation in 1915 with Theodore Roosevelt, who was also a leading proponent of preparedness. Stimson considered Roosevelt's efforts to rally the country to a stronger stand against Germany as one of his greatest moments.[34]

From the outset, Stimson saw the war as being about more than the rights of neutrals. As he had noted in his Carnegie Hall speech, Stimson perceived the fundamental issue of the war as a question of the survival of democracy and civilization. He wrote in 1914 that he was glad to see that most Americans sided with the Allies, for "they are fighting the battle of civilization to which we are committed. Germany is seeking to overthrow the fundamental postulates of that civilization." He also praised the manner by which Wilson had "phrased his expressions of neutrality." By 1916, however, Stimson believed that war was inevitable, that Wilson was not taking a strong enough stand on preparedness, and that the president would make a poor leader in the troubled times ahead. He feared Wilson would back a congressional proposal to use the National Guard as the vehicle to expand the nation's forces rather than the regular army and the reserves. When Secretary of War Garrison resigned in early 1916 over Wilson's failure to oppose the congressional plan, Stimson wrote a series of highly critical letters to the *New York Times* in which he made the case for expanding the army and pointed out the flaws in the bill to "federalize" the National Guard. Moreover, he had reached the conclusion that a German victory would be "disastrous to our foreign trade, our time-honored Monroe doctrine in the Western hemisphere, our relation to Mexico and the Panama Canal, our Republican institutions or our national solidarity as an English-speaking race." Stimson now saw Wilson's unwillingness to make an alliance with England and France as "directly postponing the cause of the world's peace."[35]

When Wilson was reelected, Stimson believed it was his duty, along with all Americans, to support the president, and willingly embarked on a two-week tour of the Midwest to speak on behalf of preparedness and the basic issues of the war. With Germany's resumption of unrestricted submarine warfare, Stimson's position and the president's once again became closely aligned. Stimson no longer spoke about neutrality as the main issue. "America," he declared, " is not going to war with Germany merely because, as one of the accidents of the great struggle raging across the water, we have suffered an incidental injury. . . . It is because we realize that upon the battlefields of Europe there is at stake the future of the free institutions of the world." The war stemmed from German autocracy, Prussianism, and an erroneous philosophy that made the use of war the basic policy of the state. Violations of the rights of neutrals were a result of this philosophy as well as the German lack of respect for or belief in individual rights versus the state. "This war had made clear," Stimson observed, "that it is the conception of the sanctity of the rights of the individual, in relation to his government, which is the life-preserver of civilization against not only absolutism but all the cruelty and barbarism" that comes from autocracy. Stimson was convinced that war was the only way to stop German militarism and, in Wilson's words, make the world "safe for democracy." Stimson fully endorsed this view and believed that "into such a struggle a man or a nation may well go with lofty faith and burning ardor."[36]

Colonel Stimson during World War I.
Henry Lewis Stimson Papers, Manuscripts and Archives, Yale University Library

Stimson, having called first for preparedness and then for war, now acted on his own advice, and at the age of forty-nine he enlisted in the army. For Stimson, this was an opportunity to overcome the disappointment of missing service in the Spanish-American War and to gain the actual combat experience that he believed would allow him to speak with more authority on military and diplomatic issues. Herbert Hoover tried to recruit him to join his relief organization, but Stimson declined. He wrote Hoover that "for six years I have been studying and thinking in terms of military problems against the inevitable crisis I have foreseen coming . . . and for two years I have been preaching to other men the duty of military service." As a result, "I could not live comfortably with my own self-respect if I did not take my share in the difficult and dangerous work that there is before this country now on the other side of the Atlantic." Using his numerous contacts in the military, Stimson was commissioned in May 1917 and assigned to the War College in Washington with an understanding that he might be able to join a field artillery unit. Stimson had, as early as 1914, and again in 1916, made serious inquiries concerning joining the army when it appeared that tensions with Mexico might escalate into armed conflict. He made arrangements through Crowder and Wood so he could gain an officer's commission and used these same channels in 1917 to obtain his new position.[37] Stimson drilled as an artillery officer early mornings and evenings while serving as a staff intelligence officer during the day. He made no secret of his extra training and his desire to become a field artillery officer so, toward the end of the summer, he was pleased to learn that his name was on the list of officers who were being recommended for promotions and assignments to the field.

The presence of a former secretary of war in the army presented something of a problem for the Wilson administration, and the current secretary of war, Newton Baker, removed Stimson's name from a list of officers recommended for field service. Even with the military expanding rapidly and a shortage of experienced officers, Baker feared that Stimson was just using his influence to gain a position for future political glory. In late August, Stimson requested a meeting with Baker and also met with Chief of Staff Hugh Scott to make his case for field service. He assured Baker that he had no political ambition and that his only desire was to serve. Within an hour of his meetings, Stimson was promoted to lieutenant colonel and assigned as second in command to the 305th Regiment, Field Artillery, 77th Division.[38]

Stimson's service with the 305th confirmed for him the correctness of all his policies as secretary of war. The military had a clear plan and was prepared to expand rapidly by training new recruits to meet the demands of the national emergency. He found the officers in his outfit, as he expected after the military reforms he passed and his experience at Plattsburgh, to be well trained, innovative, and energetic. They were able quickly to turn the conscripted soldiers, whom he found resilient, resourceful, and eager participants from all walks of life, into quality soldiers. The organization and flexibility that Stimson had provided the army was working as well as he could expect, and Colonel Stimson was anxious to lead his troops into battle and contribute to the great cause he believed the nation was fighting for.

Stimson, however, was sent to Europe ahead of his regiment first to join the 51st, a Highland Division of the British Army, for further instruction, and then to attend a school at Langres, France, for new officers. Upon completion of his training, he was reunited with his outfit in France, where they completed their final training and were ordered to the line in July 1918. Stimson's tour of duty at the front was uneventful. His unit's sector was quiet, and after only three weeks Stimson was ordered home to assume command and training of a newly formed artillery unit. Although this new assignment was a tribute to Stimson's abilities, it meant that he never faced the actual combat with his regiment that he desired. German resistance collapsed that fall, and the war ended before Stimson could return to France with his new unit. The Colonel was discharged from the army that December, greatly pleased with his service and the great military victory of his nation. Stimson would later recall that his experience during World War I was his "greatest lesson in American democracy."[39]

The vexing question for the postwar period was the means the United States should employ to best protect and further that democracy. Woodrow Wilson placed his hopes on the creation of a League of Nations that would provide the mechanism for disarmament, arbitration, and the peaceful resolution of international disagreements. Stimson, along with Root and numerous other leading Republican internationalists, also supported the idea of a League of Nations and American participation in it, but he had concerns about specific aspects of the Covenant of the League contained in the Treaty of Versailles. The main lessons of World War I were, to Stimson, easily learned. The United States could not be isolated from world affairs and must assume the responsibility of world leadership. As he wrote in February 1919, "The time is surely coming when in international law an act of aggression by one nation upon another will be regarded as an offense against the community of nations." It was important that the United States "take advantage of this time to help move the world along towards that condition of development."[40]

Stimson disagreed with Wilson over Article X of the Covenant and its provision that all member nations were obligated to "respect and preserve as against external aggression the territorial integrity and existing political integrity of all members of the League." To Stimson and Root, there were two problems with this provision. First, it appeared to them impractical, as they doubted that the United States would honor its commitment, for example, if there were a renewal of fighting in the Balkans. Such a failure would then doom the League as a viable international organization. Second, it "showed a terrible lack of appreciation of the political realities of the situation." Stimson believed that the lessons of internationalism had to be learned gradually over time by the people of the United States. This jibed with his consistent belief in gradual change, and the principle that people "are controlled not by argument or reason but by association, tradition, inheritance, habit and the consequent emotions that go with these." A more general charter, which allowed the League to develop its program and take on added obligations as it became more accepted, seemed wiser. In this manner, Stimson thought that the "slowly growing spirit of international responsibility might be fostered, unchecked by the disillusionment of broken pledges."[41]

Stimson, therefore, joined with Root to try for passage of the Treaty of Versailles and American membership in the League by attaching a series of reservations to the treaty that would address these concerns. The two men talked often throughout the first half of the year about what changes were needed to make the League of Nations acceptable to both them and the American people. In June 1919, Root submitted his reservations to the Senate, the primary one being that the United States could disclaim all obligation to honor any articles it found objectionable even while still ratifying the Treaty of Versailles and American membership in the League. Stimson was confident that moderate Republicans and President Wilson could agree on a compromise that was satisfactory to both sides. Root's reservations, however, were changed and augmented by Republican "irreconcilables." Led by Massachusetts Senator and Chair of the Senate Foreign Relations Committee Henry Cabot Lodge, the "irreconcilables" wanted to amend the treaty fundamentally and defeat its primary purpose of a United States entry into the League. Stimson found Lodge's additions wholly unsatisfactory, "very harsh and unpleasant in tone," and the Republican Party the main stumbling block to the ratification of a revised treaty.[42]

Instead of pushing the members of his own party harder for a more compromising stance, Stimson and the other leading internationalists in the Republican Party made what Stimson characterized as a "serious mistake" and a "blunder." After months of political debate, and Wilson's refusal, in the face of Lodge's challenge, to compromise on any aspects of the treaty, they decided that the best course of action toward securing American membership in the League of Nations was a Republican victory in the 1920 election. After failing to secure the nomination for Leonard Wood, Stimson and Root supported Warren Harding on the theory that his election would mean the ratification of the treaty with Root's reservations concerning Article X. Furthermore, Stimson joined with thirty other leading Republicans, including Charles Evans Hughes and Herbert Hoover, in signing a public statement drafted by Root that advised voters that the election of Harding was the surest way to obtain American membership in the League. To vote for the Democrats was to be asked to accept the League with the unlimited obligations of Article X, while a vote for Harding would mean membership with the proper reservations. As Stimson noted in his memoirs, "events soon proved that these men were deceived" and their faith in Harding unfounded. The new president had never actually supported American membership in the League, and the United States never joined. For Stimson, the "rejection of the League was . . . the greatest error made by the United States in the twentieth century."[43]

Still, Stimson could take satisfaction in what he had accomplished over the past decade. He had helped modernize the army by strengthening the position of the General Staff and the Chief of Staff's control over the service, changing the length of enlistment while creating a reserve force, and implementing a tactical reorganization of the army. Stimson had laid the groundwork that allowed for the mobilization of the vast military forces the United States fielded in 1917–1918 and would again amass in 1940–1945. As an officer during World War I, he witnessed the improvements from the clear lines of command in the American military training system he set up, and he would personally benefit from these changes during his second term as secretary of war during World War II. In addition, his achievements made him a national figure and one of the most prominent Republican policymakers in the nation and would open up opportunities for future assignments. His experiences had led to a greater maturity, confidence, and confirmation of his worldview. Although he thought the nation, and his party, had made a mistake in refusing to join the League of Nations, he held to his strong convictions concerning the responsibility of the United States to be actively involved in world affairs, and he still believed the country would eventually come to agree with him. Until such time as the country accepted the role in the world that Stimson envisioned, he would continue to work for gradual change, education of the nation, and the implementation of his ideas wherever he could have an impact. The Colonel was ready to renew his efforts when, in 1927, he was called upon for service in Nicaragua and the Philippines by the Coolidge administration.

Notes

1. Stimson, February 1911; Stimson to Barnes, 16 May 1911, Stimson Papers, reel 23.
2. Personal Reminiscences, 1911–1912, HLSD.
3. Ibid.

4. Ibid.

5. Stimson to Bannard, 6 December 1911; Stimson to Peabody, 6 February 1912, Stimson Papers, reel 7.

6. Ibid.; Stimson to Hapgood, 3 February 1912, Stimson to Stevenson, 8 February 1912, reel 7; Root to Stimson, 7 December 1911, reel 27; Morison, *Turmoil and Tradition*, 125–26.

7. Ainsworth to Stimson, 30 August 1911, Stimson Papers, reel 25: Ainsworth memorandum, 5 September 1911; Wood to Stimson, 8 September 1911; Stimson to Ainsworth, 19 September 1911, reel 26.

8. Morison, *Turmoil and Tradition*, 128.

9. Personal Reminiscences, 1911–1912, HLSD; Stimson to Ainsworth, 14 February 1912, Stimson Papers, reel 9; Stimson to Lewis Stimson, 19 February 1912, reel 28.

10. Personal Reminiscences, 1911–1912, HLSD; Stimson, 23 August 1912; Stimson to Taft, 24 August 1912, Stimson Papers, reel 8.

11. Stimson to Denison, 17 July 1912, Stimson Papers, reel 10.

12. Personal Reminiscences, 1911–1912, HLSD; Stimson, 23 August 1912, Stimson Papers, reel 8; Stimson, 1 February 1913, reel 10.

13. Stimson to Garfield, 15 February 1912, Stimson Papers, reel 7; Personal Reminiscences, 1911–1912, HLSD.

14. Stimson to Lewis Stimson, 13 February 1913, Stimson Papers, reel 31.

15. Personal Reminiscences, 1911–1912, HLSD.

16. Felix Frankfurter and George Shelton, "Secretary Stimson's Administration of the War Department: A Review," Stimson Papers, reel 140.

17. David Schmitz, *Thank God They're on Our Side* (Chapel Hill: University of North Carolina Press, 1999), 21–29.

18. Personal Reminiscences, 1911–1912, HLSD.

19. Stimson to Forbes, 1 September 1911, Stimson Papers, reel 9.

20. Stimson to Roosevelt, 18 November 1911, ibid., reel 7.

21. Personal Reminiscences, 1911–1912, HLSD; Stimson to Forbes, 1 September 1911, Stimson Papers, reel 9.

22. Personal Reminiscences, 1911–1912, HLSD.

23. Stimson to Parkhurst, 21 February 1913, Stimson Papers, reel 31.

24. Stimson, Memorandum for Taft, November 1912, ibid., reel 30.

25. Stimson to Roosevelt, 2 September 1910, ibid. reel 19; Personal Reminiscences, 1911–1912, HLSD.

26. Personal Reminiscences, 1911–1912, HLSD.

27. Stimson to Roosevelt, 7 February 1912, Stimson Papers, reel 7.

28. Personal Reminiscences, 1911–1912, HLSD.

29. Stimson to Lewis Stimson, 26 February 1912, Stimson Papers, reel 28; Stimson to Shattuck, 2 March 1912; Stimson to Gill, 15 March 1912, reel 7; Stimson to Roosevelt, 3 March 1912; Roosevelt to Stimson, 5 March 1912, reel 28; Stimson and Bundy, *On Active Service*, 51.

30. Stimson and Bundy, *On Active Service*, 53; Personal Reminiscences, 1911–1912, HLSD.

31. For an example of Stimson's letters, see Stimson to Williams, 31 December 1912, Stimson Papers, reel 8; Personal Reminiscences, 1911–1912, HLSD.

32. Stimson to Palmer, 2 June 1913; Stimson to Garrison, 9 May 1913, Stimson Papers, reel 6.

33. Stimson and Bundy, *On Active Service*, 85.

34. Stimson to Crowder, 10 December 1915, Stimson Papers, reel 42; Stimson and Bundy, *On Active Service*, 87, 91.

35. Stimson to Denison, 4 November 1912, Stimson Papers, reel 37; Stimson to *New York Times*, 12 February 1916 and 20, 21, 22 March 1916; Stimson to Root, 9 May 1916, reel 44.

36. Stimson to Grinnell, 10 May 1917, Stimson Papers, reel 48; Stimson and Bundy, *On Active Service*, 89–90.

37. Stimson to Hoover, 16 and 18 May 1917, Stimson Papers, reel 49; Stimson to Root, 23 April 1914; Stimson to Root, 7 May 1914, reel 35; Root to Stimson, 11 July 1916, reel 45.

38. Stimson and Bundy, *On Active Service*, 92–94.

39. Ibid., 95–100.

40. Stimson to Frankfurter, 30 October 1916, Stimson Papers, reel 46; Memorandum of Talk with Root, 22 December 1918; Stimson Diary, 15 February, 5 March, and 3 June 1919, HLSD; Stimson and Bundy, *On Active Service*, 103.

41. Memorandum of talk with Root, 22 December 1918; Stimson Diary, 5 March and 3 June 1919, HLSD; Stimson and Bundy, *On Active Service*, 103.

42. Stimson Diary, 3 December 1919, HLSD.

43. Stimson and Bundy, *On Active Service*, 105, 101.

3

The White Man's Burden

Stimson believed that the Caribbean area was "the one spot external to our shores which nature has decreed to be most vital to our national safety, not to mention our prosperity." Unrest and instability in the region were, therefore, a serious problem, and it was the duty of the United States, under the Roosevelt Corollary, to find a means for maintaining the order necessary to protect the Panama Canal and American investments. Unfortunately, according to Stimson, Mexico, Central America, and the Caribbean nations were the areas "where the difficulties of race and climate have been greatest."[1] This had led to the sending of American forces no fewer than twelve times and into seven different nations there during the first two decades of the twentieth century, and to the United States maintaining the financial supervision of three nations, the Dominican Republic, Haiti, and Nicaragua. Yet these actions did not solve the problems of unrest and political instability. As Stimson lamented, the situation did not improve even after American involvement. He was greatly concerned with the "bad way in which all of Latin America is showing up." Disorder was growing, "yet if we try to take the lead for them, at once is a cry against American domination and imperialism."[2]

Other American officials echoed Stimson's concerns. For example, Charles Evans Hughes, who served as secretary of state from 1921 to 1925, argued that in terms of policy toward Latin America, U.S. "interests do not lie in controlling peoples. Our interest is in having prosperous, peaceful, and law abiding neighbors with whom we can cooperate to mutual advantage."[3] Trouble kept erupting and forcing American intervention, due to the shortcomings of Latin Americans. "It is revolution, bloodshed and disorder that bring about the very interposition for the protection of lives and property that is the object of so much objurgation" and bring about the cries of imperialism by Latin Americans.[4] Stimson dismissed the charges of imperialism as a misunderstanding of the American desire to prevent revolutions and financial crises by providing leadership and order in the region.

Stimson, therefore, believed that the United States had to find new means to establish order in the region and protect American interests if it were to continue to take the lead. Military interventions had failed to provide a long-term solution and further exacerbated the problem of instability. In addition to being costly, sending American forces raised anti-U.S. sentiment in the region and fostered continued unrest. The crisis in Nicaragua in the late 1920s provided Stimson with an opportunity to carry out his ideas and implement a new approach in Latin America. President Calvin Coolidge dispatched him to Nicaragua in 1927 to mediate the civil war that had broken out and to find a long-term solution that would provide stability and order. The quest for order within a framework acceptable to Washington, but without direct American intervention, led Stimson to turn to a greater reliance on local elites, indigenous forces, and, if necessary, dictatorships in the region.

Stimson's actions were central to the development in the 1920s of the American policy of supporting right-wing dictatorships in response to the broad revolutionary challenges from the Bolshevik and Mexican uprisings. American policymakers came to support authoritarian governments that promised stability, anti-Bolshevism, and trade with the United States. In searching for a policy between continued military intervention and complete self-determination for Nicaragua, the specter of Bolshevism and the argument that the people of Nicaragua were not yet ready for complete independence were invoked to justify American actions. Stimson's decisions in Nicaragua, therefore, served as the precursor to Roosevelt's Good Neighbor policy and American behavior toward Latin America for much of the twentieth century. His approach allowed for the continuation of American dominance and imposed stability while still upholding the pledge of nonintervention.

The Coolidge administration also called upon Stimson for service in the Philippines. Tensions had been growing in America's largest colony for over a decade, with a movement for independence and criticism of American imperialism developing in both the United States and the Philippines. Stimson again dismissed the critics of American policy in the Philippines as naive or trouble-makers and set out to demonstrate what he considered the positive accomplishments brought about by the United States in shoulder-ing its proper responsibilities toward the Filipinos. He did not be-lieve that the Filipinos were ready for independence, or that any responsible person on either side of the Pacific could sincerely be-lieve that the Philippines would be better off detached from the United States. To carry out his paternalistic vision of an empire, Stimson again turned to a close collaboration with local elites to maintain order, stability, and a pro-American government.

That Stimson so often asserted American innocence of imperi-alism is telling, but the real significance lies in his narrow view of the proper relationship between the United States and the nations of Latin America and East Asia. Stimson's belief in the value of American leadership and the need to impose order, stability, and adherence to American wishes provided him with an optimism and confidence that U.S. intervention was always beneficial to other nations. Although his supreme confidence in his ideas and values, along with his unquestioned commitment to American leadership and gradual reform, had served him well both in his private life and during his tenure as secretary of war, it also closed him off from other ideas and experiences and led to inflexibility or unwill-ingness to entertain other perspectives. Stimson had an instinct for disregarding the views of those who challenged his belief in Ameri-can duty and responsibility to the world. Even though he did not know any Spanish and had never spent time studying the history or problems of Nicaragua or the Philippines, Stimson assumed he could speak for other peoples and knew what was best for them. He believed in the universal nature and application of American laws, institutions, and values, and in the need for Americans to transmit them properly to other peoples. His work in Nicaragua and the Philippines illustrated the persistence of the ideas justify-ing U.S. expansion at the end of the nineteenth century and how these ideas were adjusted and modified to meet changing condi-tions and to legitimize U.S. intervention and leadership in a postcolonial world. His service also demonstrated the limitations of Stimson's thinking about American foreign policy in Latin America and Asia, as the United States adopted its policy of sup-porting right-wing dictatorships despite its avowed commitment to liberalism and democracy internationally.

Backing Authoritarian Regimes

Since the first landing of American Marines in Nicaragua in 1912, the United States had sought to impose stability on that nation. But the direct method of military intervention was paradoxically part of the problem that created instability. Hughes sought to remedy this problem through treaties with the nations of Central America. Order and respect for international law, he hoped, would ensure protection of American security and exports to all the nations of Central America. In December 1922, Hughes sponsored a conference in Washington to discuss regional stability, guarantees for order and the protection of property, and methods for combating revolutions. It was agreed by all the nations in the region that they would not recognize any governments that resulted from coups d'etat.

Although the United States did not actually sign the treaty, it agreed to abide by this provision. Hughes hoped that the treaty would remove the necessity for continued U.S. intervention. He believed that the withholding of Washington's recognition and an always-implied threat of American intervention would deter unconstitutional seizures of power, improve the stability of the region, provide protection for existing governments, and thus promote the growth of trade and economic development. That political change was possible in most of these nations only by revolution did not dissuade Hughes. Stability, the rule of law, and increased economic activity were of primary importance. Even though Hughes recognized that the "formal processes of constitutional government are so susceptible of abuse by those holding power that revolution has frequently appeared to be the only remedy," he still thought that the 1923 Washington Treaty would "promote stability" as opposed to "the side of bloodshed and disorder."[5] Stimson was convinced that the treaty had had a positive impact. Many "a contemplated revolution has been abandoned," he argued, due to "a simple reminder by a minister from this country" that, even if successful, the new government would not be recognized. "In many more cases . . . the knowledge of the existence of the policy prevented even the preparation for a revolution or *coup d'etat*."[6]

Along with internal upheavals, another potential source of trouble in the region was Mexico. Hughes feared that Mexico was involved in a "socialistic experiment," having claimed the right to confiscate land and subsoil minerals in their 1917 Constitution.[7] Relations had broken down between Mexico and the United States during the Wilson administration, and Hughes continued the policy of nonrecognition of the Obregón government. The secretary of state could not understand the Mexican position or why Mexico City refused to follow Washington's leadership. Hughes's thinking reflected the views of all leading American officials, including Stimson. There was not, according to Hughes, "the slightest reason why there should be antagonism between the peoples or the Governments of the United States and Mexico." The nature of a friendly relationship appeared obvious to him. "Mexico is a land of great resources which need development. Citizens of the United States who are not adventurers, and are not seeking opportunities of exploitation to the disadvantage of Mexico, have capital to invest. But confidence is essential to sound economic relations."[8] The problem was that Mexico's claims and constitutional provisions threatened American property and undercut any confidence in its government.

The situation only worsened during the administration of Calvin Coolidge. His secretary of state, Frank B. Kellogg, warned that Mexico's "alien land and petroleum laws" created a serious situation, which placed that nation "on trial before the world." Coolidge's ambassador to Mexico, James Sheffield, blamed the problems in their relations on the Mexicans and their "Latin-Indian mind, filled with hatred of the United States." He believed that the "main factors are greed . . . and an Indian, not Latin, hatred of all people not on the reservation. There is very little white blood in the Cabinet."[9] By 1926 the State Department had concluded that Mexico was under Soviet influence and presented a danger to the whole region. In a report entitled "Radical and Socialistic Influences in Mexico," the Division of Mexican Affairs concluded that President Plutarco Elías Calles was the "most dangerous man for the future of Mexico." "In fact, it has been stated that he is a much redder bolshevist than Lenin ever was. . . ."[10] Undersecretary of State Robert Olds claimed in November that Mexico was "seeking to establish a Bolshevik authority in Nicaragua to drive a 'hostile wedge' between the U.S. and the Panama Canal."[11] Effective barriers to this danger needed to be erected in Central America.

The outbreak of civil war in Nicaragua in late 1926 elicited fears of Mexican influence and a renewed round of American intervention that culminated in the emergence of the military dictatorship of Anastasio Somoza García. The fighting centered on the contested presidency of Nicaragua. In 1924, a coalition party of Conservatives and Liberals had defeated Emiliano Chamorro, only to be overthrown the next year by Chamorro and his supporters. Chamorro, whom the United States refused to recognize under the 1923 treaty, was himself forced from power in 1926 and replaced by the Conservative Adolfo Díaz. The former vice president from the 1924 election, Liberal Juan Sacasa, with the support of Mexico, claimed that the presidency rightly belonged to him and began a military campaign to oust Díaz.

The United States indicated its preference by recognizing Díaz and again dispatching troops, which had only been withdrawn from Nicaragua the previous year. Coolidge told the press in December 1926 that American intervention was necessary because "there is a revolution going on there and whenever a condition of that kind exists in Central American countries it means trouble for our citizens that are there and it is almost always necessary for this country to take action for their protection."[12] Olds pointed out the historical reasons for the Coolidge administration's actions in a memorandum prepared on January 2, 1927:

> The Central American area down to and including the Isthmus of Panama constitutes a legitimate sphere of influence for the United States. . . . Our ministers accredited to the five little republics stretching from the Mexican border to Panama . . . have been advisors whose advice has been accepted virtually as law . . . we do control the destinies of Central America and we do so for the simple reason that the national interest absolutely dictates such a course. . . . At this moment a deliberate attempt to undermine our position and set aside our special relationship in Central America is being made. The action of Mexico in the Nicaraguan crisis is a direct challenge to the United States. . . . We must decide whether we shall tolerate [Mexican interference] or insist upon our own dominant position. . . . Until now Central America has always understood that governments which we recognize and support stay in power, while those which we do not recognize and support fall. Nicaragua has become a test case. It is difficult to see how we can afford to be defeated.[13]

Drawing upon Olds's analysis, President Coolidge sent Congress a lengthy message on January 10 explaining his reasons for the reintroduction of American troops in Nicaragua. The events in Nicaragua, Coolidge claimed, "seriously threaten American lives and property [and] endanger the stability of all Central America." He invoked the obligation of the United States under the 1923 treaties to support the existing government and to oppose the Liberals' efforts to remove Díaz from power. "There is no question that if the revolution continues American investments and business interests in Nicaragua will be seriously affected, if not destroyed." Coolidge concluded, therefore, that "the United States cannot . . . fail to view with deep concern any serious threat to stability and constitutional government in Nicaragua tending toward anarchy and jeopardizing American interests, especially if such state of affairs is contributed to or brought about by outside influences or by any foreign power."[14] The American economic interest at the time amounted to almost $10 million in direct investments, mainly in the ownership of vast tracts of land to produce fruit, although the Commerce Department noted that "these may be in reality worth many times that value at some future date," because many of the land holdings were not yet developed. Its estimates ran as high as $20 million.[15] Moreover, the United States controlled Nicaragua's finances, customs revenue, and railroads.

Secretary of State Kellogg rounded out the president's analysis when he delivered a report to the Senate on January 12 entitled "Bolshevik Aims and Policies in Mexico and Latin America." The "outside influences" and "foreign power" the president referred to were identified as Bolshevism and Mexico. Kellogg argued that, through Mexico, Bolshevik leaders had set out "as one of their fundamental tasks the destruction of what they term American Imperialism as a necessary prerequisite to [a] . . . revolutionary movement in the world." Thus, support for Díaz was not only support for stability and the protection of American business in Nicaragua, but also a part of stemming the tide of international Communism.[16]

Critics, led by Senator William Borah of Idaho, castigated Kellogg and the administration for drawing the specter of Communism into the discussion on Nicaragua. Borah pointed out that the civil war was a product of internal Nicaraguan politics and charged that Kellogg's only purpose in citing Bolsheviks was to provide cover for the use of marines to protect American investments. Kellogg's analysis still provided the basis for U.S. policy, but extensive criticism of the use of troops spurred the president and the secretary of state to search for a method to resolve the conflict on terms favorable to the United States without the use of force. Toward that end, they turned to Stimson, in April 1927, to find a means to end the fighting and prevent future outbreaks of civil war.

Since the end of World War I, Stimson had spent most of his time concentrating on his law practice and private affairs. His disapproval of Harding after his betrayal on the question of the League of Nations only grew with the scandals that emerged during his presidency. Stimson kept his distance, and Harding's became the only administration between Theodore Roosevelt's and Harry Truman's that Stimson did not serve in some capacity. He returned to public service first in 1926, when the Coolidge administration called upon him twice for advice. Initially, Stimson was asked by the State Department to prepare an advisory brief concerning the territorial dispute between Chile and Peru over the provinces of Tacna and Arica. His role in the eventual settlement was minor. What is worth noting is that this problem confirmed for Stimson his long-held view that "the notion of honest elections and plebiscites is not a fruitful one in most Latin American countries in any critical issue, unless those elections or plebiscites are impartially guided by an outsider agency."[17] This was a conviction he would soon act upon in Nicaragua. He was next asked to make a visit to the Philippines and report his findings to the president. He had two meetings with Coolidge upon his return, and this assignment brought him back into the official Republican fold and led to his being sent as the president's special emissary to Managua.

Olds contacted Stimson on March 31, 1927, asking him to take on a new assignment of an "important and emergent nature." He took the train that night to Washington and met with the president the next day. After lunch with Coolidge, Stimson asked if he wanted him to be his eyes and ears in Nicaragua, to just report back and nothing more. "No," replied the president, "I want you to go somewhat further. If you find a chance to straighten the matter out, I want you to do so." Appealing to Stimson's well-known sense of duty, Coolidge told him that if he did not take on this mission, the president did not "know who I can select . . . in the U.S."[18]

Stimson spent a week reading State Department papers and talking to people, with Root the most important among them, about Nicaragua. He quickly reached the conclusion that Díaz had to be retained in office and that the United States needed to supervise the next series of elections in Nicaragua and create new institutions that would provide for long-term stability. The principal problem was getting the Liberals to accept these conditions. In his final meeting with Coolidge on April 7, Stimson stated that he considered the matter of the recognition of Díaz to be settled and that any change "would be an element of weakness" to hurt his mission. The president assured him that the United States would stand by this position. Although reluctant, the president agreed to a threat of further force if the Liberals refused to stop fighting.[19]

Upon his departure, Stimson believed he understood the problem faced by the United States in resolving the difficulties in Nicaragua. According to Stimson, Nicaraguans "were not fitted for the responsibilities that go with independence and still less fitted for popular self-government." This had been the case throughout the nineteenth century to the present, with the result being "a concentration of practically all the powers of government in presidential dictators," and with revolution being the only means to change government.[20] Upon his return from Nicaragua, Stimson concurred with Root's assessment that U.S. recognition of the independence of the Latin American states had been "premature." The Latin Americans were "admittedly like children and unable to maintain the obligations which go with independence."[21] This simplistic analysis guided the Colonel as the United States helped establish the institutions of modern Nicaragua.

Once in Nicaragua, Stimson formulated three alternatives. The United States could simply use more troops, "barren or naked American intervention," to assure Díaz's continuation in power. But that "did not get to the root of the evil." Stimson noted that, "in spite of its limited economic benefits," use of force by the United States was politically damaging. Under the previous military occupation "the country learned nothing in the way of self-government and within twenty-five days after removal of marines there was a *coup d'etat*." Blatant U.S. force would just continue the cycle of revolutions. Nor did prohibiting revolution by treaty appear to work. It merely tended to "perpetuate the power of the party or individual who happened to be in control of the government." The answer, Stimson concluded, was "constructive American intervention which would endeavor to lead the country nearer to self-government." Stimson, therefore, set out to resolve the present crisis through a new election under American supervision and the establishment of a "new and impartial police force . . . to take the place of the forces which the government was in the habit of using to terrorize and control elections." This, too, would be done under American guidance. Stimson concluded that the American restructuring of the politics and institutions of Nicaragua was "the only road by which a bloody and devastating revolution could be stopped and ballots substituted for bullets."[22]

Stimson quickly set the terms for a settlement in his meetings with both the Conservatives and Liberals. He informed them that the issue of U.S. recognition of Díaz was not negotiable. He would remain president until American-sponsored elections were held in 1928. Stimson also made his biases clear. He favored the Conservatives who were willing to follow the American lead. As he recorded in his diary, the Colonel found "all conservatives, wealthy, dreadfully frightened of liberal success." They "wanted us not only to give military protection but to run their finances in absolute US control," and he found them "frank in admitting Nicaraguan incompetence and corruption."[23] He informed Washington that "Díaz has behaved well consistently and is evidently willing to entirely subordinate his own personal interests to a constructive peace program. So far as I can see no other equally intelligent and conciliatory substitute for him could be found or even desired."[24] In addition, both sides had to accept the creation of a U.S.-trained and -commanded constabulary and the continued presence of U.S. Marines until the Guardia Nacional (National Guard) was prepared to take over peacekeeping chores. In reality, Stimson was not conducting negotiations or mediating between the two sides—he was imposing a settlement.

The Conservatives, for obvious reasons, agreed immediately to all of Stimson's demands as they would maintain their power and the protection of American forces. Negotiations with Sacasa also went well, but he did not have full authority to speak for the Liberals. The key was to get the agreement of General José Moncada who led the largest contingent of Liberal forces. Moncada finally agreed to meet Stimson on May 4 in the town of Tipitapa, on the Tipitapa River that flows between Lake Nicaragua and Lake Managua. Sitting under a thorn tree, with a contingent of some five hundred marines, Stimson opened up the negotiations. Moncada was willing to accept U.S.-supervised elections and the disarming of his forces by the marines, but he balked at the retention of Díaz as president. It was against Díaz that they had begun the civil war. Moncada's soldiers had died fighting against this presidency, and he could not ask them to accept this condition. But in the end, the Liberals had little choice. In his meeting with Moncada, Stimson left no doubt as to his commitment to Díaz. He told Moncada that "forcible disarmament would be made of those unwilling to lay down their arms," and he put the threat in writing. Furthermore, following instructions from Kellogg, Stimson informed Moncada that should the United States have to resort to force, the Coolidge administration would no longer be committed to supervising the 1928 elections. With the direct threat of more American Marines entering the fighting to force acquiescence to American terms, and no chance of removing Díaz even by election if he refused, Moncada agreed to Stimson's conditions.[25] The two men met a week later to finalize the agreement, including the payment for the weapons turned in, and Moncada agreed to end the fighting.

It was during the negotiations with the Liberals that Stimson first met Anastasio Somoza. Stimson was accustomed to deferential behavior from those he thought inferior to him, and he immediately liked Somoza who sought to ingratiate himself with the Colonel. Stimson described Somoza as a "very frank, friendly, likeable young liberal," and found, because he spoke fluent English, that Somoza "impresses me more favorably than almost any other" person.[26] So impressed was Stimson that he had Somoza act as his interpreter for a few days while he negotiated with Sacasa and prepared to meet Moncada. The contrast with his views on Augusto Sandino could not have been greater.

Stimson cabled Washington on May 15 that "the civil war in Nicaragua is now definitely ended." There was also, he noted, "less danger of banditry and guerrilla warfare than I at first feared," and the small group of remaining malcontents could not disrupt the country.[27] Yet, when the agreement was reached, Sandino, one of Moncada's generals, refused to lay down his arms and vowed to continue fighting until all American troops were withdrawn from Nicaragua. Sandino's promise to continue fighting did not, however, concern Stimson. Sandino was left out of the agreement because Stimson adopted the interpretation that Sandino was "a bandit leader" who employed "plainly unprincipled and brutal activities." He explained to the State Department that his threat to use force if the Liberal forces did not disarm was "a warning to the bandit fringe."[28] Responding to Sandino's call for social change, Stimson dismissed him as a man who "came back to Nicaragua on the outbreak of the revolution in order to enjoy the opportunities for violence and pillage which it offered."[29] He saw American policy as an unqualified success "punctuated only by sporadic outbreaks from the bandit Sandino."[30]

Stimson's views of both Somoza and Sandino were soon adopted by other American officials and shaped all American policy toward Nicaragua. Charles Eberhardt, the American Minister in Managua, wrote Kellogg that Sandino "preached communism . . . and death to the Americans until the rabble of the whole North Country joined him in his plan to massacre Americans there and to set up his own government."[31] The State Department denounced Sandino for using the "stealthy and ruthless tactics which characterized the savages who fell upon American settlers in our country

150 years ago."[32] In 1933, the State Department was still referring to Sandino and the movement he led in these same terms. A departmental overview of American policy toward Nicaragua discusses Sandino's "career in banditry" and the "chronic bandit depredations" of his followers.[33] Somoza, on the other hand, emerged as a favorite of the Americans in Nicaragua. In 1932, General Calvin Matthews, the commander of the United States training mission in Nicaragua and also the current head of the Guardia Nacional, and Matthew Hanna, the U.S. Minister to Nicaragua, backed Somoza for the position of director of the Guardia upon the approaching withdrawal of the U.S. Marines at the beginning of 1933.

Although Moncada and the Liberals won the 1928 election, stability in Nicaragua still rested with the marines and the National Guard, not the electoral process. The central goals of American policy were the elimination of Sandino and the creation of a force that could maintain stability and a friendly government once American forces were withdrawn. A democratically elected government would be a good, but not an essential, part of this policy. When Brigadier General Frank McCoy, whom Coolidge had placed in charge of the American electoral mission in Nicaragua, asked for additional troops and absolute control over both supervising the elections and training the National Guard in 1928, his requests were quickly granted. Robert Olds clearly set out the State Department priorities when he instructed McCoy that the creation of the National Guard to replace American forces was the "most vital feature of the entire [American] program." The Guard would be the "cornerstone of stability for the whole country long after the election" was over.[34] The most important institutions of modern Nicaragua, the Guardia Nacional and the National Bank of Nicaragua, Limited, whose board of directors was dominated by U.S. citizens and met in New York, were being installed along with the election rules. From this would be created a new type of military leader whom the United States would support.

Stimson retained these same views and carried through on his policy when he became secretary of state under Hoover in 1929. After the onset of the Great Depression, however, Hoover and Stimson tired of the costs and the role of direct intervention and began the gradual withdrawal of American troops. Stimson concluded that the National Guard could handle Sandino and provide stability. In 1931, over the protests of American businessmen in Nicaragua, Stimson announced that the remaining marines would be withdrawn by 1933 despite Sandino's continued attacks. In addition to his desire to end the intervention and criticisms at home and abroad, larger international problems were forcing the secretary's hand. As he wrote in his diary, a continuation of the marines' presence or other American interventions "would put me in the absolute wrong in China, where Japan has done all this monstrous work under the guise of protecting her nationals with a landing force."[35] The stability in Nicaragua was still, however, a militarily imposed one. It was now local forces and elites friendly to the United States who were in direct control, with the United States providing financial and military support.

In Nicaragua, the Americans working with the government found it difficult to get along with President Moncada. His violent temper, heavy drinking, and desire to use the Guardia Nacional against his political opponents forced them to seek out other contacts in the government. The man they turned to was Anastasio Somoza. The selection of Somoza as the head of the National Guard put him in charge of the most important institution in the country. The U.S. Marine leadership in Nicaragua worried that the Guard had no senior officers who had not been involved in previous civil wars and that the graduates of the officer Academia were young and lacked the leadership experience needed to take over from the Americans. Therefore, the American Legation suggested that the position of Jefe Director and other senior positions should be filled by the winner of the 1932 presidential election from a list of those who had had previous military experience. Political position and ties to the winning party would thus determine who became Jefe Director.

American officials backed Somoza for this position. Hanna wrote the State Department that he was the "best man in the country for the position"; General Matthews and others agreed.[36] The leading student of the formation and history of the Guardia Nacional, Richard Millett, has concluded, "The United States had given Nicaragua the best trained and equipped army it had ever known, but it had also given that nation an instrument potentially capable of crushing political opposition with greater efficiency than ever before in the nation. . . . In addition, the danger of a break between the new Jefe Director and the Nicaraguan President existed before either of them had even taken office. This represented the real heritage left by the United States when the Marines turned over command of the Guardia."[37]

Only one obstacle remained in Somoza's path to complete power: Sandino. With the withdrawal of American forces, Sandino agreed, as promised, to enter into negotiations with the government. His main requests were that the National Guard be disbanded and that power rest with the elected officials. In 1934, Somoza issued orders for Sandino to be killed. Somoza's men trapped him on the road after a meeting with Sacasa, took him and two of his generals to a field, and shot them. Somoza claimed the order had received the approval of Arthur Bliss Lane, the U.S. Minister in Nicaragua. Lane denied the charge and produced evidence that he had learned of the plan and warned Somoza not to attack Sandino. Nonetheless, even after the assassination of Sandino, Somoza remained the man the United States supported in Nicaragua. Even if the State Department did not endorse this specific act, it continued to support him.

When, in 1936, Somoza decided to take over the presidency, even though he was prohibited as the leader of the Guard, Washington did not protest. Franklin Roosevelt's Secretary of State Cordell Hull rejected pleas from Nicaraguan civilian leaders that the United States protect them from the military. He wrote that the "special relationship" between the United States and Nicaragua had ended with the final evacuation of the marines and to intervene would be in violation of the Good Neighbor policy. To act now would be interfering in Nicaragua's internal affairs.[38] Indeed, the withdrawal of American forces had made it easier for Somoza to solidify his control over Nicaragua. Fighting broke out in May 1936, and Somoza quickly seized political power. The Roosevelt administration recognized the new government and extended it economic assistance. The United States wanted stability in the region and a government that would protect American economic and strategic interests. It was the job of the National Guard, and not the elected government, to do that once the marines were withdrawn.

For Stimson, the solution had always rested on the collaboration between local elites and the United States and the creation of a force that would prevent the return of civil war in Nicaragua. The supervision of elections had apparently just furthered unrest. Turning to the local military force solved the dilemma of how to maintain order, protect American interests, and defeat Mexican-sponsored Bolshevism without having to deploy the marines. By supporting Somoza, American officials resolved the contradiction between nonintervention and retaining stability while allowing ostensible self-determination. The decision created a new type of leader in Latin America that the United States relied upon in times of upheaval. There were never free elections in Nicaragua without the U.S. Marines, and Somoza and his two sons ruled Nicaragua with American support until 1979. Stimson held to an analysis of events to the south that transformed a complex nationalistic revolt into an upheaval by irresponsible groups influenced by Communist agitators. Moreover, he believed that the Nicaraguans were unable freely to govern themselves and needed a strong hand to guide them. Within that framework, the appropriate and necessary course of action seemed clear, and Stimson saw his mission in and policy toward Nicaragua as one of his successes.

Governor General

Stimson applied the same assumptions to the Philippines. Rudyard Kipling's famous 1899 poem, "The White Man's Burden," opens with the following stanza.

Take up the White Man's Burden—
Send forth the best ye breed—
Go, bind your sons to exile
To serve your captives' need;
To wait in heavy harness
On fluttered folk and wild—
Your new-caught, sullen peoples,
Half devil and half child.

Kipling's subtitle was "The United States and the Philippine Islands." Stimson agreed with Theodore Roosevelt, who noted that it was "very poor poetry but made good sense from the expansion point of view." Since the taking of the Philippines in 1898, Stimson had fully supported American control and the idea of a national duty to "civilize" the islands' inhabitants. It fully fit his sense of noblesse oblige, of the better classes of people taking care of those less fortunate. When he was once told that his attitudes and benevolent imperialism were Kipling's notion of the "White Man's Burden," Stimson responded, "Yes, that's what it comes down to and I believe in assuming it."[39] In 1927 he would have his opportunity to act on these beliefs and carry out his ideas for bringing civilization to those he saw as his inferiors. At the age of sixty, he was not the young son sent into exile, but the willing imperialist who fully believed in his mission to serve his captives' needs.

Stimson agreed to be governor general because he was dismayed at the course the American colony had taken since his service as secretary of war and wanted to prove that with the right policies the United States could succeed in its mission to the archipelago. He believed that the United States was not fully living up to the commitments it had made in 1899 "to establish on said islands a government suitable to the wants and conditions of the inhabitants . . . , to prepare them for local self-government, and in due time to make such disposition of said islands as will best promote the interests of the citizens of the United States and the inhabitants." In addition, Stimson had now retired from the practice of law and saw the chance to go to Manila as a last adventure.[40] Little did he know that instead of being just an exotic way to begin his retirement, his service in the Philippines would lead to his return to service in Washington, D.C., as secretary of state and that his greatest contributions to the nation were still ahead of him.

Stimson believed that the Roosevelt and Taft administrations had made remarkable progress after the suppression of the Philippine insurrection by pursuing the "great political objective" of "educat[ing] the Filipinos to a constantly growing measure of democratic self-government." As he recalled in his memoirs, "Perhaps no group of white men has ever accomplished so much with a colonial people as the American officials, educators, and missionaries who went to the Philippines in the early twentieth century." He saw progress in health and sanitation, education, and economic advancement. Still, he thought more needed to be done, and that the Philippines had to remain under the care and direction of the United States. Stimson urged the Wilson administration not to change policy. As he wrote in 1912, "With all the progress of the decade, our work in the Philippines has but just commenced. Along no line, moral, mental, or material, can it be counted as completed." The effort at Americanization of the Philippines had to continue. A release from direct American supervision "would not merely retard progress . . . but would inevitably mark the beginning of a period of rapid retrogression." He concluded, "Until our work in the archipelago is completed, until the Filipinos are prepared not only to preserve but to continue it, abandonment of the Philippines, under whatever guise, would be an abandonment of our responsibility to the Filipino people and of the moral obligation which we have voluntarily assumed before the world."[41]

The Wilson administration did take a different course, and one that Stimson saw as a complete failure. The new governor general, Francis Burton Harrison, had abandoned Republican policy for one of rapid Filipinization of the governing of the islands. Harrison broke up the American control over the civil service, appointed Filipinos to numerous government posts, and allowed local officials enormous powers in making governing decisions. Stimson characterized all of this as "an astonishing abdication of the Governor General's supervisory and executive functions." Moreover, the Democrats favored granting the Philippines independence, in the words of the Jones Act of 1916, "as soon as a stable government can be established therein." Stimson believed that the administration "deliberately prostituted and debased [the] work" being conducted in the Philippines, and in so doing Wilson had "done more than any President in my recollection to debauch the national sense of duty and conscience of our own people." The result of the changes that allowed the Filipinos to take more control in their own governing and over the civil service, and to entertain the idea of independence, Stimson believed, was that "the Malay tendency to backslide promptly made itself felt with disastrous consequences," for business, banking, and the currency.[42]

The return of Republican control over policy led to efforts to reverse the actions of Harrison and to stabilize American domination over the Philippines. General Wood was sent to the islands in 1921 to reassert American sovereignty and return power within the government to American officials. As Wood saw the problem, the negative developments in business and corruption in government stemmed from "bad example, incompetent direction . . . political infection of the services, and above all to lack of competent supervision and inspection. This has been brought about by surrendering, or failing to employ, the executive authority of the Governor General." When Stimson visited the Philippines in 1926, at Wood's request, he found that Wood had been only partially successful in reestablishing the ultimate authority of the governor general, and that in the process of attempting to redirect policy, Wood had come into constant conflict with local officials who hampered his ability to govern. As Stimson reported, the effort to restore fully the power of the governor general "necessarily could only be partial. The 'Big Brother' method was gone forever as the admirable force of American civil servants who had been brought to the Philippines . . . during the first fifteen years had been dismissed." Wood had brought about "a gradual rehabilitation" of his powers, but "it has been a most difficult and ungrateful task. Powers of supervision over any race or people once abandoned can be re-established only with the utmost difficulty." Still, Stimson found that Wood had undone most of the "damage done by the reckless experiment of the Harrison administration," particularly by restoring the currency and improving the business climate.[43]

Stimson found that the Filipinos remained unprepared not only for independence, but even for limited self-rule. The problem, as he saw it, was simply a matter of race. Stimson recorded a conversation with Wood during his 1926 visit that fixed where they placed the Filipinos on their scale of people. Wood found the "pure Malays . . . superior to pure *Mexican Indians* . . . in self governing possibilities–*but probable* [sic] *inferior to Porto Rican and Cuban*, owing to *white blood in latter*; thinks them *far* superior to negro and probably far simpler here owing to lack of negro blood." They were "in development thus farther than West Indian islands where there is a negro element." Stimson offered no objections to these conclusions. Rather, he saw the political problem of the Philippines, "with a shock of happy recognition . . . to be one for which his own political thinking of the previous decade suggested a tailor-made solution."[44]

Governor General Stimson with unidentified Filipino leaders. *Henry Lewis Stimson Papers, Manuscripts and Archives, Yale University Library*

In his meeting with the leaders of the Philippine Congress, Manuel Quezon, Sergio Ozmeña, and Manuel Roxas, Stimson made it clear that he opposed independence. That, he argued, would only leave the islands in political chaos and vulnerable to domination by another power. They were not prepared for self-rule much less self-defense. Moreover, he stated that the American mission to train the population and bring progress was not finished, and that it was the duty of the United States to stay until "the attitudes of mind which would permit the unsupervised survival of free democratic institutions" were ingrained. Concerned about the deadlock between Wood and the Congress over how to govern effectively, Stimson proposed a cabinet government be established that would

bring leading Filipinos from the Congress into the executive offices. This, he believed, would be the "most direct step toward securing co-operation between [the Congress] and the executive."
This, however, could only be done if the Filipinos provided a full
recognition of the ultimate authority of the governor general. His
offer was rejected due to the "bad faith and unsympathetic attitudes" between Wood and the Filipino elites, and Stimson left the
islands with the deadlock unresolved. He was convinced, however,
"that there remained only personal reasons" for the impasse, and
that they could be overcome in time.[45]

Wood died suddenly during the summer of 1927. While Coolidge was still considering whom to name to replace him, Quezon
and Ozmeña came to the United States to urge the appointment of
Stimson. On the one hand, given Stimson's frank and publicly expressed attitudes concerning the inferiority of Filipinos, their inability to govern themselves, and the necessity that all final
authority should rest with the governor general, it is surprising
that these men would recommend him. On the other hand, Quezon
and Ozmeña were sympathetic to Stimson's proposal for a cabinet
government and believed he would allow local elites a say in most
matters. Thus, Stimson could help them solidify their own power.
The visitors promised Stimson their full cooperation, as leaders of
the legislature, in carrying out his policies. Stimson considered this
a great opportunity to implement his ideas on benevolent control
through cabinet government and working with local elites. He
would carry forward the tradition of Theodore Roosevelt and Elihu
Root, representing his nation not only as the man who had the final authority and responsibility for governing, but as the conser-
vator of belief in the duty and responsibility of the United States to
provide moral and material leadership to the less fortunate areas
of the world.

Stimson made it clear from the outset that his concerns would
be economic development and education and that he saw all political questions not only as closed, but also as a distraction for the
Filipino people. In his first meeting with Filipino leaders, Stimson
explained that he "did not intend to discuss" the question of independence, but "desired to draw the attention of the people here
away from that thought." Rather, as he noted in his inaugural
speech, he would "lay particular stress upon industrial education
and economic progress." Both could be obtained only through cooperation with the United States, "for it was a necessary condition
of economic growth that large quantities of foreign—presumably

American—capital be attracted to the Islands." Political stability was, in turn, a prerequisite for attracting and protecting American investments.[46]

The question was how to obtain this stability and attract American capital. Like his proposal for Nicaragua, Stimson outlined three possible courses of action: direct force, rational argument and local control, or proper outside leadership, direction, and cooperation with local elites. The first two were rejected as outdated or impractical. Stimson believed that to govern the "Oriental races . . . the old methods of force were obsolete and also the idea of intelligent persuasion could not be used."[47] This left only firm American guidance through executive power in collaboration with local authorities. Stimson remained convinced "that the Filipino people were immature in matters of Government and required for that reason the supervision and control of the Governor General."[48] He, therefore, set out to make sure his authority was unquestioned and that he had the mechanisms needed to carry out his mission.

To achieve his first objective, Stimson set out to establish his governance on the basis of cooperation with the local elites. He believed that Wood's biggest difficulty was his unwillingness to demonstrate trust in the Filipinos with whom he worked. For example, Wood never met with any Filipinos without another American present. This led to challenges to his power and rulings. On his first day as governor general, Stimson met with Ozmeña and Roxas (Quezon was still in the United States receiving treatment for tuberculosis) to discuss various matters of concern; he was establishing a precedent of regular meetings with them that would be held throughout his term. Stimson opened up his residence, Malacañan Palace, to Americans and Filipinos alike for both business and social occasions, and often dined alone with Quezon who became a close personal friend. Quezon was later to comment that Stimson never showed any reservations in talking to him and "made me feel that he gave me his entire confidence exactly as he would have done if I had been an American sitting at his council table."[49] Even given Stimson's paternalistic beliefs concerning the Filipinos, he still saw no threat in meeting with the people. Indeed, he was determined to model proper behavior and to share his ideas so that the Filipinos could profit from his example. Stimson had concluded that the only way to earn trust was to demonstrate trust in others. Any signs of caution or fear would only result in misunderstandings, ill will, and damaging conflicts.

Still, Stimson believed he needed certain structures to govern effectively. First, he obtained, through the passage of the Belo Law in 1928, a new level of advisors responsible only to him to assist in governing the islands. They were mainly technical experts and assistants who served as the eyes and ears of the governor general by investigating problems and implementing his plans for greater industrial education and economic development. He emphasized that these experts allowed him to stay well informed about the actual workings of the government and enabled him to grant greater freedom to the Filipino administrators as he could understand the activities of different agencies. Second, Stimson implemented his main reform. He created a cabinet government in which its members had seats on the floor of the Congress as well as executive duties. Thus, the executive branch was strengthened relative to the Congress, and power was further concentrated in the hands of a few men.

Although Stimson saw these changes as necessary for creating the only type of governing structure that could succeed in a nation such as the Philippines, they also served his purposes of cooperation with local elites and promotion of economic development. He believed greater executive authority and power would guarantee order and attract investors as well as divert the attention of the people from the issues of politics and independence. Final independence could be granted only after the proper "economic foundations which must underlie it" were firmly established. Although Stimson acknowledged that for some "industrial development has been dreaded as if it were inconsistent with the liberties of a people," he believed "that no greater error could be made." The Filipinos should concentrate on the more practical matters of training, education, and sanitation until they reached political "maturity." Thus, Stimson set out to reform the Philippine corporation laws on foreign investment, even though this "flew squarely in the face of the natural prejudices which Filipinos shared with most colonial peoples." There was nothing Stimson was "more proud [of] than his success in winning Filipino approval of a more liberal corporation law" and opening up the flow of American capital to the islands.

When Stimson left the Philippines in January 1929 to become secretary of state under Herbert Hoover, he believed he had established a solid foundation for the governing and development of the islands and the continuation of American control. Yet he had misread the cooperation he received as abandonment of the desire for independence by Filipino leaders and the people. When the issue of limiting free trade between the United States and the Philippines arose in early 1929, Stimson was surprised to discover that most Filipinos sought a fundamental change of relations with the United States and a promise of independence. The Timberlake Resolution that sought to impose a tariff on Philippine goods forced Stimson to have his first discussions of independence with Filipino leaders. Quezon told the governor general on January 6, 1929, that the "tariff issue was probably the greatest crisis that the Philippine Islands had met since the American occupation and that it opened up the entire question of the future relations of the Islands with the United States." He informed Stimson that, if the United States continued to hold the islands without free access to the American market, it would "destroy his faith in the attitude of the American people and the United States Government," and that he would have to "go home and teach [my] boy to be a rebel." Indeed, the only alternative to a tariff was independence.

Stimson replied that he did not think the United States would take such a step, but that he feared "that when the dilemma was presented between a tariff against the Philippines on one side and independence on the other, the American Congress remembering the long-continued demands for *immediate independence* by the Filipinos" would grant independence "and disregard the real harm and cruelty which this would do to them." Quezon agreed that this was the danger at hand. He said that if he "could get a dominion government with free trade advantages," he would "do so at the price of giving up all agitation for independence." This appealed to Stimson as an ultimate goal, analogous he said to the "basis of an honorable marriage where the Islands like a woman are persuaded that it is for their best interest to make the connection."[50] Stimson continued to believe that "complete independence from the United States was the wrong final goal for the Philippines." It was impractical, dangerous, and not in the interest of either party. Filipinos needed American guidance and protection, "while America's political position in the Far East was greatly strengthened by the existence in the Philippines of an outpost of American civilization." Continuing to believe that he and his nation knew best, Stimson found the notion of independence "a misnomer for the legitimate and natural Filipino aspiration toward full self-government."[51]

Quezon returned less than two weeks later to inform the governor general of his findings from talks with other Filipino leaders.

The consensus of the business community was that even if the threat of an end to free trade were defeated this time, there would be a "constant uncertainty and danger." Politicians agreed. The "unanimous opinion expressed was that if they had to choose between free trade and independence, they would take independence," and that there was no measure that could prevent "agitation if the tariff threat was continued." This was the only benefit of American rule from their perspective, and it must be maintained or the relationship would have to change. Stimson, however, adamantly rejected any talk of independence, condescendingly informing Quezon that "he was the only Filipino I knew with a sufficient Anglo-Saxon mind to fill the job at present" of Filipino president.[52]

As secretary of state, Stimson fought against both the Timberlake Resolution and Philippine independence. Twice in 1929 he blocked passage of the tariff measure. But with the onset of the Great Depression, the political climate in America began to change in favor of protection, and the opponents of Philippine imports joined the supporters of independence to create a majority in support of both measures. Stimson kept up the fight until he left office in 1933, but he knew the end was near. As he noted with despair in February 1932, the "selfish interests which want to get rid of the Philippines so as to get rid of their competition . . . have got evidently a majority in both houses [of Congress] pretty well pledged for [independence]. The poor Filipinos themselves have at last realized their danger and are almost pathetic in their desire to escape, but of course they are tied hand and foot by their previous slogans and they do not dare to change for fear of political death in the Islands."[53] Over President Hoover's veto, Congress passed the Hare-Hawes-Cutting Act in 1933 that called for the granting of independence to the Philippines. It, however, could not go into effect without Filipino approval. Quezon was able to block this measure, but not the Tydings-McDuffie Act of 1934, which established the Philippines Commonwealth Government and scheduled complete independence for 1946.

To the end, Stimson thought that his nation had made a mistake in granting Philippine independence. He did not believe that the Filipinos could govern themselves or properly manage their economic affairs. Most of all, he was disappointed that Americans were unwilling "to continue to recognize their responsibility for Philippine prosperity."[54] But he was hopeful as well. The movement toward Philippine independence changed the nature of the relationship, but not, from Stimson's perspective, the Filipinos' need for the United States' protection and guidance. Here, Stimson's ability to work closely with local elites, such as Quezon, provided solace. So long as they could stay in power and continue to rely upon the United States, stability, order, and economic progress could be maintained. The Philippines needed a firm government to maintain order and promote the economic changes that would allow for the development of a more "mature" and disciplined population.

Stimson's service in Nicaragua and the Philippines confirmed his paternalistic attitudes and the conviction that the United States was justified in using its strength, both military and economic, to intervene in the affairs of other nations and safeguard those who, he thought, needed protection from themselves. Throughout the 1920s, the United States developed the logic and rationale for supporting right-wing dictatorships, and Stimson played a large role in the creation and implementation of this policy. His work for the Coolidge administration also expanded his thinking about the world beyond Europe, providing him with a global perspective that brought all of Asia and Latin America into his vision and demonstrated the continuity of American ideas about the world over time. Even when Stimson had to yield on the issue of maintaining a formal colony in the Philippines, he never questioned that the United States knew what was best for other nations and was destined for greatness and international leadership. The persistence of these attitudes made Stimson's service as secretary of state pivotal in the formation of American foreign policy. The challenges he faced and his responses provide the link between the foreign policy-makers of the 1890s and those of the post–World War II period who adopted Stimson's internationalist assumptions and views about the world.

Notes

1. Stimson, "The United States and the Other American Republics," 6 February 1931 (Washington, DC: Government Printing Office, 1931).

2. Stimson Diary, 11 November 1932, HLSD.

3. Quoted in Merlo Pusey, *Charles Evans Hughes* (New York: Macmillan, 1951), 531.

4. Charles Evans Hughes, *Our Relations to the Nations of the Western Hemisphere* (Princeton: Princeton University Press, 1928), 4, 50.

5. Ibid., 46, 50.

6. Stimson, "The United States and the Other American Republics."

7. Memorandum of Conversation Between Hughes and Lamont, 26 September 1921, Thomas W. Lamont Papers, Baker Library, Harvard University, Box 195.

8. Hughes, *Our Relations to the Nations of the Western Hemisphere*, 45–46.

9. Quoted in Michael Krenn, *U.S. Policy Toward Economic Nationalism in Latin America, 1917–1929* (Wilmington: Scholarly Resources, 1990), 44, 58, 62.

10. James J. Horn, "U.S. Diplomacy and 'The Specter of Bolshevism' in Mexico," *Americas* 32 (July 1975), 37.

11. Quoted in Hodgson, *The Colonel*, 108.

12. Donald R. McCoy, *Calvin Coolidge: The Quiet President* (New York: Macmillan, 1967), 352.

13. Memorandum by Undersecretary of State Robert Olds, 2 January 1927, 817.00/4350, Record Group 59, Records of the Department of State, National Archives (hereafter RG59).

14. Calvin Coolidge, "Conditions in Nicaragua," 10 January 1927, in *Foreign Relations of the United States* 1927 (hereafter *FRUS* followed by year), 3:288–98.

15. Eder to Hoover, 8 January 1927, "American Interests in Nicaragua," Commerce Papers—Nicaragua, Box 449, Herbert Hoover Presidential Library, West Branch, Iowa.

16. Frank B. Kellogg, "Bolshevik Aims and Policies in Mexico and Latin America," 12 January 1927, reel 34, Frank B. Kellogg Papers (microfilm edition), Minnesota Historical Society (Minneapolis); see also *New York Times*, 13 January 1927, 1.

17. Stimson and Bundy, *On Active Service*, 110.

18. Stimson Diary, 31 March 1927, 1 April 1927, HLSD.

19. Ibid., "Memorandum of a Conference with the President, The Secretary of State, Colonel Olds, and Mr. Stimson, Thursday, April 7, 1927."

20. Stimson, *American Policy in Nicaragua* (New York: Scribner's and Sons, 1927), 6–10.

21. Stimson, "Memorandum of Conference with Mr. Root, July 6, 1927, Re Nicaragua," Stimson Papers, reel 71.

22. Stimson, *American Policy in Nicaragua*, 18, 59–61; "Memorandum of Talk with Minister Eberhardt," 19 April 1927, HLSD.

23. Stimson Diary, 23 April 1927, HLSD.

24. *FRUS* 1927, 3:331–32.

25. Stimson, *American Policy in Nicaragua*, 65–77; *FRUS* 1927, 3:337–38, 339–42; Kellogg to Stimson, 4 May 1927; Stimson Diary, 21 May 1927, HLSD.

26. Stimson Diary, 3 May 1927, HLSD.

27. Ibid., 15 May 1927.

28. Stimson and Bundy, *On Active Service*, 115; Stimson, *American Policy in Nicaragua*, 114–15.

29. Stimson, *American Policy in Nicaragua*, 85.

30. Stimson and Bundy, *On Active Service*, 183.

31. Eberhardt to Kellogg, 20 July 1927, Box 211, Stimson Papers.

32. Quoted in Hodgson, *The Colonel*, 119.

33. Paul H. Boeker, ed., *Henry L. Stimson's American Policy in Nicaragua* (New York: Markus Wiener, 1991), 233–35.

34. Frank McCoy to Kellogg, 12 September 1927, 817.00/5028, RG 59; Andrew Bacevich, "American Electoral Mission in Nicaragua, 1927–28," *Diplomatic History* 4 (1980), 253.

35. Stimson and Bundy, *On Active Service*, 182.

36. Hanna to White, 28 October 1932, 817.1051/701 1/2, RG59.

37. Richard Millett, *Guardians of the Dynasty* (Maryknoll, NY: Orbis Books, 1977), 139.

38. *FRUS* 1936, 5:844–46.

39. Roosevelt, quoted in Schmitz, *Thank God They're on Our Side*, 23; Stimson, quoted in Current, *Secretary Stimson*, 120.

40. Stimson and Bundy, *On Active Service*, 117–18.

41. Ibid., 118–20.

42. Stimson to Fischer, 29 September 1916, Stimson Papers, reel 45; Stimson and Bundy, *On Active Service*, 121; Stimson, "Future Philippine Policy Under the Jones Act," *Foreign Affairs*, April 1927.

43. Stimson, "First-Hand Impressions of the Philippine Problem," *Saturday Evening Post* (19 March 1927), 6–7.

44. Stimson Diary, 22 August 1926, HLSD (emphasis in the original); Stimson and Bundy, *On Active Service*, 124.

45. Stimson Diary, 9 September 1926, HLSD; Stimson and Bundy, *On Active Service*, 125–26, 135.

46. Stimson Diary, 2 March 1928, HLSD; Stimson and Bundy, *On Active Service*, 139–40.

47. Stimson Diary, 18 March 1928, HLSD.

48. Ibid., 21 August 1928.

49. Stimson and Bundy, *On Active Service*, 138.

50. Stimson Diary, 6 January 1929, HLSD (emphasis in the original).

51. Stimson and Bundy, *On Active Service*, 146.

52. Stimson Diary, 16, 17 January 1929, HLSD.

53. Ibid., 10 February 1932.

54. Stimson and Bundy, *On Active Service*, 151.

4

Spears of Straw and Swords of Ice

Having been out of the country for almost two years, Stimson had played a very small role in ongoing Republican Party politics or the presidential election of 1928. As far as he could see, Herbert Hoover's victory over Al Smith would allow him to stay on in the Philippines and continue his work until he decided it was time to go home. Stimson was, therefore, quite surprised when a cable arrived in Manila on January 26, 1929, from his law partner, George Roberts, asking for his views on a possible appointment to Hoover's cabinet as either attorney general or secretary of state. Stimson replied that he would gladly accept the State Department, but made it perfectly clear that he had no interest in the Justice Department post. Four days later, Hoover announced that Stimson would replace Frank Kellogg as secretary of state. Stimson was not Hoover's first choice. Indeed, beyond Hoover's effort during World War I to recruit Stimson as chief counsel for his food relief agency, the two men barely knew each other and had never worked together. But Stimson was the candidate of the internationalist wing of the party, in particular, of Elihu Root, Charles Evans Hughes, and William Taft, and he met the president's criterion for a candidate with experience and knowledge of world affairs.

When Stimson sailed home from the Philippines to become secretary of state, the United States was at peace and domestic prosperity was at an all-time high. In Europe, Republican internationalists, led by Hughes, had worked throughout the 1920s to overcome the rejection of the Treaty of Versailles and to increase American cooperation with the powers of Europe by negotiating a series of disarmament and debt-reduction agreements. Although they avoided any political commitments by the United States to Europe, American officials believed their actions would reduce the danger of war and provide greater political stability while also promoting American trade and prosperity. Moreover, the Republicans continued the policy of nonrecognition of the Soviet Union and attempted to isolate that nation from world affairs. U.S. policy toward Latin America was guided by the Roosevelt Corollary to the Monroe Doctrine, efforts to promote regional stability, and protection of American trade and the Panama Canal. In Asia, the United States pursued the Open Door policy in China, naval limitation, and the easing of imperialist rivalries in the region. Stimson endorsed all the efforts made to improve American relations in Europe and modify the financial burdens imposed by Versailles and hoped to continue to provide American leadership in the areas of disarmament, debt reduction, and the peaceful resolution of international conflicts. Moreover, he sought to modify policy toward Latin America by ending direct U.S. intervention there and the use of force. Stimson took office convinced that the world would remain at peace because of its revulsion against the Great War and the growing interdependence among nations.

The coming of the Great Depression and the international economic collapse of 1931 completely changed the context for American foreign policy and introduced a host of new crises and challenges. The failure of the central banks of Austria and Germany plunged Europe into an economic crisis that destroyed the agreements of the prior decade, led to rising nationalism, and returned the danger of international conflict to the fore. With the growing political crisis in Germany and the rise of the Nazis came the twin dangers of war and revolution. The rapid drop of world prices for raw materials created economic problems throughout Latin America that stimulated new political upheaval and growing opposition to American intervention in the region. These conditions raised the question of the most effective means for the United States to protect its interests while promoting stability and preventing the spread of Communism in the region. In the Far East, fighting broke out in 1931 with Japan's invasion of Manchuria. Japan's aggression threatened the political integrity of China, stability throughout all of East Asia, and America's Open Door policy and interests in the region.

Although these problems were unexpected, Stimson responded to them in a manner consistent with his past actions and his views of America's proper role in the world. He continued to push for disarmament, debt reduction, and the upholding of treaties in Europe, ended the use of American forces in Latin America, and led the international condemnation of and opposition to Japan's aggression in China. Yet Stimson was frustrated time and again by what he saw as Hoover's unwillingness to exercise the necessary world leadership and by the constraints of U.S. public opinion that supported only policies he deemed too limited and misguided.

Stimson's years at Foggy Bottom were, therefore, difficult and often unhappy ones because of the international crises, the domestic depression, and his often tense relationship with Hoover. Still, he took solace in the effective work of his staff, in his enjoyment of his Washington estate Woodley, in his confidence that the policies he pursued were the correct ones for the nation and the world and that he had achieved as much as he could given the president's timidity and the nation's isolationism. Stimson maintained the principle of debt reduction and fought for disarmament as he upheld international commitments and continued efforts at negotiated settlements in Europe. He implemented what would be termed the Good Neighbor policy under Franklin Roosevelt in Latin America and established a long-standing U.S. policy with his refusal to recognize Japanese aggression in Manchuria. Still, only in Latin America did Stimson believe he was able to carry out his policies fully and achieve complete success. Not until the outbreak of World War II were the positions and policies Stimson advocated as secretary of state adopted as the official policy of the United States in Europe and Asia.

A Bath of Ink

The key problem that faced American foreign policymakers in the wake of World War I was how to create stability and order in the world, particularly Europe, while promoting and protecting American trade and investments. The United States had emerged from the Great War as the world's leading creditor, greatest industrial producer, and its most powerful nation. Republican officials drew several lessons from World War I that guided the formulation of their policies. They did not believe that the League of Nations was adequate to deter future aggression and wars. The only means to peace were political stability and economic prosperity that would allow the great powers to cooperate and recognize their common goals. The war proved the interdependence of the world's economies and

that American prosperity was, therefore, tied to the economic recovery of Europe. As Hughes stated in 1921, "The prosperity of the
United States largely depends upon the economic settlements which
may be made in Europe." The next year he noted that "the economic conditions in Europe give us the greatest concern. . . . It is
idle to say that we are not interested in these problems . . . as our
credits and markets are involved. . . . We cannot dispose of these
problems by calling them European, for they are world problems
and we cannot escape the injurious consequences of a failure to
settle them."[1] Central to European economic health was a revived
and vital German economy. This meant that there would have to
be economic adjustments to the punitive reparations imposed by
the Treaty of Versailles to facilitate German recovery. In addition,
European nations owed billions of dollars in war debts to the United
States that were proving to be a significant drain on their economies. These debts, although never directly linked to reparations
payments, would be lowered along with reparation payments to
promote economic recovery. Although Republican leaders continued to reject political involvement in the affairs and disputes of
Europe, the 1920s were characterized by vigorous American efforts
to use its economic power to assist Europe's economic recovery
and create a cooperative international system on the continent while
continuing to isolate the Soviet Union.

The main problems blocking Europe's and Germany's recovery were the agreements in the Treaty of Versailles and France's
intransigence regarding any revisions that aided Germany. Republican officials saw the Versailles settlement, in particular, the high
reparations payments, as too harsh on Germany. They feared that
Germany would never be able to recover fully from the war if it
met its full obligations, and that this would not only hold up European recovery, but create political instability and the possibility of
revolution. This anxiety was compounded by France's policies of
enforcing the Treaty of Versailles while simultaneously spending
enormous sums on defense and forming hostile alliances to encircle
Germany. In the face of Paris's refusal to entertain any treaty revisions and its efforts to collect Germany's full payments, there was
little the United States could do. Germany, however, was unable to
make all of its scheduled payments, and France, strapped by its
military overspending, moved to force German compliance in 1923
by sending its forces into the Saar Basin to collect at bayonet point.
The Germans responded with passive resistance, and the French
occupation had disastrous consequences for both the French and

German economies, with France losing its credit due to a drastic devaluation of the franc and Germany beset by hyperinflation.

This crisis allowed the United States to take action and impose a settlement on American terms. An American delegation, headed by the banker Charles Dawes, traveled to Europe with the goal of stabilizing French and German finances and setting up arrangements to promote economic recovery. For any plan to work, France would have to accept a downward revision in reparations payments. In order to gain agreement from Paris, American bankers extended loans to France to restore the value of its currency and to offset its loss in revenues from scaling back the reparations. Moreover, American officials promised to negotiate a reduction in the debts owed to the United States once the economies of Europe were stabilized. American loans were made available to Germany as well to finance recovery, spur investments, and increase German imports.

The Dawes Plan worked as it was expected to. Between 1924 and 1929, Germany's economy recovered—and with it the rest of Europe—and Berlin resumed its reparation payments. The United States negotiated agreements with all of the European nations to lower the war debts owed it, based on a formula of capacity to pay. By 1925, U.S. trade with Europe was up to $2.6 billion annually, and in the first five years of the Dawes Plan, American bankers lent Germany over $1.3 billion. That plan was quickly followed by the Locarno Pact that guaranteed respect for all existing political borders in Western Europe. In 1929, a second American delegation, headed by Owen D. Young, negotiated a second series of reparation and war-debt reductions and new loans designed to fine tune the 1924 arrangements. These two plans together appeared to demonstrate that prosperity and security were best secured in a cooperative, integrated economic system.

In addition to these financial arrangements, the United States promoted disarmament after World War I as a means to solve various problems, particularly in Asia. Through the so-called Washington System, the United States negotiated a series of treaties that limited naval shipbuilding, sought to protect China's territorial integrity and the Open Door policy, and attempted to integrate Japan into a Western-led international system. It was hoped that disarmament would reduce the amount of capital used for weapons and lessen the chances of international conflict. The money saved on armaments would help promote economic recovery, while the reduction in military forces would persuade nations to settle their differences through negotiation and arbitration rather than conflict.

By disengaging Japan from China, while providing for Japan's economic and security needs and eliminating her efforts to expand, East Asian political stability could be achieved.

In 1922, Secretary of State Hughes opened the first Washington Naval Conference with the pledge that the United States would scuttle all the ships it was currently building and called upon the other leading naval powers to take similar steps. The results of these negotiations were that the allowed tonnage of capital ships was fixed at the ratio of U.S. and U.K. 5: Japan 3: France and Italy 1.25. The Washington Naval Treaty was followed by the Nine-Power Treaty that provided for formal recognition of the Open Door and China's control over its territory through the elimination of the extraterritorial arrangements of various powers. Throughout the 1920s, China's Kuomintang Party struggled to unite China under its rule, with the protection of the Washington System, while the United States continued to promote China's independence and efforts at international cooperation in the Pacific.

Stimson had closely followed the development of these policies throughout the decade and found no pressing international issues that demanded his immediate attention. He, therefore, delayed his departure from the Philippines to oversee a special session of the Philippine Congress. Stimson finally arrived in Washington, D.C., on March 26 and was sworn in as secretary of state on March 28. The Colonel was determined to continue the well-established policies of his predecessors in Europe and Asia, and further American efforts at debt reduction, disarmament, and international cooperation. Only in Latin America did he seek any fundamental changes in policy, but he believed there was plenty of time to act. His first order of business was to get to know Hoover better. Stimson spent his first ten days as secretary of state living at the White House and meeting with the president. Stimson was quickly impressed with Hoover's intellectual prowess and "capacity for assimilating and organizing information."[2] They talked over a wide range of issues, found themselves in general agreement on the major points, and grew to trust each other's words and intentions. The two men would soon discover, however, that they were temperamentally different, had conflicting ideas on leadership, and, when the series of international crises brought about by the Great Depression erupted in the next few years, often disagreed over policy.

Stimson was by nature and training an advocate and one who sought to study a problem and then take action, "confident that

Secretary of State Stimson, 1930. *Henry Lewis Stimson Papers, Manuscripts and Archives, Yale University Library*

aggressive executive leadership would win followers." Hoover, on the other hand, tended to study problems for longer periods of time, and as Stimson noted, had a tendency toward "seeing the dark side first." Stimson once lectured Hoover, an engineer, that political leadership was "not like building a bridge" in that not every stress could be calculated. "In the movements of the great currents of human opinions . . . you could make your plans only for a certain distance. . . ." Trying to consider all angles led to vacillation and weakness. When in doubt, Stimson argued, you "march toward the guns."[3]

Given these differences, their relationship, and Stimson's term as secretary of state, survived only because of the fundamental trust established between the two men and Hoover's confidence in Stimson's unwavering loyalty.

While Stimson was settling in on his new job, he had to organize his office and find a suitable place to live in Washington. Unlike all his other positions, here Stimson had far less control over selecting his staff. Still, he did insist on appointing his own undersecretary of state, naming the attorney and his long-time friend Joseph Cotton to the position. Cotton served Stimson well as both an advisor and confidant until his untimely death in March 1931. Cotton was replaced by William Castle, a career officer and a friend of Hoover's whom the president had strongly urged Stimson to appoint. This was a decision Stimson quickly regretted. He could never fully trust Castle to carry out his instructions or to demonstrate loyalty to him, and he suspected that Castle was talking to Hoover behind his back. Stimson, therefore, had to rely on others for counsel. The rest of the senior administration was made up of career officers until 1931, when Stimson appointed a number of new men to assist him with the economic collapse in Europe. Most important, to replace Cotton as his personal confidant, he named his law partner Allen Klots as a special assistant. To provide him with economic advice, Stimson brought in Harvey Bundy, a Boston attorney with experience in finance as an assistant secretary, and the economist Herbert Feis as his economic advisor.

Stimson's search for a home lasted until summer, when he purchased the Woodley estate in the Rock Creek Valley for $800,000. Woodley, the former summer home to four presidents, was a large southern colonial house situated on twenty acres that provided the Colonel a commanding view of Washington, D.C., and plenty of opportunity for riding. This was the closest the Stimsons could come to their beloved Highhold estate and still live in the city. Stimson would spend many hours of his workweek at Woodley playing paddle tennis with various staff members as they discussed the issues confronting them. Stimson kept the house until 1946 when, upon his final retirement, he donated it to Andover.

Stimson's first year in office was dominated by his preparation for and participation in the London Naval Conference of 1930. This meeting was critical for two reasons. First, Stimson saw it as a means to address the shortcomings of the Washington Treaty and to build on the achievements of the past decade. Second, it could further peaceful international cooperation, particularly between the United

States and Great Britain, and, along with the Young Plan, create a context for a more comprehensive settlement of Europe's remaining problems. As he began planning for this meeting in 1929, Stimson could not know that the crash of the American stock market and the ensuing international financial crisis would make London's the last disarmament agreement of the post–World War I period.

Although the parties to the Washington Treaty had honored their commitments, competition reappeared in new categories of ships, the most important among them the heavy cruisers of 10,000 tons with 8-inch and 6-inch guns and great speed, which were not covered in that agreement. On five different occasions after 1922 negotiators had failed to solve this problem, and the construction of these cruisers continued to threaten a renewal of naval rivalries and another round of arms buildups. The London meeting convened on January 17 and lasted until April 22. Agreement was quickly reached between the United States and Great Britain on the limitation of cruisers with 8-inch and 6-inch guns. Having accomplished his first and primary goal of improved relations with London, Stimson turned his attention toward Japan. Tokyo was demanding concessions that raised its Washington treaty ratio of battleship strength vis-à-vis the United States and Great Britain to 7:10. Stimson considered this demand an unacceptable threat to the whole structure of disarmament, and held to the 6:10 ratio in heavy cruisers and battleships. To gain Japanese agreement, Japan was granted its desired ratio in other naval categories and, for submarines, parity. Moreover, the United States agreed not to complete its heavy cruiser program until 1936, after the treaty's expiration date. This allowed for a reopening of the question before Japan faced the complete buildup of the American Navy.

Stimson was not concerned that the meeting failed to reach a settlement on the size of the French and Italian navies. He had accomplished in London all that he set out to do. The specific reductions were not so important to him as the fact that there was an agreement to control building by the three leading powers, and that a first step toward greater international cooperation had been taken. Most important, for Stimson, was the improvement of relations with Great Britain. He saw the London Naval Conference "as a method of bringing the British and the Americans together." Stimson was always a "confirmed believer in the vital importance of firm Anglo-American friendship," and the improvement of relations between London and Washington was "a cardinal objective" of his service as secretary of state.[4] It was also, however, the last time that Stimson would achieve complete success in his European policy.

The beginning of the depression elicited new efforts to, in the words of one of the promoters of a new tariff, make the nation's economy "self-contained and self-sustaining." Recalling the difficulties that tariff policy had caused President Taft, Stimson stayed out of the public debate over the Hawley-Smoot Tariff Act of 1930. Although Stimson completely opposed the excessively high barriers the tariff established, the most restrictive in the nation's history, he did not want to spend his prestige and influence over this volatile political issue. He understood that shutting off American markets from foreign trade, while politically attractive at the outset of the Great Depression, would make it more difficult for other nations to earn dollars to pay back their debts and for American producers to sell their goods abroad. Stimson attempted to persuade Hoover to veto the bill, but his arguments concerning the tariff's damage to international finances failed to persuade the president to oppose this popular protectionist measure.[5]

At the same time, Stimson sought to impose his own values on the conduct of American foreign policy. The Colonel had long acted on the principle that the only way to make people trustworthy was to trust them. He was, therefore, surprised to learn that the State Department, through its so-called Black Chamber, was routinely reading the communications between foreign embassies and their home governments. For a man who held trust as the highest value, these actions were inexcusable, and Stimson closed down the State Department's code-breaking office. He thought this was necessary to demonstrate his commitment to international cooperation and good will. Stimson would later defend his action by stating that "gentlemen do not read each other's mail."[6]

As the economic depression that began with the crash of the New York Stock Market in October 1929 spread to the rest of the world in 1931, pressure mounted on the Hoover administration to help relieve the financial burdens on Germany and the rest of Europe by taking action on their debts to the United States. As conditions worsened, social strife increased in many European nations, thus raising the fear of political instability and the spread of Communism. In May, the Austrian Credit Anstalt (Central Bank) failed, precipitating a banking crisis over all of Central Europe, with bank runs mounting through May and June. Germany soon announced that it was no longer able to meet the payments on its debts to foreign nations, creating the danger of a general default on all intergovernmental debts. There was the danger of a return to the Ruhr crisis of 1923, with its political upheaval and repudiation of international obligations. These developments propelled Stimson to the center of world politics for the remainder of his term as secretary of state.

The economic collapse of Central Europe's banking had serious implications for both European and American politics. American banks had extended enormous amounts of credit to Germany under the Dawes and Young plans and any complete collapse of German finances guaranteed repercussions across all the nations of Europe and in the United States. On June 5, Hoover raised the idea of a moratorium on all intergovernmental debts for a year or two, by which the United States, as the largest creditor, would declare a holiday on all these payments in order to allow nations and banks to stabilize their finances. For Stimson, Hoover's idea was just the right approach. He had never supported the repayment of the Allied war debts and would later endorse the outright cancellation of all remaining obligations. He saw Hoover's proposal as "a bold emphatic proposition to assume leadership himself, and I, myself, felt more glad than I could say that he was at last turning that way."[7] As the administration worked out the details of the plan, Stimson compared the atmosphere to that of being at war, with Central Europe as "the front," and the news from there getting consistently worse.

Hoover, however, immediately began to have doubts as to whether he should take the lead in responding to this situation. For the next two weeks, Stimson had to prevent the president from "seeing the dark side" of the issue and persuade him to go forward with his original idea. Hoover worried that a moratorium might appear to connect war debts with reparations and that the American people would never accept such an arrangement out of fear that it would "drag us into the European mess." Stimson and the president argued many times, with the secretary of state urging action despite this hazard. The Colonel understood that it was impossible to separate the financial connection between reparations and war debts owed the United States.[8]

While Hoover vacillated, Stimson continued to push for action. He cautioned "that there is the greatest danger that a situation is going to arise which will produce a very prompt financial crisis in Germany and ultimately a most serious economic crisis there." If the United States did not take quick steps, it would lose control over the situation, and the solution "may be put to us in an even more dangerous form, the general suspension by Germany of all payments." A United States failure to take the initiative and "to meet the situation in advance is likely to confront us with a problem infinitely greater and more difficult to solve at some later date." The "whole question of debts and reparations is going to be presented to our Government" as connected. If that occurred, Stimson warned that "it will be too late for us to give curative treatment," and thus it would have a further significant negative impact on the domestic economy.[9]

With his staff and members of the Treasury Department, the secretary of state prepared a paper that demonstrated that inaction by the United States was even more damaging than a moratorium proposal. On the evening of June 18, Stimson, accompanied by Ogden Mills of the Treasury Department, went to see the president to make a final case for a moratorium. Hoover was tired and brought up all the negative possibilities of the proposal. "It was," Stimson observed, "like sitting in a bath of ink to sit in his room." In the end, however, Stimson persuaded Hoover to act, and he would provide the key assistance to the president in his lobbying efforts with both Congress and the European nations.[10]

On June 20, Hoover announced a one-year moratorium on all intergovernmental debts, including German reparations, in order to strengthen Germany's finances and protect all of Europe's banks and credit. Despite initial French opposition, all the European nations ultimately accepted the moratorium. Stimson believed that the moratorium staved off the possibility of a revolution in Germany and the collapse of Europe's finances. Although Hoover had not gone as far as Stimson would have liked as to cancel the remaining debts, Stimson did see the moratorium as "one of the best things Mr. Hoover ever did." It was the one time that he demonstrated the "bold executive leadership" that Stimson "considered the central requirement of effective democratic government."[11]

In July, Stimson departed on a previously scheduled trip to Europe to meet with various leaders. The original purpose was to discuss disarmament and exchange views on the economic depression. But coming so soon after the financial crisis in Central Europe, Stimson's trip became primarily an opportunity for him to observe at firsthand Europe's economic and political problems. He hoped to discover whether there were any further actions the United States could take to follow up on the debt moratorium and further ease the economic problems of Europe. As he planned for the trip, the secretary of state was increasingly concerned with the renewed strength of Communism in Europe and the growing appeal of the Soviet Union to workers and others hurt by the Great Depression. The perceived Bolshevik threat further complicated the already complex problems in the making of policy toward Europe, and Stimson was determined to continue the nonrecognition and isolation of the Soviet Union. At one point, the secretary exhibited his quick temper in response to the consistent intrusion of the subject of the Soviet Union and Communism on all discussions of Europe. In an April conversation with his law partners and George Roberts of the Federal Reserve Bank of New York (FRBNY), Stimson declared that "if there was no economic depression nobody would be thinking of Russia." Yet the Colonel was thinking about Communism and Russia regularly. On his way home to Huntington for a rest before his trip, Stimson brought with him extensive reading material on the Soviet Union and the economic conditions in Europe.[12]

While at Highhold, Stimson went into New York City to discuss the economic problems of Europe, and in particular, of Germany, with George Harrison of the FRBNY and Montague Norman of the Bank of England. Both bankers expressed serious concerns over the developments of the past year and worried that the worst problems were still ahead. Furthermore, Norman noted that he believed that "Russia was the very greatest of all dangers" because of the alternative example it provided to all nations struggling with the depression. The Soviet Union could only benefit from their troubles to the detriment of the rest of Europe. The three men noted that Germany and Eastern Europe were the areas of real concern because they were not receiving enough "help from the capitalist system to stand the expense of remaining capitalistic . . . and all the time while they wobbled and wavered Russia was beckoning to them to come over to her system."[13]

Stimson's first stop on his highly publicized tour of Europe was Italy. Since the Fascist takeover in 1922, the United States had supported Mussolini's regime. Fascism in Italy was seen as a necessary "strong hand" in a nation unprepared for democracy, a defense against Communism, and a modernizing force for the Italian economy. Before the March on Rome, American leaders feared that postwar upheavals in Italy would lead to a Communist victory. Mussolini's seizure of power ended the threat of Bolshevism and, in the words of Elihu Root, led to "a revival of prosperity, contentment and happiness under a dictator, who was the man of the hour to seize upon the fact that the Italians had undertaken to govern themselves without having quite learned the hang of it." The United States negotiated the most favorable debt-reduction plan with Italy, and American banks extended substantial loans to the Italian government. Stimson saw no reason to challenge any of these assumptions. He perceived Mussolini as "a sound and useful leader," and "one of the most ardent and least inconsistent advocates of disarmament in all of Europe."[14]

Secretary of State Stimson meeting with Benito Mussolini in Rome, 1931. *Henry Lewis Stimson Papers, Manuscripts and Archives, Yale University Library*

While in Rome, Stimson held a series of meetings with Italian Foreign Minister Dino Grandi and had one long formal conversation with Mussolini and Grandi together. The three men discussed disarmament, the depression, and the threat of Communism in Europe. Grandi reaffirmed Italy's support for the debt moratorium, going so far as to predict that it would bring an end to the depression. Stimson noted that this was his hope and that he believed the crisis was caused "by the lack of confidence which made people withdraw their credits from Germany." The Colonel told Grandi that he saw it as essential "to restore the confidence and set aside the psychology of fear" that was causing the continued problems. Both Grandi and Mussolini assured Stimson that Italy also continued to support disarmament as a means to ease the financial crisis. Stimson told Mussolini that he thought it was critical that the nations agree to further arms reductions, arguing that "either Europe will change or go to the cycle of competition and war." Stimson, however, agreed with Grandi that the settlement of Europe's political problems rested first with a solution to the continent's economic problems.[15]

In his meeting with Grandi, Stimson raised the question of Bolshevism and the political unrest in Europe. Grandi reported that there was little danger of Communism in Italy and no signs of political turmoil. Although Stimson was glad to hear this, he told Grandi that he found Fascism to be "a form of government foreign to the American spirit" and wondered if the continuation of the dictatorship and nonconstitutional rule might sow the "seeds of grave danger." Grandi quickly defended Mussolini's rule by arguing that strong governmental control was necessary in Italy for the maintenance of order and stability. He told Stimson that Italy was on the brink of ruin, ready to fall to Communism prior to the Fascist takeover. The foreign minister explained that he had joined the Fascists because "he saw the whole framework of society collapsing under attack from the left." Stimson responded that "Americans could understand from their frontier experience that in a time of lawlessness there might be a need for vigilantes" as part of the development of the nation.[16]

From Rome, Stimson traveled to Paris where he confronted a new financial crisis in Germany. The moratorium, weakened by France's delay in agreement, had not stopped private creditors from withdrawing their German assets, and Germany was faced with bankruptcy. After consultations with Hoover, Stimson crossed the Channel to London to organize a meeting of European leaders to discuss this new problem. The secretary of state gained the acceptance of a standstill agreement on private debts that prevented the further removal of foreign capital from Germany. This ended the immediate crisis, and Stimson left the issue of further assistance to Germany in the hands of private bankers.

It was in this tense atmosphere that Stimson arrived in Berlin for meetings with German Chancellor Heinrich Bruening. The Germans, along with American Ambassador Frederic Sackett, sought to impress upon the secretary of state the dire nature of Germany's economy and the danger of revolution and Bolshevism in Germany. Bruening told Stimson that Germany was witnessing "a considerable increase" in Communist activity and voting and that, unless

Germany obtained more relief from the restrictions of the Versailles Treaty, the threat of revolution would grow. Sackett informed Stimson that he agreed with Bruening concerning the danger of Communism and that the Germans believed that the whole question of the spread of Bolshevism throughout Europe would soon reappear. "In this maelstrom," Sackett reported, "Germany will be the buffer state and must be ready to defend itself and the rest of Europe against Bolshevism."[17]

These arguments placed Stimson in a bind. He, too, worried about the spread of Communism and the future of Germany, and he wanted to help more, by extending the debt moratorium for another year and cancelling war-debt payments to America. President Hoover, however, refused to endorse either of these proposals. Still, Stimson also wondered if the Germans were not exaggerating the danger to attract greater support from the United States for their efforts to modify the Treaty of Versailles and to improve on the economic arrangements provided for by the debt moratorium and the standstill agreement. Allen Klots advised Stimson that "the Germans can do much to remedy this situation themselves." Stimson concurred, noting that he thought there were steps the German government could take domestically to ease its economic problems. In any event, the United States could not deliver any formal changes to Versailles. Stimson informed the Germans that the United States "had confidence in Germany and that the American government has shown this" through its efforts to stabilize German finances. Restrained, however, by Hoover's reluctance to take further action, he knew the United States could not solve all of Germany's problems. "In the final event," Stimson told his hosts, "Germany could be saved only by her own efforts and the German people must show the requisite courage and confidence which will persuade the banking institutions of the world that it will be safe to lend her their resources."[18]

In a little over a month, Stimson had succeeded in persuading Hoover to propose a moratorium on debts and establish the standstill agreement on private credits. On top of his achievement of a naval disarmament agreement the previous year, this was an impressive set of accomplishments for the secretary of state under the most difficult of circumstances. Yet, Stimson returned from his European trip pessimistic about the economic conditions and political future of the continent. The secretary could not see how Europe was going to survive without American leadership and greater efforts at disarmament, debt reduction, and reduced government spending. That the Hoover administration, to Stimson's frustration, had no new policies to offer only compounded the problem. Stimson did what he could to convince the French of the "impossibility of the Versailles Treaty stabilizing" Europe, and claimed that "it would be much wiser to try to stabilize the situation at a median position" rather than continuing to use their power to keep Germany at a disadvantage. He and the president both saw France as the major obstacle to solving the problems of Europe, and believed that, "if Germany collapses, if Germany has a revolution, it would affect France" more than any other European nation. Still, Hoover "did not see how the United States could take the leadership" in resolving this problem. He believed most Americans recognized the sacrifices made during the Great War by the United States, "yet Europe was in a worse condition than she was before the war." In that context, the American public wanted little more to do with European affairs.[19] Try as Stimson might, he could not persuade the president to offer more relief to Europe.

In 1932, Stimson made one more effort to persuade Hoover to extend further American aid to ease Europe's economic problems and to end the unwise efforts to collect European war debts. In June, the Hoover administration attempted to break the deadlock in disarmament negotiations. The so-called Hoover Plan called for a one-third reduction of all armies beyond the level required to preserve internal order. Although its purpose was to encourage the nations of Europe to act in concert and reduce their spending on armaments, the effort failed to gain European acceptance and was met with criticism at home and abroad. Critics argued that disarmament talks were a distraction from the work of solving the world's economic problems. Moreover, the Hoover Plan was proposed at the same time as the opening of the Lausanne Economic Conference. At Lausanne, the nations of Europe agreed to repudiate both reparations by Germany and inter-Allied debts in a bid to ease the economic crisis, provided that a similar agreement could be reached with the United States on their war debts. It was hoped that the United States would follow suit and cancel the remaining debts owed by Europe.

Stimson believed that the Lausanne settlement "might really be the beginning of a recovery" and that the United States had to provide its complete support. Hoover, however, refused to link the debts owed to the United States to reparation payments. "He told me," Stimson noted in his diary, "that he entirely differed with me, in fundamentals, that we really had no common ground; that he thought the debts owed to us could and should be paid." Stimson replied that they "were indeed on such different ground" that he could not give him much good advice and offered to resign.[20]

To Stimson, Hoover was wrong for both economic and political reasons. The repayment of the war debts served only to further unbalance international trade, and cancellation "would certainly have a considerable reviving effect on world trade, and even a very small gain of this sort would more than balance the payments lost by the United States." Stimson saw even greater political value in reaching an agreement to end the payment of the war debts. He believed "it would restore an atmosphere of good feeling and confidence between the United States and western Europe" at a crucial time. But Stimson was unable to persuade the president to budge, and the effort to obtain cancellation fell through.[21]

This episode represented to Stimson all the shortcomings of Hoover's policies and all the difficulties of working with him. He believed the president's refusal had undone "all the benefits of the good will that we have been laboring so hard for the past three years." He noted that he was "trying to make it as easy as possible" for the European debtors, but "my zone of operations has been a very narrow one, for the President has been perfectly set in his policy." What Stimson wanted was for the United States to assert leadership in getting "these damn debts" out of the way. Stimson had tried to convince Hoover that there was little chance of recovering the debts anyway, and that, when a nation such as France took the risk of giving up reparations from Germany "in spite of all the feeling in France arising out of the war on behalf of those reparations, . . . it seems preposterous to think that we should be able to keep our debts."[22]

As the crisis in Germany worsened, Stimson could offer no new proposals or aid. The ambivalent response to Adolf Hitler's becoming chancellor on January 30, 1933, was clearly a reflection of Hoover and Stimson's position as heads of a lame-duck administration. The president saw Hitler's government as "monarchical and reactionary," but also "bitterly hostile to the Communists" and "curiously enough committed to a very radical . . . program." Stimson thought the Nazis were more "a protest" than a party, and that it was not clear in which direction they would go.[23] Yet, given the state of affairs in Europe and his inability to get Hoover to assert American leadership to solve the economic crisis, Stimson was also full of foreboding about the future. He believed that the events in Europe were similar to an unfolding Greek tragedy, where one saw the march of events and knew what action should be taken, but was powerless to prevent "its marching to its grim conclusion."[24]

Creating the Good Neighbor Policy

The negative impact of the Great Depression was not limited to Europe. Latin American nations, with their heavy dependence on the export of raw materials, quickly felt the impact of the spreading world economic crisis. In 1930 and 1931 alone, there were ten revolutions in the twenty nations of the region, creating growing concern in Washington about stability and order to the south. These numerous changes of government not only raised the question of recognition of the new governments, but also the best means for the United States to ensure its goals of stable neighbor nations friendly to the United States and open to American trade and investment. Stimson recognized that direct U.S. intervention in various nations had, "instead of promoting feelings of friendship . . . initiated feelings of hate and hostility towards this country."[25] He believed that good relations with Latin America were hindered "by several historic sore spots," such as sending the marines into Mexico, Haiti, and Nicaragua, "which have been obstinately interfering with the growth of good will and friendly relations between us and our neighbors to the south." American actions were misperceived, Stimson stated, and "have all suffered from distortion in South America unwarranted by these events as we understood them. Each has been used by the enemies and critics of the United States as proof positive that we are an imperialist people prone to use our power in subverting the independence of our neighbors." These accusations, which Stimson found "unjustifiable," had nonetheless "damaged our good name, our credit, and our trade far beyond the apprehension of our own people."[26]

Stimson asserted that the American interventions had been in the best interests of both the United States and these nations, and he declared in 1931 that American policy toward Latin America "has been a noble one." He was confident that a "calm historical perspective" would refute the charge that American actions in the Western Hemisphere were a "manifestation of a selfish American imperialism" and demonstrate that the United States had respected the legal rights of all the other countries. The United States only intervened to uphold principles and international law in an area "where the progress of these republics has been most slow" and "where the recurrence of domestic violence has most frequently

resulted in the failure of duty on the part of the republics themselves and the violation of the rights of life and property accorded
by international law to foreigners."[27] Still, Stimson was forced to
acknowledge the growing nationalism and criticism that these actions had engendered.

The secretary, therefore, sought to continue the policy he first
developed in Nicaragua of removing American forces from the region, while finding indigenous means of maintaining stability and
a favorable environment for American business. As he noted in regard to Cuba, it was necessary to develop policies so "that less and
less pressure would be necessary on the part of the United States
to keep matters straight."[28] Recognizing that American actions had
aroused more anger than gratitude, Stimson officially overturned
the Roosevelt Corollary with the publication, in 1930, of a memorandum prepared by J. Reuben Clark of the State Department. This
statement rejected U.S. intervention in the internal affairs of its
neighbors. Stimson explained that the change was warranted because "the Monroe Doctrine was a declaration of the United States
versus Europe—not of the United States versus Latin America."[29]

This, however, was not an easy step, as events in El Salvador
would soon demonstrate, and it led to a greater reliance than ever
by the United States on the military rulers in the region to enforce
stability and protect trade and investments. Stimson continued to
hold his paternalistic views of nonwhites and was unwilling to
consider Latin American nationalists seriously. For example, at one
point during negotiations between Bolivia and Paraguay in Washington, D.C., Stimson noted that he was trying to assist "in settling
the irritating difficulties between those two little nonsensical republics."[30] By 1933, dictators ruled fifteen of the twenty Latin
American republics, most of them having come to power in the
previous two years and enjoying the support of the United States.
They were seen as necessary and useful rulers who served to protect American interests by preserving order, controlling radical reform movements, and protecting American investments while they
obviated the need for direct U.S. intervention.

The military's overthrow of the government in El Salvador created a crisis for the Hoover administration at the same time that it
was trying to respond to the economic collapse in Europe and the
Japanese invasion of Manchuria. Events in El Salvador challenged
the Republican adherence to the 1923 Washington Treaty of nonrecognition of governments that came to power by revolution in
Central America and, in 1932, brought a reversal of that policy.

Responding to what the State Department viewed as a Communist revolt in January 1932, the United States informally recognized the government of General Maximiliano Hernández Martínez because he was seen as necessary to stability and anti-Communism in the region. Martínez took power after the overthrow of El Salvador's first democratically elected president, Arturo Araujo, in December 1931. In keeping with the 1923 Washington Treaty, the State Department initially refused to recognize Martínez. After a peasant revolt in January 1932, this policy came into conflict with the overriding desire for stability. The department's interpretation of the domestic unrest in El Salvador as Bolshevist incited, and an assessment of the people of El Salvador as inferior and in need of a firm hand, led Stimson to ignore Martínez's responsibility for the *matanza* [massacre] that killed thirty thousand El Salvadoreans and to accept the murderous Martínez as the ruler of El Salvador. As he had done in Nicaragua, Stimson relied on the military to enforce stability and order. The Roosevelt administration, acting under the Good Neighbor policy, accepted the policies of the Republicans in Central America and extended formal recognition to Martínez in January 1934.

El Salvador, because of the domination of the so-called forty families (the oligarchy), had been one of the most politically stable nations in Central America. Coffee, which had been introduced there in the mid-nineteenth century, was the dominant crop, accounting for over 90 percent of all exports by the 1920s. The oligarchy's power rested in its control of the *haciendas*, which control had been solidified in the 1880s when the government abolished all town communal land holdings in the name of private property. The costs of these actions to the peasants were high. Tens of thousands were displaced from the lands they farmed, and the production of staple crops, such as maize and beans, was dramatically cut. During the 1920s, the amount of land devoted to coffee production increased 34 percent, and El Salvador became dependent on food imports from the United States. While most peasants had survived on seasonal work and subsistence wages, the price of maize increased 100 percent and beans 225 percent during the 1920s. Sporadic peasant unrest was met forcefully by the Guardia Nacional. In addition to selling staple foods to El Salvador, U.S. banks lent $21 million to the government and appointed a fiscal agent to supervise the collection of trade duties. The coming of the Great Depression only worsened the situation. Coffee prices had dropped from $15.75 per hundred kilograms in 1928 to $5.97 by 1932, a devastating blow to a nation that got over 80 percent of its national income from coffee. The income of plantation workers, which had barely reached subsistence levels in 1928, was cut in half by 1932. Life for the *campesinos* was reaching a point of starvation and desperation. These were the key factors in the peasant revolt of 1932.

The domination of El Salvador by the oligarchy had provided political stability there in contrast to the unrest in Nicaragua. The oligarchy had established the custom of having each president personally designate his heir, thereby preventing internal factions from contesting for power. The presidents were "thorough-going dictators who ruled with an iron hand" in the interests of the oligarchy and the military.[31] In 1927, the candidate "elected" was Pío Romero Bosque. Romero Bosque, however, turned out to be a reformer who desired to open up the political process and hold free elections for the presidency. When the time came, he refused to name a successor. The American Embassy in San Salvador feared problems in Dr. Bosque's attempt to broaden the political process, a step embassy officials did not believe El Salvador was ready for. Given U.S. support of the oligarchy and the stability it imposed on El Salvador, the economic advantages it provided Americans, and the paternalistic views of State Department leaders that portrayed Latin Americans as incapable of democracy, the department saw no reason for change.

The onset of the Great Depression and the fall of coffee prices, coupled with the now open presidential race, brought about rising and widespread vocal opposition to the oligarchy's rule and the status quo in El Salvador. Most of the opposition came from unorganized peasants and the trade unions in San Salvador. In addition, the Partido Comunisto de El Salvador (PCS), headed by Agustín Farabundo Martí, was founded in 1929. This party, however, never grew much beyond the students and intellectuals in the capital. The crash of coffee prices set off a series of protests in the nation. Eighty thousand people marched in San Salvador on May Day, 1930, demanding a minimum wage for agricultural workers, an end to unemployment, and better working conditions. Smaller demonstrations followed in both the capital and small towns, particularly around Izalco in the San Sonate Province. The government moved quickly to put an end to these protests. President Bosque banned all demonstrations and the distribution of "leftist" literature. Mass arrests were made, and in the four-month period leading up to the election, twelve hundred people were jailed. The government's actions curtailed the number of demonstrations but did not eliminate unrest in the nation.

In March 1930, the new American chargé, W. W. Schott, wrote to Stimson to report on the first upsurge of protest. Although there was some cause for concern, he believed that prompt government action would quickly return calm to the nation. He did not think "radicalism extends widely in the capital nor that the Government, by prompt and decisive measures, could not eradicate it entirely." Unfortunately, "it has not seen fit" to do so. Ignoring the conditions that prompted the protests or the demands being made, Schott laid the blame at the feet of "agitators" who were "spreading subversive doctrines." Even after reporting cases of violence on the large estates, the chargé stated that the ordinary Salvadorean "does not incline toward change." The danger was that, given their ignorance, they could be aroused by the PCS toward actions they did not understand. Still, the "situation could be controlled by no great energetic action."[32]

By August, the chargé's reports indicated that El Salvador's problems had passed.[33] Given such reporting and the prevalent views of American officials, it is no wonder that the State Department concluded in 1931 that El Salvador's political situation was the best and most stable in the region, and would remain so as long as no one tried to institute too much change. The president needed only to maintain the support of the army and the oligarchy. The key to El Salvador's stability was that the Assembly was under the complete control of the president and approved whatever he wanted. This meant, the Division of Latin American Affairs concluded, that "in general the Governments of Salvador have been fairly good, not oppressive to the people and with very little danger of being overthrown by revolution."[34] The Secretary of State agreed. Stimson noted in his diary that El Salvador's stability made it the "second best" of the Central American republics.[35]

In this climate of unrest and repression, the first genuinely free elections were held in El Salvador in January 1931. Six candidates entered the race, three from the now-divided oligarchy, two generals, including General Martínez, and Arturo Araujo. While the other five represented the status quo and the interests of the oligarchy, Araujo campaigned as a liberal reformer. Even though he was a large landowner, he was known to pay his workers twice the normal wage. Labor and the peasants, lacking any political organizations of their own, supported Araujo. After a bitter campaign, and a last-minute withdrawal by Martínez to become Araujo's vice president, Araujo led all the candidates with over 100,000 votes to 62,000 for the second candidate and 53,000 for the other three combined. Lacking a majority, the election went to the Assembly where Araujo's election was ensured when the third-place candidate supported him.[36] Araujo's promises of land reform and legalized trade unions proved popular with the masses and indicated that many people in El Salvador desired change more than American officials had believed.

Inaugurated on March 1, 1931, Araujo's government lasted only nine months. The new government was ill-fated from the outset. On the one hand, the oligarchy went on "strike." Unwilling to accept the election results, El Salvador's elite refused to allow their supporters to take any government jobs. This deprived Araujo of most of El Salvador's experienced professionals. On the other hand, having raised the expectations of the poor, Araujo found he could not satisfy his supporters. By July, martial law was declared and Araujo was relying on traditional methods to maintain his authority. In the fall, Araujo lost the support of the army, and on December 2, 1931, the army ousted him and established General Martínez as the new president.[37] Because he was vice president and minister of war in Araujo's government and was thought to have played a role in planning the coup, the State Department, in the midst of the Manchurian crisis, invoked the 1923 Washington Treaty and denied recognition to Martínez.

From the outset of the army rebellion, the actions of the new American minister, Charles Curtis, frustrated Stimson. Curtis had failed to inform the leaders of the revolt that the United States would uphold the "Hughes doctrine," as Stimson called it, of not recognizing any revolutionary government. "This was a lost chance," Stimson wrote in his diary, "because we have often been able to prevent a revolution by notifying the conspirators that even if they were successful, they wouldn't get any recognition."[38] Stimson wired Curtis that he needed to make this policy clear to the leaders of the revolt.[39] He found the situation in El Salvador "critical" and instructed Curtis to ascertain how General Martínez believed "a regime which can be recognized can be brought into office."[40]

Nonrecognition placed the United States in a difficult position. Martínez had the support of both the military and the oligarchy and thus the power to defy American wishes and remain in power. Without the threat of military intervention, clearly out of the question given Stimson's position regarding Japan's actions in Manchuria, his efforts to withdraw American forces from Nicaragua, and the publication of the Clark Memorandum, how could the United States effectively influence events in El Salvador? The problem could be solved only through a change in policy.

In his first effort to resolve this problem and arrange a government in El Salvador that the United States could recognize, Stimson sent Jefferson Caffery to San Salvador on December 19, 1931, as a special representative of the Department of State. Caffery, who was currently the U.S. Minister to Colombia, was a former minister to El Salvador and enjoyed Stimson's confidence. Despite protests that the United States had no desire to interfere in the internal affairs of El Salvador, the Caffery mission was designed to obtain Martínez's removal and the creation of a new government headed by somebody, civilian or military, who could be recognized by the United States under the terms of the treaty.

Caffery immediately sought Martínez's resignation. He told the general directly that "under no circumstances could [the United States] recognize him."[41] His initial meetings, however, brought no movement by the president. Caffery informed Stimson that "unfortunately the better elements here are now supporting General Martínez because he offers for the moment a stable government."[42] With Martínez refusing to step down, Caffery realized that further efforts designed to secure a voluntary resignation were futile; he turned his attention instead to the young officers who had organized the December 2 revolt. Caffery sought, in effect, another coup to remove Martínez and replace him with somebody who was not associated with Araujo's government and was, therefore, eligible for U.S. recognition. Caffery was able, so he believed, to persuade the officers to "force Martínez out and replace him with someone" who was eligible under the treaty.[43] He informed the officers that the "Department of State would be glad to recognize anyone not debarred by the treaty." Responding to the "tactfully" expressed concern relating to the "well known charges regarding the United States forcing its will on the smaller Latin American countries," Caffery assured them that the United States "had not the slightest desire of doing anything of the kind; 'we are backing no candidates.'"[44]

Caffery returned to Washington, D.C., on January 8, 1932. Stimson termed his "rescue mission" a success because it had persuaded the "people who are in control there . . . to abide by . . . our views of the situation."[45] Caffery, however, had been unable to obtain a commitment from the officers to a specific time or a person who would replace Martínez, and they made no move to oust the general. More than likely, they had told Caffery what he wanted to hear, not what they intended to do. Accustomed to the U.S. domination of events in the region, Stimson believed El Salvador would have to yield to American desires.

The failure of Caffery's mission did not signal the end of American pressure. Stimson wrote the newest chargé, William McCafferty, on January 13 that "under no circumstances [could Martínez] be recognized," and that the department hoped that an acceptable "government may be established in Salvador at the earliest possible moment."[46] Lacking a military threat or economic lever, there was little more Stimson could do. A gradual shift, however, in the American position was beginning to appear. Equating all unrest with Communism, the danger of a Communistic uprising began to become a regular feature in embassy reports. This fear led to a re-evaluation of Martínez. Summarizing the concerns of the embassy staff, McCafferty reported on January 20 that, for the "past three years and especially during the Araujo administration, communism has been permitted to spread throughout Salvador." The leaders, particularly the "notorious Agustin Marti," had "succeeded in inciting the farm laborers to take over control of several large coffee plantations," and only government force had kept control of the situation. Labeling the problem "serious," McCafferty was genuinely worried about a revolt.[47]

On January 22, 1932, thousands of Salvadorean peasants, armed mainly with machetes, attacked local government and army outposts in the western coffee regions of El Salvador. They briefly held a few towns, the largest being San Sonate, a town of twenty thousand and a commercial center for the coffee area. The government quickly crushed the rebellion. The insurrection had led to the killing of a hundred people, but the *matanza* that followed claimed up to thirty thousand lives. Unions and all other political organizations were banned in the country. The U.S. government justified this severe repression on the grounds that the peasants who revolted were Communists.[48]

McCafferty set the tone with a report on January 23. He ironically urged the State Department to help the government "in any way," as it "might prevent the threatened establishment of a communistic state here accompanied by much bloodshed." The chargé requested American warships be sent to El Salvador and that financial aid be extended to the government.[49] Two days later he reported that the "large landowners against whom the venom of the Communists is naturally directed" remained scared.[50]

The chargé's reports created alarm in Washington. Stimson dispatched three American warships carrying marines from the Special Service Squadron in Panama to El Salvador. Although he hoped that the marines would be unnecessary, "for it would make a bad impression in Latin America," they were sent as a precaution should the government lose control of the situation.[51] The State Department informed the press that there had been a genuine Communist revolt, not a popular rebellion, and that its leaders had come from Mexico. The situation had been serious, but the Martínez government was taking energetic action to suppress the rebellion.[52]

Martínez's actions not only strengthened his position domestically, as he was declared constitutional president by the Assembly on February 5, but also brought about a reversal in American policy. Stimson's changing position was apparent immediately when he noted on January 25 that the "communistic revolution in Salvador . . . produces a rather nasty . . . problem, because the man who is president and who is the only pillar against the success of what seems to be a rather nasty proletarian revolution is Martínez, whom we were unable to recognize under the 1923 rule."[53] Stimson moved to resolve this dilemma. He wrote the U.S. minister in Guatemala that the question of recognition was now "a difficult one," because "Martínez appears to have strengthened his position . . . as a result of having put down the recent disorders and he apparently has a favorable majority in the recently elected Salvadorean Congress."[54]

By the beginning of February, McCafferty was reporting that the government was firmly in control, and that order would be maintained as long as there were "sufficient funds to pay the armed forces."[55] He argued that the department should relax its legalistic opposition toward Martínez. The general was willing to give up the formal position of president while retaining actual control of the government. He would appoint the First Designate as president, return to the vice presidency, and, therefore, be able to "resume the Presidency" should the First Designate resign in "say 6 or 7 months."[56] Stimson replied that the United States could not support Martínez's proposal. "It is clear that the plan contemplates an evasion of the terms of the Treaty" and would consist of U.S. recognition of Martínez's government. Yet Stimson wanted it made clear to Martínez that the department's actions were "not motivated by any unfriendliness against General Martínez for whom it has great regard." McCafferty informed Martínez that he believed the only thing he could do was resign outright.[57]

In early March, Stimson was willing to accept a different plan that allowed for recognition of a government in which Martínez maintained power. On March 8, McCafferty telegraphed Stimson that "Martínez had decided to resign the Presidency outright." He would, instead, become the minister of war in the new government. Stimson responded that the State Department had no objection to that arrangement.[58] When McCafferty met with Martínez on April 2 to discuss why the promised change had not occurred and when he could inform the State Department to expect the reorganization, Martínez replied that a change at that time would be a disaster. He argued that Communism remained a serious problem, that the army wanted him to remain, and that he had the support of the public. On June 8, Martínez announced that he was no longer going to try and find an arrangement to satisfy the 1923 treaty and that he would remain in office until the end of his term in 1935. Stability and the desire of the overwhelming majority of the people were his stated reasons for this move. McCafferty reported that nonrecognition was not seen as a problem by Martínez and his advisors.[59]

Stimson was faced with the decision of withdrawing the chargé and closing the legation or leaving McCafferty in San Salvador and thereby extending informal recognition to Martínez. Not removing McCafferty, supporters argued, would destroy the 1923 treaty and undermine U.S. ability to influence events in the region short of military intervention. It was, in effect, a choice between increasing American pressure and forcing Martínez out, or accepting him in power. Stimson had, however, already reached the conclusion that Martínez was necessary for stability in El Salvador. Not surprisingly, the secretary of state decided to keep the legation open. To do otherwise, he believed, would be seen as a signal of disapproval of Martínez. Stimson preferred to end the American commitment to a treaty the United States had never signed and have the United States "resume its freedom of action and . . . judge each case upon its merits."[60] On that basis, Stimson saw the continuation of Martínez's rule as necessary for the stability and development of El Salvador and the protection of American interests in the region.

In a review of its accomplishments at the end of Hoover's presidency, the State Department continued to label the uprising in El Salvador as a "communist revolt." The *matanza* was ignored. Instead, the report noted only that the "government . . . suppressed the uprising with utmost severity in a relatively short time and succeeded in restoring order. *This display of efficiency strengthened Martínez' position in the republic."*[61] Instead of hurting his standing with the United States, the *matanza* bolstered Martínez's position. It did not incite condemnation and statements that it was proof that the United States was correct in not backing such a government, but rather a growing approval of the general and proposals for skirting the legal problem of recognition. Finding no such method, the State Department simply quit its efforts to "retire" Martínez, and, in June 1932, informally recognized his regime. The dictator was now seen as essential for social peace and the development of El Salvador. The perceived benefits of stability, trade, and anti-Bolshevism called for the continued American support of authoritarian rulers throughout the hemisphere and overrode the problems of constitutionality and the desire to help limit arbitrary power in Central America.

Stimson believed that his policy toward Latin America was an unqualified success. As he wrote upon leaving office, he had managed to improve relations with all nations in the hemisphere by pursuing a policy of nonintervention. The United States had renounced forceful interventions and "the use of military pressure to collect business debts in foreign countries," and was "withdrawing our marines as rapidly as possible from Santo Domingo, Haiti, and Nicaragua." In addition, the administration "reestablished the sensible practice of our forefathers as to the recognition of new governments in conformity with their rights to regulate their own internal affairs, and, in view of the economic depression, and the consequent need for prompt measures of financial stabilization, have accorded to them recognition under this policy with as little delay as possible in order to give them the quickest possible opportunity for recovering their economic poise."[62] Franklin Roosevelt would gain most of the credit for this policy with the announcement in his inaugural address that U.S. relations with the other American republics would be based on the "policy of the good neighbor . . . who resolutely respects . . . the rights of others." Yet the Good Neighbor policy was first practiced by Stimson as based on his perhaps not overly neighborly policy. Moreover, having renounced the use of force, the Good Neighbor policy was dependent on strong authoritarian rulers who imposed order and stability, received U.S. backing, and blocked nascent reform efforts that challenged American policy and economic interests in the region.

The Stimson Doctrine

On September 18, 1931, fighting broke out in the Manchurian city of Mukden. The Japanese claimed that the rail lines had been bombed and that they were responding to Chinese provocations. In reality, the Japanese staged the incident in order to begin a military operation that would lead to their complete control over China's most northern province by the beginning of the next year. Thus began the decade-long aggression by Japan that would culminate in the December 7, 1941, attack on Pearl Harbor. It fell to Stimson to forget the first attempts by the United States to deal with this new aggression and rally international action to protect both China and American interests in East Asia. In the course of the crisis, Stimson moved from a cautious effort to warn the Japanese to respect China's territory and their international agreements to a policy of nonrecognition, the Stimson Doctrine, that placed the United States in the lead of a world too divided and distracted by the Great Depression to uphold collective security and take any more forceful action. Stimson knew that nonrecognition would not deter Japan. At the same time, he was determined to make it clear that Japan's attack was wrong and that the United States would use its influence to oppose such actions. The Stimson Doctrine was not, therefore, empty idealism, but the first, if still insufficient, step in awakening world opinion against Japan and to the growing danger of war.

The United States had struggled since the announcement of the Open Door policy at the end of the nineteenth century to preserve the territorial integrity of China against the efforts by Europeans and the Japanese to gain concessions and possibly divide China into colonies. At the end of World War I, China was more a name than an actual political entity. The last dynasty had collapsed in 1911, and the country was a patchwork of areas governed by the Kuomintang Party (KMT), warlords, and foreign nations with extraterritoriality arrangements over various ports and transportation lines. As part of the Washington System designed to bring stability to international relations in East Asia, the United States sponsored both the Five-Power Washington Naval Limitations Treaty and the Nine-Power Treaty that called upon all nations to recognize China's rights and the nationalist government once it established effective control. In keeping with its efforts to support Chinese nationalism, the United States was the first nation to recognize the KMT as the government of China.

By the 1920s, Japan provided the greatest threat to China. After the United States had forced the opening of Japan in the 1850s, Japanese leaders concluded that the only way to prevent their nation from being conquered was to adopt the West's economic system. As a result, Japan became the first non-Western nation to industrialize. Yet Japan's road to industrialization was beset with significant problems. The first was geographical. Japan lacked many of the raw materials necessary for a fully developed industrial economy and had to import much of its fuel and other basic items. Second, Japan suffered from overpopulation and an inability to produce enough food on the home islands to feed its people. Again taking their cue from the Western powers, the Japanese sought a solution to these problems through colonial conquests, most notably, Korea and Taiwan, and by gaining control over parts of China. This allowed for both access to raw materials and the settlement of Japanese citizens abroad.

Washington and Tokyo, therefore, were pursuing conflicting policies regarding China. The United States was trying to protect the Open Door, access to China, and Chinese nationalism, while Japan was attempting to increase its influence in the area. These difficulties were furthered by Japan's dissatisfaction with the Versailles Treaty and its failure to gain control over the former German concessions in China. The United States needed to find some mechanism that protected China and kept Japan from making a protectorate out of large portions of its territory, while still recognizing legitimate Japanese security interests and needs for markets and raw materials.

The Washington System appeared to satisfy the goals of both sides. The United States gained naval limitations, agreement to the Open Door policy, and assurances that differences would be worked out through negotiations. Japan, growing ever more dependent on the United States for oil, lumber, and other products, and fearful of a U.S.-U.K. alliance, agreed to seek its security and prosperity through international cooperation. Its leaders concluded at the time that Japan could not afford to be isolated and would gain more through cooperation with the United States. Throughout the 1920s, relations between Washington and Tokyo were friendly, and the system appeared to work as designed. The KMT gained greater control over China, spending on arms was limited, and Japan's trade with both the United States and China increased, with the United States alone taking more than 40 percent of Japan's exports. This trade allowed Japan access to the foodstuffs and raw materials on which its prosperity depended.

As it had in Europe, the coming of the Great Depression undercut the programs established by the United States during the 1920s. With access to American funds ended by the crash on Wall Street and with the disastrous Hawley-Smoot Tariff Act cutting Japan's exports to the United States in half, the Washington System quickly unraveled. The British, French, and Dutch also closed off their empires from foreign trade, leaving Japan unable to obtain many of the imports it needed. The militarist faction in Japan, which had always questioned the policy of cooperation with the West, now gained the upper hand. The military argued that the United States had upheld the Open Door only when it was to Washington's advantage and had used it to control Japan. For Japan to prosper, the militarists believed, it would have to act unilaterally to secure markets, materials, and wealth. In September 1931, Japan made its first move by taking control over Manchuria by force.

From the outset, Stimson opposed the Japanese military seizure of Manchuria. Yet, in the first days of the crisis, it was not clear to Stimson whether the attacks on Mukden and other strategic points in the province were caused by "the Army . . . acting under a plan of the Government or on its own."[63] The Japanese ambassador reported that the incident was "a great surprise to him" and that Baron Shidehara, the Japanese foreign minister, was trying to "isolate" the situation.[64] Stimson saw the event as stemming from a split within the Japanese government between moderates who wanted to continue to pursue international cooperation and extreme nationalists who wanted the glory of conquest. He thought, on September 21, that the foreign minister and cabinet were "sitting tight and . . . doing their best to prevent the Ministry of War from running amok." His policy, as he outlined it the next day, was "to let the Japanese know that we are watching them and at the same time to do it in a way which will help Shidehara, who is on the right side, and not play into the hands of any Nationalist agitators on the other." Stimson concluded that the "evidence in our hands pointed to" allowing Shidehara "an opportunity, free from anything approaching a threat or even public criticism, to get control of the situation."[65]

Stimson believed that his policy of patience and reticence provided the best chance for a quick and peaceful settlement of the crisis. He also thought that any other course of action, while there was still hope that the Japanese government might reverse the military's course, would lead either to failure or war. Stimson soon realized, however, that his assumptions about the split within the Japanese government were wrong, and that the military campaign in Manchuria was part of what he termed "a widely extended movement of aggression" that was carried out "only after careful preparation with a strategic goal in mind."[66] He, therefore, began the process of seeking new measures for gradually building up pressure against Japan to force a modification of its policy, and then mobilizing world opinion in the hopes of making his policy work. In early October, he noted that the situation in Manchuria was "rapidly getting bad" and that he was afraid that the United States would have to "take a firm ground and aggressive stand toward Japan. It is a very ticklish situation and I am much troubled by it."[67]

In the wake of the Japanese bombing of Chinchow on October 9, Stimson sought Hoover's approval for more direct warnings to Japan about upholding its treaty obligations and closer U.S. cooperation with the League of Nations. Hoover worried that the Europeans would try to dump the problem in the American lap, and he did not want to be put "into a humiliating position" of making threats "in case Japan refused to do anything" to honor what he called America's "scraps of paper." Hoover's view greatly troubled his secretary of state and led to sharp words between the two men. First, Stimson informed the president that he had been trying to persuade the League of Nations to take action on China's behalf. He noted that it was his "policy to encourage the League" and to provide moral support for its efforts so as to not "leave it in our lap." As to the notion that treaties were merely "scraps of paper," Stimson responded that, from his point of view, "This fight has come on in the worst part of the world for peace treaties." The agreements of the Western nations "no more fit the three great races of Russia, Japan, and China," Stimson declared, than "a stovepipe hat would fit an African savage." Nevertheless, the whole world was watching to see if the treaties would have any power. "If we lie down and treat them like scraps of paper nothing will happen, and in the future the peace movement will receive a blow that it will not recover from for a long time," if Japan were allowed to run wild and do whatever it pleased by force. After both men cooled down, Hoover informed Stimson the next day that he approved of his policy.[68]

The movement toward greater cooperation with the League in applying pressure on Japan stemmed from Stimson's desire to mobilize public opinion as a means to modify Tokyo's actions and bring about a negotiated settlement to the crisis. The League had issued a call for the removal of Japanese troops from Manchuria and agreed to establish a committee, later to be called the Lytton Commission, to investigate the incident of September 18 and determine who was responsible for the fighting. Stimson believed "that the public opinion of the world is a live factor which can be promptly mobilized and which has become a factor of prime importance in the solution of the problems and controversies which may arise between nations."[69] He recalled using public opinion when he was U.S. Attorney to assist him in his prosecutions of corporations and thought that it could again serve him in carrying out his policy of ending Japan's efforts at conquering Manchuria.

Within Hoover's cabinet, Secretary of War Patrick Hurley raised objections to these new departures. On November 13, he argued that the administration was making "a mistake to get into it at all; that the Japanese were going to seize Manchuria anyhow, and we are simply letting our country in for a rebuff and a loss of prestige." The only policy that would work was using force. The president, however, had ruled out that option as early as 1929 when he stated in an Armistice Day speech that "neither our obligations to China, nor our own interests or dignity require us to go to war " over Japan's violations of China's sovereignty, and he had not changed his position. Stimson was sympathetic to Hurley's position, but he also knew that it was not feasible. Therefore, the "only alternative when this thing came up was either to lie down and destroy all peace treaties, or else to do the best we could with the force of public opinion." He pointed out that when the United States rejected the League, it "had deliberately chosen to rest solely upon treaties with the sanction of public opinion alone." Thus, American policy had to be one based on upholding the Nine-Power Treaty and the Open Door, or the administration would be "letting down our country on its determined policy."[70]

As Japan continued to expand its control in Manchuria, Stimson concluded that his original policy was not working. The question now was what could the United States do short of war? In early November, Japanese forces took Tsitsihar, 370 miles northwest of Mukden. This attack ended any pretense that Japan was simply putting down local disorders and protecting its interest in the Manchurian railroad. Stimson saw this attack as "a flagrant violation of the spirit and probably the letter of all the treaties." Moreover, he believed that the "Japanese Government which we have been dealing with is no longer in control," and that "the situation is in the hands of virtually mad dogs."[71] In response, he raised for the first time the possibility of an economic boycott against Japan to try to force it to stop its conquest. Although Hoover rejected sanctions, and the secretary of state was not yet willing to push him on this option, Stimson's approach to the crisis was hardening by the day. As Assistant Secretary of State Harvey Bundy recalled, "Stimson was prepared to go a long way in applying sanctions to the Japanese for their conduct in Manchuria," but Hoover "was very reluctant to go forward." The secretary of state "had been brought up in the Teddy Roosevelt tradition and believed in the exercise of power, and not waiting. . . . He believed in taking the bit in his teeth and going forward." The Colonel "was on his horse and ready to shoot the Japanese at sunrise," but he did not have the support of the president or the nation.[72] He, therefore, had to continue to push for other measures to try to reverse Japan's action.

In early December, the secretary of state again raised the question of an economic boycott, first with his senior advisors in the State Department and then with the president. Stimson's staff all acknowledged that there was "the danger of an embargo going further and leading to . . . war," but everyone except Castle thought that a Japanese collapse was much more likely. Stanley Hornbeck, chief of the Division of Far Eastern Affairs, argued that Japan could not withstand a boycott for "more than a very few days, or weeks." On Sunday afternoon, December 6, Stimson visited Hoover in the White House to see if he could persuade him to call for a cutoff of all trade with Japan. Stimson explained to Hoover that he was trying to "start from the same fundamental proposition that he did"; that economic action would create ill will and bring about the threat of a larger war. But these considerations had to be weighed "against the terrible disadvantages which Japan's action was doing to the cause of peace in the world at large and the danger that Japan was setting on foot a possible war with China which might spread to the entire world." Much to Stimson's surprise, he found that Hoover "was not absolutely and to the last resort against a boycott." The president did say, however, that it would have to be done under the auspices of the Nine-Power Treaty, not through the League, and only after a meeting of the signatory nations.[73] Hoover, however, quickly changed his mind. He was fearful that the imposition of economic sanctions would lead to war, and for a second time overruled Stimson on this matter.

On December 10, Japan's government fell, and the militarists took complete control over Japanese policy. Within days, Japan began its final push to conquer all of Manchuria. On January 2, 1932, the army took Chinchow and destroyed the last vestige of Chinese authority in the province. Now Stimson was confronted with a new problem. If the United States could not condone the violation of treaties and the president was unwilling to take any military or economic action to uphold the treaties, what could the United States do in the face of Japan's taking of Manchuria? Stimson, after spending a sleepless night pondering this question, got up on January 3 with his "mind clarified on what [he] wanted to do." He concluded that, with any resort to force or boycotts out of the question, the only viable answer was the nonrecognition of Japan's conquest. He needed to go back to the realm of public opinion and make sure that Japan was clearly branded as the aggressor and that its actions were not rewarded. His plan was to notify the other powers that the United States would not recognize any agreement that gave Japan control over Manchuria, and he would propose to the signatories of the Nine-Power Pact that they also refuse to recognize as legal any territorial changes that resulted from Japan's actions since September.[74]

The idea for what became the Stimson Doctrine had first been suggested by President Hoover back in November when he mentioned to his secretary of state that he was beginning to conclude that the "main weapon is to give an announcement" that if, to end the crisis, a treaty between Japan and China "is made under military pressure we will not recognize it or avow it."[75] Stimson spent most of the next two days working with his staff to prepare his note. On the evening of January 4, he brought the draft to the president where he received Hoover's approval of his course of action. The note was finally completed on January 7 and sent to Japan, China, and the other members of the Nine-Power Treaty. The Stimson Doctrine stated that, in light of Japan's most recent military actions and the destruction of the last remaining administrative authority of the Chinese government in Manchuria, it was the duty of the United States to inform both Japan and China "that it cannot admit the legality of any situation *de facto* nor does it intend to recognize any treaty or agreement entered into between those Governments . . . which may impair the treaty rights of the United States or its citizens in China, including those which relate to the sovereignty, the independence, or the territorial and administrative integrity of the Republic of China, or to the international policy relative to China, commonly known as the open door policy."[76]

Stimson believed that nonrecognition could effectively serve many American interests. It was a moral weapon designed to express the opposition of the United States and its people to the Japanese action and to shape world opinion on the issue. Moreover, it was intended to reassure China and protect American interests in East Asia. Stimson wrote in 1936 that he was aware of "the incalculable harm which would be done immediately to American prestige in China and ultimately to the material interests of America and her people in the region" if, after so many years of working to assist China and securing the "covenant of all the great powers, including ourselves, 'to respect her sovereignty, her independence and her territorial integrity,' we should now cynically abandon her to her fate when this same covenant was violated."[77]

Stimson did not profess to be able to check Japan's move or bring about a reversal of its course. But he did want to provide a mechanism for the whole of world opinion to weigh in on the side of China's integrity and against the use of force as a legitimate instrument of national policy. The Japanese had to be made to realize that, no matter what their success in Manchuria, they still had to contend with the opinion and power of the rest of the world. Faced with the choice of sanctioning Japan's dismemberment of China or not recognizing it and aligning American influence against aggression, Stimson found his course of action clear. With the world too divided to intervene against Japan, the Stimson Doctrine was the best alternative available for taking the leadership in condemning Japan's behavior and awakening the world to the potential dangers that would lie ahead. With the announcement of his nonrecognition doctrine, Stimson became the leading advocate of American opposition to aggression, a position he would hold down through World War II.

The Stimson Doctrine failed to attract any immediate support from other nations. Most disappointing to Stimson was Great Britain's rejection of it. While he understood that "poor old England is having so many troubles," he had hoped it would stand with the United States, and he knew that without London's support no other powers would endorse his policy. This did not really surprise the Colonel, because he realized that there was a great deal of sympathy for Japan among the European powers that found it difficult to condemn Japan without calling into question their own imperial policies. He could not, however, help comparing his action with those of the other leaders. It took, Stimson wrote, "a good deal of courage to keep up the necessary firm front not to compromise the rights of one's government during a period of general depression and discouragement." It was this failure of nerve that Japan was counting on to protect it. Stimson did not intend to "have some of my successors find that we yielded to it during this time" and failed to demonstrate resolve and leadership.[78]

On January 28, the crisis in China flared again with the Japanese bombing of Shanghai, a major port and center for international business. This assault, which directly threatened all of the Western nations' holdings in the International Settlement of that city, created a brief moment of united opposition. Stimson was outraged by Japan's actions and again sought to increase American pressure on Tokyo. With the president's approval and in conjunction with Great Britain, Stimson augmented American military strength in Shanghai to protect American interests. Both nations made it clear to the Japanese that they took the spread of fighting to other parts of China seriously. Stimson was, in Allen Klots's words, ready to run "a calculated risk of going to war with Japan, to take a strong stand," but President Hoover was still not willing to take economic or military action. Stimson told Hoover that the United States should use its economic and military strength to force Japan to comply with the treaties and American opinion. He quoted Theodore Roosevelt's statement that the nation had to "speak softly and carry a big stick!" The secretary of state did not necessarily want to put the threat into writing. It was better "to rely upon the unconscious elements of our great size and military strength" that he was sure "Japan was afraid of." Hoover, however, made it clear that he saw it as "folly" to get into a war with Japan, and "that such a war could not be localized or kept in bounds." He would fight to defend United States territory, but that was all.[79]

Still, Stimson believed he had to take some action. He did not want to send a note to the Nine-Power Treaty members due to his fear of the "yellow-bellied responses" he would receive and he did not want to make a speech on the issue. Stimson, following a technique he recalled Theodore Roosevelt using, decided to write an open letter to Senator William E. Borah of Idaho of the Senate Foreign Relations Committee. Sent on February 23, the letter served as a restatement of the U.S. commitment to the Nine-Power Treaty and the Open Door policy and its continued adherence to the principles set out in the Stimson Doctrine. What was new was Stimson's argument that the Nine-Power Treaty was a part of a series of agreements reached during the 1920s concerning disarmament and nonaggression, and that all of these arrangements were interrelated and interdependent. "No one of these treaties could be disregarded without disturbing the general understanding and equilibrium which were intended to be accomplished and effected by the group of agreements arrived at in their entirety." Any modification or abrogation of the terms relating to the territorial integrity of China automatically opened up the question of how binding all the other commitments were on the various signatory nations. In particular, it raised the question of American willingness to continue to limit its battleships or further fortify its naval bases in the Pacific.[80] In other words, Stimson was pointing out to Tokyo that, if Japan continued to violate the Open Door policy and the treaties designed to protect it, the United States would be free to rebuild its navy and take any other appropriate action to protect its policies and interests in the region.

Japan responded to this thinly veiled threat by arguing that it was not violating any treaties because the Imperial Government did not and "cannot consider that China is an 'organized people' within the meaning of the Covenant of the League of Nations."[81] As Stimson presciently noted, the lines were clearly drawn. "At present," Stimson wrote on March 9, "it seems to me that if Japan keeps up this attitude in which she now is, we are shaping up an issue between the two great theories of civilization and economic methods." Japan was not content with industrialization and trade, and was seeking to "make markets for herself in China by force, which means that she must permanently exploit China and impose the suzerainty of a dominant race upon another race." Stimson was convinced that Japan would fail, that China was too big and "the better race." In the meantime, Japan's policy would increasingly challenge American interests in the region, making it "almost impossible that there should not be an armed clash between two such different civilizations."[82]

Stimson still found himself in the minority. Similar to his observations concerning Europe as a Greek tragedy, he again was able to see the difficulties and challenges arising from international developments, but was once more frustrated by his inability to convince the president or his fellow citizens of the necessity for stronger action. He found himself armed with only "spears of straw and swords of ice," yet forced to carry out a policy that in the end he knew was weak and inadequate.[83] Stimson was gratified that the Lytton Commission report, which was published in October 1932, found Japan fully responsible for the crisis in Manchuria, and he worked hard during his remaining time in office to secure the League's adoption of its findings and recommendation to refuse to recognize the Japanese puppet state of Manchukuo. The League's agreement in February 1933 finally brought it in line with the policy Stimson had pursued for over a year. Still, the situation in Manchuria was not changed, and Japan, refusing to accept this judgment, left the League of Nations.

Hoover's defeat in the 1932 presidential election was something of a relief to Stimson. He noted on the day after the election that he had "a greater sense of freedom than I have [had] for four years." He did not know what he would do come March, but he was sure he would continue to speak out on international affairs and put to good use all he had learned during his term as secretary of state. What was unclear was what platform he would have and whether or not he would have access to the new administration. His party had just been defeated, and he had made some speeches highly critical of Roosevelt during the campaign. His fate was "in the lap of the gods, and only the future will tell what we can do." The immediate task ahead of him was to assist Roosevelt in the transition and "make sure that whoever comes in as Secretary of State after me shall have a fair chance to understand the policies we have been working out during this time, and, as far as possible, not do something to reverse them unnecessarily."[84]

The president, however, was very bitter over his defeat and distrustful of Roosevelt. The first effort at cooperation between the Hoover administration and Roosevelt went poorly when, in late November, the president-elect refused to promise his support for any actions Hoover might take concerning war debts. Roosevelt, wary of tying himself to any new actions by the administration, took the position that he could not intervene in the matter and that it was the responsibility of the men still in office to conduct policy. A second effort by Hoover in December ended on a similar note, with both Hoover and Stimson angry with Roosevelt over his unwillingness to endorse their idea of a new interlocking commission to work on debts, disarmament, and the depression. Stimson thought the plan would be a "great contribution . . . for it brings together all the elements of the problem," and he found Roosevelt's message of December 21 that he could not share responsibility for the creation of such a body a small act that left the administration "with nothing except to show that we have done our best."[85]

With negotiations seemingly at an impasse, Stimson received a call the next day from Felix Frankfurter, who was in Albany visiting Roosevelt. He told Stimson that, in the middle of their conversation, Roosevelt "suddenly out of a clear sky said, 'Why doesn't Henry Stimson come up here and talk with me and settle this damn thing that nobody seems to be able to do?' " Frankfurter told Stimson that the president-elect "feels very badly that all cooperative efforts had been broken off," and saw the disagreements over the war debts as "a terrible misunderstanding." Roosevelt wanted to cooperate, and if Stimson called Roosevelt, he would invite the secretary up to meet with him at his home in Hyde Park, New York. Hoover, however, was against it "from the first," and Stimson had to tell Frankfurter that he could not meet with Roosevelt. Stimson thought Hoover's position was wrong, that it made no sense to "deprive the incoming President of the United States of important information about foreign affairs," and he hoped it would not prevent a meeting later.[86]

Frankfurter came down to Washington on December 28 to give Stimson his impressions of Roosevelt and to extend a new invitation for a meeting between the two men. The portrait he painted of the New York governor "was a more attractive picture than we have been getting from the other side," and it convinced Stimson that he should meet with Roosevelt. When Hoover returned to Washington after the holidays, Stimson told him that he wanted to see Roosevelt, that it was his responsibility to give him the information he sought concerning the nation's foreign policy. Hoover said that Roosevelt was "a very dangerous and contrary man and that he would never see him alone." He could not be trusted. Stimson responded that it was his experience that if you showed trust to someone, that person usually proved worthy of the effort. Hoover conceded that it was possible that Stimson could have some influence on Roosevelt, and the next day he agreed to let the secretary of state go to New York to meet with him.[87]

Stimson's meeting with Roosevelt on January 9, 1933, in Hyde Park lasted for six hours. The two men covered all areas of American foreign policy and found themselves in substantial agreement concerning every major aspect of current policy. The first, and most important point to Stimson, was Roosevelt's understanding and support of his Manchurian policy. Roosevelt noted that he "fully approved" of Stimson's actions and "that his only possible criticism was that we did not begin it earlier." Concerning Latin America, Roosevelt inquired about the stability of Cuba and Haiti and indicated his agreement with the policy of removing American forces from the region as a means of reducing tensions. On the questions of disarmaments and debts, Stimson thought that Roosevelt underestimated the problems, but that "none of the President's forebodings" were realized. The two New Yorkers, who, oddly enough, given their connections to Theodore Roosevelt, had never met before, got along well. Roosevelt publicly endorsed the Stimson Doctrine the next week and in a follow-up meeting with Stimson in Washington remarked, "We are getting so that we do pretty good teamwork, don't we?" Stimson agreed, and was confident from these meetings, and subsequent ones with the new secretary of state, Cordell Hull, that the nation's foreign policy would not change under the new administration. Moreover, Stimson had established a personal relationship with Franklin Roosevelt that would grow throughout the 1930s and lead to his final service to the nation as secretary of war during World War II.[88]

For a number of reasons, as McGeorge Bundy recalled from conversations with the Colonel, Stimson "did not really enjoy running the State Department." He found working with Hoover to be a trying experience. This problem was compounded by his appointment of Castle as undersecretary of state, a dour and arrogant man who always took Hoover's position and who, Stimson believed, was at times reporting to the president behind his back. The burdens of conducting foreign policy at the outset of the Great Depression, and then the emergence of the European financial crisis and Japanese aggression, made it a difficult and unhappy four years and made being secretary of state Stimson's least favorite job. But most troubling was the president's unwillingness to support "any form of political action overseas."[89]

In late November 1932, Stimson's frustration with his job and the course of events got the better of him. As he recorded his own outburst: "I broke out and said that I was living in a world where all my troubles came from the same thing, not only in finance but in all matters, where we are constantly shut in by the timidity of governments making certain great decisions, for fear that some administration will be overthrown. . . . I said that the time had come when somebody has got to show some guts."[90] Stimson continued to see the policy of nonrecognition as correct, but he also knew full well that it was insufficient for upholding international agreements and deterring aggression. Moral outrage and the stands on principles were sound, and they helped begin the process of awakening public opinion, but the politics and restraints of the time would not allow Stimson to do any more.

In the final evaluation for Stimson, foreign policy did not have to be a Greek tragedy, with the outcome inevitable. He always believed that political leaders could have and should have acted with greater alacrity and force to deal with the financial crisis in Europe and to counter Japan's aggression in Asia. It was for Stimson "a tragedy of foolish nations and inadequate statesmen."[91] The issues he faced reinforced all of his assumptions about the need for the United States to take up the role of world leader. As the crisis of the 1930s continued to grow, and as aggression spread in Europe, Africa, and Asia, Stimson would try to counter the tragedy of timidity by pointing out the dangers and calling on his nation and others to take bold action to prevent the war he saw coming long before most of his contemporaries. His stance would make Stimson the leader in the call for collective security throughout the decade and prompt Franklin Roosevelt to ask Stimson, at the age of seventy-two, to run the War Department once again. This time, his proposals and ideas would be adopted as U.S. policy during the war and into the postwar period.

Notes

1. Quoted in Schmitz, *Thank God They're on Our Side*, 10.
2. Stimson and Bundy, *On Active Service*, 161.
3. Ibid., 196; Morison, *Turmoil and Tradition*, 257.
4. Stimson and Bundy, *On Active Service*, 164, 174.
5. Morison, *Turmoil and Tradition*, 256.
6. Stimson and Bundy, *On Active Service*, 188.
7. Stimson Diary, 5 June 1931, HLSD.
8. Stimson and Bundy, *On Active Service*, 204–205.
9. Stimson Memorandum, 12 June 1931, Stimson Papers, reel 126.
10. Stimson and Bundy, *On Active Service*, 204–205.
11. Ibid., 208.
12. Stimson Diary, 1 April 1931, HLSD.
13. Ibid., 8 April 1931.
14. Root, quoted in David Schmitz, *The United States and Fascist Italy* (Chapel Hill: University of North Carolina Press, 1988), 84; Stimson and Bundy, *On Active Service*, 268–70.
15. Stimson Diary, Memorandum Conversation with Grandi and Mussolini and Memorandum Conversation with Grandi, 9 July 1931, HLSD.
16. Ibid., Memorandum Conversation with Grandi, 9 July 1931; Stimson and Bundy, *On Active Service*, 268–69.
17. Stimson Diary, 26 July 1931, 27 August 1931, HLSD.
18. Stimson to Grandi, 20 August 1931; Klots to Stimson, 21 August 1931, Stimson Papers, reel 81.
19. Stimson Diary, 18 November 1931, HLSD.

20. Ibid., 11 July 1932.
21. Stimson and Bundy, *On Active Service*, 214–15.
22. Stimson Diary, 23 November 1932, 4 December 1932, HLSD.
23. Ibid., 31 January 1933.
24. Ibid., 17 April 1932.
25. Ibid., 15 September 1930.
26. Stimson and Bundy, *On Active Service*, 183.
27. Stimson, "The United States and the Other American Republics."
28. Stimson Diary, 18 September 1930, HLSD.
29. Morison, *Turmoil and Tradition*, 258.
30. Stimson Diary, 7 December 1931, HLSD.
31. Thomas P. Anderson, *Matanza* (Lincoln: University of Nebraska Press, 1971), 7.
32. Schott to Stimson, 30 March 1930, 816.00B/11, RG59.
33. Ibid., 14 August 1930, 816.00B/15.
34. Cruse, "Central America: Political," 24 September 1931, 813.00/1257, RG59.
35. Stimson Diary, 4 December 1931, HLSD.
36. Anderson, *Matanza*, 40–63.
37. Ibid., 49–63.
38. Stimson Diary, 4 December 1931, HLSD.
39. Stimson to Curtis, 4 December 1931, 816.00Revolutions/11, RG59.
40. Ibid., 11 December 1931, 816.01/17A.
41. *FRUS* 1931, 2:206.
42. Ibid., 203.
43. Caffery to Stimson, 1 January 1932, 816.01Caffery Mission/14, RG59.
44. *FRUS* 1931, 2:210–12.
45. Stimson Diary, 8 January 1932, HLSD.
46. *FRUS* 1932, 5:613.
47. McCafferty to Stimson, 20 January 1932, 816.00B/44, RG59.
48. Anderson, *Matanza*, 134.
49. McCafferty to Stimson, 23 January 1932, 816.00Revolutions/60 and 816.00Revolutions/62, RG59.
50. *FRUS* 1932, 5:618–19.
51. Stimson Diary, 25 January 1932, HLSD.
52. Department of State, Press Releases, 30 January 1932; *New York Times*, 26 January 1932.
53. Stimson Diary, 25 January 1932, HLSD.
54. *FRUS* 1932, 5:574–75.
55. Ibid., 619–20.
56. Ibid., 579–80.
57. Ibid., 581, 584–86.
58. Ibid., 584–86.
59. Ibid., 593–94, 602–603.
60. Department of State, "Review of Accomplishments," vol. 1:40, President's Cabinet Offices, Box 49, Herbert Hoover Presidential Library, West Branch, Iowa (hereafter HHL).
61. Ibid., 75 (emphasis added).
62. Stimson, "Bases of American Foreign Policy During the Past Four Years," *Foreign Affairs* (April 1933), 394–95.
63. Stimson Diary, 19 September 1931, HLSD.

64. Morison, *Turmoil and Tradition*, 308.

65. Stimson Diary, 21 September, 22 September 1931, HLSD; Stimson, *The Far Eastern Crisis: Recollections and Observations* (New York: Harper & Brothers, 1936), 34.

66. Morison, *Turmoil and Tradition*, 313.

67. Stimson Diary, 8 October 1931, HLSD.

68. Ibid., 9 October, 10 October 1931.

69. Morison, *Turmoil and Tradition*, 307–308.

70. Stimson Diary, 13 November 1931, HLSD; Hoover, quoted in Hodgson, *The Colonel*, 156.

71. Stimson Diary, 7 November, 19 November 1931, HLSD.

72. Harvey Bundy, Oral History, Columbia University Oral History Project.

73. Stimson Diary, 6 December 1931, HLSD.

74. Ibid., 3 January 1932.

75. Ibid., 9 November 1931.

76. *FRUS: Japan, 1931–1941*, 1:76.

77. Stimson, *Far Eastern Crisis*, 90.

78. Stimson Diary, 7 January 1932, HLSD.

79. Klots, quoted in Morison, *Turmoil and Tradition*, 326; Stimson Diary, 26 January 1932, HLSD.

80. Stimson Diary, 21 February 1932, HLSD; Stimson's letter to Borah is reprinted in Stimson and Bundy, *On Active Service*, 249–54.

81. Stimson and Bundy, *On Active Service*, 255.

82. Stimson Diary, 9 March 1932, HLSD.

83. Stimson and Bundy, *On Active Service*, 256.

84. Stimson Diary, 9 November 1932, HLSD.

85. Ibid., 17 December, 18 December, 21 December 1931.

86. Ibid., 22 December, 23 December, 24 December 1932.

87. Ibid., 28 December 1932, 3 January, 4 January 1933.

88. Ibid., 9 January 1933; Stimson, "Memorandum of Conversation with Franklin D. Roosevelt," 9 January 1933; Stimson Diary, 19 January 1933.

89. Author's interview with McGeorge Bundy, 16 January 1996.

90. Stimson and Bundy, *On Active Service*, 281.

91. Ibid., 280.

5

The Only Deadly Sin
Is Cynicism

L eaving the State Department at the age of sixty-five,
Stimson, reasonably enough, thought he was retir-
ing from public service for good. His party had suffered
a resounding defeat at the polls and he was at an age when
most people hope to retire. The Colonel was looking forward to some time off, rest, traveling, and more time with
his wife. He returned to New York, where he rented offices in his old law firm in order to practice his profes-
sion part-time, but kept the Woodley estate so he would
have a place to live during his frequent visits to Washington. Although Stimson fully intended to continue
speaking out on international issues and informally to
provide advice to President Roosevelt and Secretary Hull,
he could not foresee that he would return to Washington
seven years later for his longest and most exacting job in
government. As the former secretary of state, he was in
demand for his views on foreign policy and had access to
the national media. In 1934, Stimson delivered a series of
lectures at Princeton University that became a book, *Democracy and Nationalism*, and in 1936 he published *The Far
Eastern Crisis* about events in Manchuria and his policy
concerning them. The following year, Stimson was elected
president of the New York Bar Association, and in 1938
he took on the single largest law case of his career. Still,
Stimson found that the law could not hold his attention
or fully satisfy him, and he missed being at the center of
the nation's foreign policy.

Beginning in 1935, international affairs again began
to claim much of his and the world's attention. Crisis
built upon crisis with an increasing tempo, as one event

overtook the next in the rush to war. Germany's announcement that it was rearming and Italy's fall invasion of Ethiopia threatened war might return to Europe. These events were quickly followed in 1936 by the outbreak of the Spanish Civil War and the German occupation of the Rhineland. Although events seemed to stabilize in Europe the next year, Japan launched a full-scale attack on China. Nineteen thirty-eight brought the German *Anschluss* with Austria, followed by the crisis over the Sudetenland and the dismemberment of Czechoslovakia in the wake of the Munich Conference. By 1939, American officials began their "death watch" as Germany first took the rest of Czechoslovakia and then issued demands for new territory from Poland. Great Britain and France's guarantees to defend Poland did little to deter Germany. After the signing of the Nazi–Soviet nonaggression pact in August, war finally came on September 1, 1939, with the German attack on Poland and the British and French declarations of war two days later.

Stimson watched these events unfold with increasing horror and determination to get his nation to act. In general, he supported Roosevelt's approach to foreign policy even if he opposed much of his domestic New Deal program. He had spoken out against the neutrality acts that Congress began to pass in 1935, which were designed to insulate the United States from war, and called for greater cooperation with Great Britain, active opposition to Germany and Japan, and military preparedness. Indeed, he was the leading national advocate of American support for Great Britain and supplying those countries opposing German and Japanese aggression. The Colonel fully appreciated the restraints on President Roosevelt, and even he did not call for direct American participation in a war. But Stimson believed that isolationist opinion could be overcome by more aggressive executive action and a clear declaration of the American stake in the fighting overseas. He was confident his views would eventually be adopted, holding to his principle that "the man who tries to work for the good, believing in its eventual victory, while he may suffer setback and even disaster, will never know defeat. The only deadly sin I know is cynicism."[1]

With the outbreak of fighting in 1939, Roosevelt searched for a stance that allowed for greater American military preparedness but stopped short of open belligerency. This meant he needed someone running the War Department who was capable and trustworthy. Simultaneously, with the president's decision to seek a third term in office, he sought to make foreign policy a less divisive issue in the campaign. This led him to the decision to form a "war cabinet" that included leading Republicans in key positions. For these reasons, Franklin Roosevelt summoned Henry Stimson to assume leadership of the effort to prepare the nation for war. Roosevelt remembered well their work together during the transition in 1933, appreciated Stimson's support on foreign policy, and shared most of his views on international events. Moreover, he knew that Stimson would approach the office in a bipartisan manner and that his loyalty would be dedicated to carrying out the policies of the administration.

Loyal Opposition

As Stimson recalled in his memoirs, he "found Mr. Roosevelt's basic view of foreign affairs" similar to his own, and for the first two years out of office he was guardedly optimistic about international affairs. He met with the president a number of times to discuss world affairs and supported all of Roosevelt's initiatives. In particular, Stimson supported Roosevelt's recognition of the Soviet Union and efforts to build up the navy as "useful complements to the continued firmness of the American stand in the Far East." In 1934, Stimson threw all his weight behind the administration's Reciprocal Trade Agreement bill that was designed to lower tariffs and increase international trade. Stimson had always supported lower tariffs, and he believed that the United States, as a creditor nation, had to increase its imports. In addition, the bill called for greater executive authority to make changes in the tariff. This proposition was consistent with Stimson's philosophy of government with greater executive control over foreign affairs. That April, he gave a national radio speech endorsing the proposal that appeared in many newspapers across the country.[2]

Stimson had no difficulty supporting this Democratic initiative and considered Republican opposition to it shortsighted and unfounded. He noted that "Republicans on the whole were very angry" at him for making the speech and lending support to Roosevelt, "for it contravened their rather stupid policy of indiscriminate opposition." Stimson saw the matter as an opportunity "to assist the policy of the conservative advisers of the President and to oppose that of the radicals" who sought more government control over the economy rather than free trade. Roosevelt invited Stimson to the White House in May to congratulate him on his speech. He told Stimson that his support "was the chief influence in securing the probable passage of the bill." While Stimson knew that Roosevelt was engaging in exaggeration and flattery, he also realized how closely their views coincided and that his action had earned him the further respect of the president.[3]

As Stimson's comments make clear, there were parts of Roosevelt's New Deal program that he supported, but other areas that he opposed. As an old Progressive, Stimson supported many of the reform measures implemented by Roosevelt. He applauded FDR's banking bill designed to restore confidence and stave off more radical measures. Referring to his days as a United States Attorney, he wrote Roosevelt in 1935 that he was always "on the side of national efficiency." He considered himself "a Hamiltonian in my belief in a strong central American government" and saw the fundamental economic problem as how to "preserve the essentials of real competition while curbing the evils of cutthroat competition; — to secure the stabilization of modern industry, the prevention of unfair practices, and the prohibition of the exploitation of labor." He, therefore, had also supported the National Recovery Act (NRA) and its codes and regulations designed to regulate business and stabilize the economy.[4]

Yet Stimson thought that, in many areas, the New Deal was going too far. He opposed the Tennessee Valley Authority as government ownership of business, feared that the unbalanced budgets necessary to pay for work programs were a danger to the nation's financial stability, and was alarmed by the campaign rhetoric appealing to class antipathy. He worried that Roosevelt was "building up an irresponsible bureaucracy" in the place of proper government regulation. Although he mainly kept these concerns private, Stimson publicly criticized the 1935 Wagner Act that established the rights of unions to bargain collectively and Roosevelt's 1937 attempt to pack the Supreme Court. The Colonel saw the Wagner Act as granting too much power to the government and a "wholly unbalanced and unfair piece of legislation." But his most vehement criticism was reserved for the Supreme Court Bill of 1937, a measure Stimson worked actively to defeat. Stimson saw this as a direct threat to the Constitution and its checks and balances among the three branches of the federal government. Although he was sure Roosevelt had no intention of making himself a dictator, Stimson did comment to Hull that this was exactly the type of course that dictators used in seizing power.[5]

Despite his growing disapproval of the New Deal, Stimson played no role in the 1936 presidential campaign because of his opposition to the Republican Party's stance on foreign affairs and its demand for a high tariff. In these areas, he found his views remained closely aligned with Roosevelt's. His 1934 lectures at Princeton provided him an opportunity to speak publicly about world affairs and to attempt to stave off the pessimism that was so prevalent concerning the events in Central Europe.[6] Stimson was uncharacteristically optimistic concerning events in Germany. He had told Roosevelt back in March 1933 that he "did not think the situation was nearly as dangerous" as most newspapers reported and that no nations, including Germany, wanted war.[7] He did not believe that the Nazis would last if they attempted to rearm and follow a policy that radically challenged the status quo. Germany needed increased foreign trade and credits for economic prosperity. Thus, policies such as the Reciprocal Trade Agreement Act would serve to maintain interdependence, promote economic recovery, and restore stability. This, Stimson believed in 1934, "offers a fairly safe guarantee against unrestrained violence against her neighbors on the part of Germany." Still, Stimson remained wary enough of events to warn that the United States, as "the world's most powerful nation," had to play a central role to help the world "in its vital struggle to protect our common civilization against war." Should the United States resort to isolationism, the international "peace machinery will be infinitely weakened," and the world will again be faced with a war that "may be as disastrous to us and to our own civilization as to that of the rest of the world."[8]

With the passage of the first Neutrality Act, Germany's rearmament, and Italy's invasion of Ethiopia in 1935, Stimson abandoned his guarded optimism and began to speak out concerning the danger of international developments to the United States and America's obligation to assist the world in preventing war. "Everything," Stimson noted in March, "seemed to be going to Hades."[9] Trying to prevent this descent increasingly commanded Stimson's time and energy for the remainder of the decade. He identified several interrelated problems that had to be overcome in order to rouse greater U.S. opposition to German and Japanese aggression. All were expressed in the neutrality acts. The rejection of the Versailles Treaty and of American cooperation with any collective security efforts by the other powers had led the United States to deny any responsibility for the problems in Europe. This, coupled with the refusal to link war debts to reparations, led many people to believe that the United States could obtain its goals while remaining independent of any political commitments. The Great

Depression and the desire by many to focus only on domestic matters reinforced these positions. Stimson rejected these views, but he fully understood their popularity among many in Congress and the general populace. For many Americans, the dubious legacy of World War I remained highly influential. They could see only revolution, economic crisis, and a Europe seemingly ungrateful for America's assistance. This, combined with the Nye Committee hearings that concluded that the U.S. entry in the war stemmed from the machinations of bankers and the munitions industry, led to the passage of the 1935 Neutrality Act that barred American loans and trade with belligerents as a means of avoiding future wars.

For Stimson, this was pure folly. In April 1935, he addressed the subject of neutrality in a speech before the American Society of International Law. He asserted that there was much confusion over the term "neutrality." What most people desired, Stimson maintained, was that the United States keep out of war. Neutrality was, however, inconsistent with that goal. War was the central evil that had to be avoided. Once war began, the United States, as a result of the interconnectedness of the world economy and the increasingly destructive power of weapons, would suffer heavily whether it was a belligerent or not. "War," Stimson declared, "is no longer a contest between two nations which the rest of the world can stand by and look at. . . . People who think they can stand aside and can look at war from a distance without ultimately becoming involved . . . are not realists but dreamers." The belief that the United States could save itself "by isolation is today an economic fantasy—worthy of the ostrich who thinks that he is hidden when he buries his head in the sand." Thus, for the United States the "real problem is to prevent war from arising—not how to act after it has arisen." Stimson believed that war could be avoided only by international cooperation and collective security. If the "world knew beforehand that in case of an emergency the United States could be counted upon to act," it would prove to be a powerful deterrent to aggression. Stimson concluded that neutrality offered no road to peace. "The only certain way to keep out of a great war is to prevent that war from taking place, and the only hope of preventing war . . . is by the earnest, intelligent, and unselfish cooperation of the nations of the world towards that end. Until America is willing . . . to do her part . . . the life of our whole modern civilization may be at the mercy of the next war."[10]

Following the Italian invasion of Ethiopia, Stimson further criticized neutrality legislation and called for greater executive action.

Speaking on national radio in October, Stimson noted that, on the one hand, the law concerning the list of goods the president could restrict was too narrow, allowing for no discretion among various belligerents and types of goods. This legislation would prevent any effective cooperation with other nations should they seek to impose economic sanctions or an embargo. On the other hand, as the events on the Horn of Africa were demonstrating, neutrality was a failure that could not prevent war and was "likely to do more harm than good." Roosevelt needed to move out from behind the congressional action and speak out concerning the issues at stake. He had to take the lead in arousing and marshaling public opinion against aggression, making it clear that there was a moral issue at stake in opposing Italy's actions. Moreover, the president should also make clear that the United States supported collective security over international anarchy. "Such an announcement from America would by its encouragement of the earnest efforts of the nations of the world in their struggle for peace go a long distance toward insuring the eventual success of that struggle."[11]

Stimson returned to these arguments and his efforts to change public opinion while prodding the administration to greater and more positive action two years later, when Japan began its full-scale war against China. On October 5, 1937, Roosevelt delivered his famous "Quarantine Speech" in response to Japan's actions. His remarks went well beyond any of his previous statements on foreign affairs, but lacked specific recommendations. He declared that "a reign of terror" now confronted the world. Those nations that desired peace would have to "make a concerted effort in opposition to those violations of treaties and those ignorings of human instincts which today are creating a state of international anarchy." Without naming any nations, Roosevelt called for a "quarantine" against those countries trying to spread unrest.[12]

Writing to the *New York Times* the next day, Stimson recounted American efforts to support Chinese independence, Japan's violations of the Open Door and the Nine-Power Treaty, and its conquest of Manchuria. Yet Japan's aggression in 1931–1932, Stimson argued, was finally halted as it realized world opinion was against its actions. The current crisis emerged because Japan was encouraged by developments in Europe and the policy of appeasement. "The Fascist dictators of Italy and Germany have boldly and successfully carried through coups invoking in Ethiopia, the Rhineland, and Spain acts of treaty violation and indefensible aggression." Meanwhile, the West has yielded to all of these actions, and appeased the aggressors, in the vain hope of avoiding war. Stimson was most critical of his own nation. While others had reason to fear immediate war, "In America, occupying the most safe and defensible position in the world, there has been no excuse except faulty reasoning for the wave of ostrich-like isolationism which has swept over us and by its erroneous form of neutrality legislation has threatened to bring upon us in the future the very dangers of war which we now are seeking to avoid."[13]

Stimson was encouraged by Roosevelt's remarks. They marked a clear endorsement of the policy he originated in 1932. Still, he sought more concrete proposals that would hinder the Japanese. He rejected military intervention as "impossible" and "abhorrent to our people." It was up to China to fight for itself, "But that is very far from saying that the only alternative is inaction or a passive and shameful acquiescence in the wrong that is now being done." Stimson called for a trade embargo against Japan, noting that it was "peculiarly dependent upon the outside world for her ability to attack China," and, therefore, "extremely vulnerable" to such action. He recalled hearing Theodore Roosevelt comment that "he put peace above everything except righteousness," but Stimson was afraid that the United States had reversed this principle and was "trying to put peace above righteousness," and in the process was endangering itself. The recent neutrality laws were the most obvious example of this flawed thinking. Stimson concluded that "such a policy of amoral drift by such a safe and powerful nation as our own will only set back the hands of progress. It will not save us from entanglement. It will even make entanglement more certain."[14]

What Stimson was calling for was an extension of the Stimson Doctrine to include an economic embargo. In November he wrote the president a five-page letter outlining his thoughts with the aim of encouraging Roosevelt to back up his words with actions that would enable the United States to take the lead and use its influence short of war in East Asia. For Stimson, the time for action and presidential leadership had arrived. He began by contrasting China, which he characterized as a peaceful people "headed by a government largely influenced by American education and traditions" with a Japan guided by "a feudal military inheritance and . . . wholly guided by military purposes . . . seeking to overthrow that Chinese government and replace it with one more amenable to Japan's own purposes and interests." Japan's goals were "inherently hostile" to the United States and its interests; China was "fighting our battle for freedom and peace" in the region. American national purpose, he continued, must be to "alleviate the disparity under which China is fighting" by imposing sanctions on Japan. Finally, Stimson called upon Roosevelt to provide greater leadership and to use the influence of the United States, both "moral and material," to aid China and the cause of peace. The Colonel acknowledged that the problems in East Asia were connected to those in Europe. Yet war had broken out only in Asia, and time was running against the United States. "Incalculable harm may be done," Stimson concluded, "by an American failure of principle, to the ultimate decisions of hundreds of millions of minds now in flux."[15]

Roosevelt asked Hull for suggestions on how to reply. He noted that they would both "wholly" agree with Stimson, "but we still have not got the answer." He wrote Stimson that his letter had stated "considerations which are ever present in my thoughts," but failed to provide an acceptable course of action. The Europeans were looking for leadership from the United States, but he was not sure that the "people of this country nor Congress" would support any measures of pressure. In the end, Roosevelt did not follow up his quarantine address with any new initiatives, and Stimson, although finding that he and Roosevelt still agreed on the fundamental issues, remained frustrated by the inaction of the administration in the face of the growing crisis and the president's unwillingness to challenge and direct public opinion. Still, he recognized that his proposed course of action might lead to war and understood the political restraints that Roosevelt operated under.[16]

Throughout 1938, most of Stimson's time and energy were taken up by the Blaustein case, a major suit involving Standard Oil that lasted until 1944. While he continued to follow international events with growing concern in 1938, he made no further efforts to influence the administration or public opinion. By early 1939, however, Stimson had concluded that war was inevitable in Europe. The Munich agreement was merely a temporary respite. Germany had been allowed to gain strength at the expense of the West, and along with Italy and Japan posed "an overwhelming threat to Western Civilization."[17] The divide between the democracies and the dictatorships was now impassable, and the aggressors could not be stopped by any means short of armed resistance by other nations. With these thoughts in mind, Stimson could no longer remain silent.

In January 1939, Stimson wrote a letter to the *New York Times* urging President Roosevelt to lift the trade embargo imposed upon

Spain and to resume the shipment of goods to the Republican government, the legal and recognized government of Spain. Nonintervention by the United States and the other Western democracies had denied the Loyalist government arms while Germany and Italy were supplying the Fascist rebels. Stimson argued that the nature of the Spanish government was an internal affair, but what was at stake was the principle of a government being able to purchase arms for its self-defense.[18] Roosevelt finally lifted the embargo two months later, but it was too late to reverse the outcome of the Spanish Civil War. Stimson regretted that he had not spoken out sooner on this matter as he saw the Fascist side "was incomparably more dangerous to us; more active in their proselytizing, more outrageous and intolerant of international law and methods" than the Loyalists and their supporters.[19]

As Roosevelt's action in Spain indicated, Stimson believed the president was beginning to "turn the American people toward the enemy" and was moving to apply pressure against the aggressors by methods, as Roosevelt put it in January, "short of war, but stronger and more effective than mere words."[20] Stimson did do all he could to assist the president by making two major statements on foreign affairs in March and April. These represented the clearest statements of his convictions and outlined the views that would guide his thinking throughout World War II. In a March 6 letter to the *New York Times,* Stimson urged Americans to support continued positive action and a direct military understanding among the United States, Great Britain, and France. If there were any hope of peace short of war, it would come only through a united opposition to Germany by the democracies and a "timely and vigorous warning of the dangers which they [the Germans] will thereby certainly incur." Such an affirmative policy would not drag the nation into war. Stimson dismissed that belief as being based upon "undue timidity." The United States could not avoid the negative consequences of the war or stay out of it once it came. It was, therefore, time for the United States to take an active role in shaping policies that would encourage resistance to further aggression.[21]

The false hope that the United States could stay isolated and remain safe within its own hemisphere or continental boundaries was, Stimson argued, based on an erroneous understanding of the Fascist governments. The Axis powers were not traditional autocracies; rather they represented "a complete reversal of the whole trend of European civilization." Fascism was "a radical attempt to reverse entirely the long evolution out of which our democracies of Europe and America have grown, and . . . it constitutes probably the most serious attack on their underlying principles" to date. These governments "reject freedom . . . scorn the principles of government by discussion and persuasion instead of force," and seek to destroy their neighbors who hold such values. Furthermore, Stimson continued, "Fascism has involved a serious moral deterioration; an increasing and callous disregard of the most formal and explicit international obligations and pledges: extreme brutality toward helpless groups of people" along with the destruction of free speech and thought. For Stimson, all of this "suggests that in our modern interdependent world Lincoln's saying holds true, that a house so divided against itself cannot permanently stand. Today the neighbors of a fascist nation are compelled to live in anticipation of immediate forceful attack."[22]

The conclusions were obvious to Stimson. He was "opposed to the doctrine preached in many quarters that our Government and our people must treat the nations on both sides of this great issue with perfect impartiality," because it was clear to the Colonel that the United States was "confronting an organized attack upon the very basis of our civilization." The time for action had arrived. To wait any longer would imperil the safety and well-being of the nation. "We cannot," Stimson declared, "ignore the fact that at almost any moment an armed attack may be aimed by the fascist group of powers" against Great Britain and France, the two nations "upon which today rest in large part the safety of our own civilization." In that event, only full U.S. support could "save the present hard-earned civilization upon which our own national welfare rests." Should the United States attempt to remain isolated, the results would be disastrous for all nations. [23]

The Colonel again condemned the neutrality laws in April. Testifying before the Senate Foreign Relations Committee, he urged Congress to modify the law to allow for presidential discretion as to when a trade embargo should be enacted and against which nations. In the present emergency, the president needed the power to discriminate between the aggressor and the victim and to impose an embargo on the former. Stimson dismissed those who worried that such presidential authority would be abused, as this executive power had been national policy up until 1935, and he believed the president needed this freedom to conduct foreign policy effectively. Moreover, he argued that the problems facing the United States were unique and that the situation was becoming critical. Neutrality provided a green light to the aggressors to continue their actions, and was a clear contributor to the fall of the government in Spain. He repeated the arguments he had now made many times about the world being interconnected and the United States not being able to avoid the negative consequences of war. It was clear who the aggressors were, and it was time to shape policies that allowed for the United States to punish those nations. It was time to deny Germany, Japan, and Italy access to American resources while keeping them available to those who opposed their aggression. Using this "economic weapon" was the safest means of protecting the nation. The neutrality laws served "in very large part to stimulate" the activities of the aggressors. Stimson told the senators that this "does not strike me as very intelligent behavior."[24]

With the outbreak of war in September, Stimson again called for a repeal of the arms embargo, thereby allowing the president full authority to impose sanctions against Germany and Japan. In a reply to Senator Borah, who claimed that a repeal of the automatic arms embargo provision would lead the United States into war, Stimson drew the opposite conclusion. He argued that "repeal of those provisions constitutes perhaps the last remaining hope of our avoiding being so dragged in." More important, it was time to recognize that "a group of nations has arisen in the world by whom the practice of military aggression upon their neighbors has become a well developed art." Unfortunately, according to Stimson, the United States, "though with the best intentions, has played into the hands of that group and has made more difficult the defense against their skillful aggression by the nations whom they have attacked."[25]

Stimson returned to these themes again on October 5 in a national radio address. The embargo, he argued, had encouraged aggression and, thereby, endangered the nation. But Stimson now added something new to his public arguments. For the first time he raised directly the issue of U.S. military action. The ultimate issue was not "how to keep the United States out of war," and the framing of the question in that manner had led to the irresponsible neutrality legislation. The "ultimate end" was the safety of the nation. In that view, repeal was both the moral and materially correct course of action in order to assist Great Britain and France who were fighting America's battle. Moreover, the nation had to realize that "a time might well come when the only way to preserve the security of the people of the United States would be to fight for that security."[26]

Secretary of War Again

Once again, Stimson was ahead of most of the country in seeing the dangers ahead and calling for early action. The nation needed to realize that this was a "novel and critical situation, a new kind of war with our civilization hanging by a thread." The aim of the war had to be the ousting of the "Nazi system as recreant to and destructive of" Western society. Steady pressure was necessary, and Stimson called for a buildup of American forces, compulsory military service, and greater aid to Great Britain and France to allow them to hold the line and drive Hitler from power. While his primary focus was on events in Europe, Stimson did not ignore Asia. Having helped obtain the repeal of the automatic embargo legislation in the fall, Stimson, in January 1940, called for legislation to bar the export of arms, munitions, and raw materials to Japan. He found it both remarkable and inexplicable that the United States continued to supply goods that were used to "assist unprovoked aggression against China" and to "facilitate acts of inexcusable cruelty toward unoffending Chinese civilians." Such an export ban would seriously damage Japan's ability to wage war and "would show that this nation recognizes its responsibility for making efforts toward the restoration of law and order, and that wherever its peaceful influence can effectively be thrown it will be thrown on the side of independence and freedom and against militarized aggression."[27]

Germany's lightning attack in May 1940 into the Low Countries and France was, Stimson recalled, "a nightmare" that changed the whole nature of the war, leaving Great Britain to fight alone. An immediate American response was essential. While he was heartened that Germany's attack helped secure congressional approval of greater military appropriations, Stimson was frustrated that the question of America's proper role was still a matter of debate. It was inconceivable to him that others did not see the battle against Hitler as America's fight. On June 18, he repeated on national radio his views and recommendations in an effort to persuade others as to the proper course to resist Germany short of a declaration of war. Stimson's opening remark was as dramatic as it was accurate. "The United States today," he declared, "faces probably the greatest crisis in its history." Only the British Navy stood between the United States and a Nazi-controlled Europe. It was imperative that the United States do everything in its power to ensure Great Britain's survival. Specifically, Stimson called for the repeal of the last remaining parts of "our ill-starred so-called neutrality venture" that had shackled the nation for the past five years, and for making all American ports available to British ships for fueling, repairs, and supplies and for sending planes and munitions to England for its defense. At home, Americans had to "combat the defeatist arguments . . . being made . . . as to the unconquerable power of Germany." Moreover, the nation had to adopt a system of universal compulsory military training and service to demonstrate its resolve and willingness to act. Stimson believed the American people were "ready to take their proper part in this threatened world and to carry through to victory, freedom, and reconstruction."[28]

Stimson's comments again placed him well ahead of Roosevelt's public remarks and the administration's policy. It, therefore, came as something of a surprise when Roosevelt called him the next day to ask him to assume the position of secretary of war and informed him that he was asking Frank Knox to become secretary of the navy. It was no secret that the president was unhappy with the current secretary of war, Harry Woodring, and the lack of leadership in the department at a time when military spending was growing rapidly. Stimson had learned earlier that month that friends, in particular, Felix Frankfurter and Grenville Clark, had recommended him to Roosevelt. As the crisis in Europe deepened, Roosevelt revived an idea he had originally expressed in 1939 of bringing leading Republicans into his cabinet. Frankfurter had met with Roosevelt on June 3 to recommend Stimson as secretary of war. Roosevelt, given his previous experience of working with Stimson and agreement with his views, was receptive to the idea, but expressed some concern about his age and health. To counter these worries, Frankfurter obtained assurances from Stimson's personal physician that he was in excellent health. In addition, it was arranged that Robert P. Patterson would be named as assistant secretary to provide the necessary energy for conducting the day-to-day business of the department.[29]

When Roosevelt called, Stimson made it clear that he would take the position only under certain conditions. He would not participate in domestic politics and he would be free to appoint his own staff. After consulting with his wife and partners, Stimson called the president back later that evening. He wanted to be sure that the president had read his radio speech from the day before and that the views he expressed in it, particularly on military ser-

Secretary of War Stimson, 1940. *Collection of the Huntington Historical Society, Long Island, New York*

vice, would not cause him any embarrassment. Roosevelt replied that he had read it and was in "full accord" with Stimson's views. It was agreed that Patterson would be appointed as Stimson's principal assistant and that Stimson would have a free hand in running the department. Learning that Knox had already accepted, Stimson did the same and prepared to return to Washington for the most demanding job of his long career.[30]

From Roosevelt's point of view, he was gaining a highly respected elder statesman whose positions he generally concurred with and whose advice he trusted to head up the most critical wartime executive department. As a Republican, Stimson's advocacy of aid to Britain, U.S. naval convoys of supplies, and compulsory military service would help Roosevelt move the country in the direction he believed it had to take. For Stimson, it was an opportunity he never expected to have again—the prospect of serving the nation in a time of peril and making his ideas policy. He did not worry that he might be helping Roosevelt win reelection. His only concerns were the correctness of his views and the necessity of the job ahead.

It was for the very reasons that Roosevelt nominated Stimson that he faced criticism and opposition from his own party. Republican leaders, most notably Senators Robert Taft and Arthur Vandenberg, dismissed the appointment as a political trick. Simultaneously, and seemingly without seeing the contradiction, the two stalwart isolationists also took the appointment as an indication that Roosevelt intended to follow Stimson's advice and take the nation to war. Harvey Bundy recalled that the more volatile isolationists, led by the *Chicago Tribune,* "called him a war-monger, and then a senile old man." They saw Stimson "as a renegade" and effectively read him out of the party. He remained unfazed and was able to establish a department that was "completely non-political" when it came to appointments and policy formation.[31] Stimson's appointment was easily confirmed, and after the war he delighted in quoting Roosevelt that his appointment was the "best idea Felix [Frankfurter] had."[32]

The Road to War

Stimson faced enormous tasks when he assumed his post on July 10, 1940. He had to assemble his staff while learning about an administration that had been in office for more than seven years. The rearmament program was just getting under way, and Stimson had to identify whom to work with in other agencies and where the problems lay in increasing war production. Equally challenging was preparation of the military for unprecedented expansion. Tied to these issues there was the need to provide as much aid as possible to Great Britain to ensure its defense while simultaneously formulating policies to counter continued Japanese expansion in Asia. Finally, there was the task of trying to persuade the nation of its obligation for leadership in the global crisis. Although many would find such a list daunting at any age, Stimson was eager to get started. That first day, he began to appoint his new staff and he persuaded Roosevelt to add a statement concerning a compulsory service bill to his message to Congress. The Colonel was already fully in control.

The issues of establishing his office personnel and gaining passage of the Selective Service Bill dominated Stimson's work for the first two months. The most important member of the "best staff he ever had" was already in Washington, Chief of Staff General George C. Marshall. The two men fully trusted each other and worked closely together for the next five years, making sure there were no divisions or problems between the civilian and military members of the War Department. Patterson, as previously arranged, had been appointed assistant secretary and was given responsibility for the army procurement program. The rest of the staff roster was filled over the course of the next nine months. John J. McCloy was appointed as a special assistant who handled a wide variety of tasks from lend-lease to relations with Congress and served as the department's troubleshooter as new crises emerged. Stimson appointed Robert A. Lovett to be his air assistant, overseeing all matters relating to the air forces from the building of the planes to their deployment in the different theaters of war. When Patterson was promoted to the new position of undersecretary, McCloy was named assistant secretary, and Lovett assistant secretary for air. Finally, in April 1941, Stimson brought Harvey Bundy back to Washington to work with him as a special assistant. He served as the administrative chief of the department, the secretary's liaison with various government committees, and as Stimson's personal advisor and counsel.[33]

Stimson trusted these men and their judgment, instilled them with a sense of common purpose, and delegated most of the tasks of running the department on a day-to-day basis to them. These four assistants, in turn, demonstrated unfailing loyalty to Stimson and served the nation with distinction throughout the war. The were not merely subordinate staffers. As Bundy noted, loyalty did not "mean that you couldn't talk back to the Secretary, but you had to be direct. . . . He might give you hell for disagreeing with him, and then the next day he'd call you up on the telephone and apologize."[34] It was their responsibility to mobilize the people and industry of the nation for the war. Stimson provided the initial efforts and the general direction for these programs, but once they were inaugurated, he turned them over to his subordinates and concentrated on the larger questions of strategy and oversight of the Manhattan project that developed the atomic bomb.

The immediate passage of a selective service bill required Stimson's full energies throughout July and August. A peacetime draft was unprecedented in American history, and Stimson had to overcome this legacy along with opponents' arguments that it was a measure that would increase the chances of war. In his appearance before the House Military Affairs Committee, Stimson pointed out that the rate of voluntary enlistment had left the army far short of its authorized strength. Selective Service, he argued, was the only fair, democratic, and effective way to raise a modern army without disruption of the nation's life. Concerning a draft in peacetime, Stimson noted that Congress had already acknowledged the need for preparation by securing equipment with its large appropriations for weapons. "It would be well to recognize also that it takes a long time to secure and train the men to use such arms." These arguments and the War Department's tireless advocacy proved effective, and President Roosevelt signed the Selective Service Act on September 16, 1940. Stimson, with Roosevelt looking on, drew the first number for the draft on October 29.[35]

Secretary of War Stimson pulls the first draft number on October 29, 1940. *Henry Lewis Stimson Papers, Manuscripts and Archives, Yale University Library*

With the new legislation calling for an expansion of the army to 1.4 million, the next problem was finding the large number of officers necessary to lead such a force. Stimson and Roosevelt originally favored the adoption of officers' camps modeled after the

Plattsburgh camp Stimson had attended prior to World War I. Marshall, however, disagreed, arguing that officers should come from the army's own ranks. Stimson yielded to his chief of staff, and the army established Officer Candidate Schools to train its larger officer corps. Moreover, Stimson allowed Marshall the control of the promotion of senior officers, restricting his involvement to reviewing the lists prepared by the military and passing along its recommendations to the president.

With the question of the expansion of the army settled, Stimson turned his attention to supplying these forces. The problem was not funds; Stimson never had to worry about appropriations throughout the war. The difficulty was getting business to convert to the making of weapons. Businesses were reluctant to expand their facilities into new areas of production, fearing that they would be left once the emergency ended with enormous plants of little value. What business wanted was tax relief to write off the expenses of new construction. Many in Congress, however, were concerned with excess profits and sought to pass stringent new laws to tax any windfalls. The whole debate frustrated Stimson who wanted the bill passed as quickly as possible in order to get production moving. Moreover, Stimson believed that "if you are going to try to go to war . . . in a capitalist country, you have got to let business make money out of the process or business won't work, and there are a great many people in Congress who think that they can tax business out of all proportion and still have businessmen work diligently and rapidly. That is not human nature."[36]

This would not be the last time that Stimson opposed efforts at reform during the war. He took a pragmatic view of the war and was single-minded in his support for measures that would aid production and bring about victory at the earliest possible moment. The disagreement was finally compromised, and the Office of Production Management was established to oversee purchasing and schedules. Although it was reorganized many times during the war, this agency met Stimson's requirements for a governmental authority to make decisions and handle the priority allocation of resources to wartime production.

Initially, this urgent need for military equipment was greatest for providing assistance to Great Britain. The problem was that, although the United States now had vast production programs under way, it would be months before a significant volume of finished weapons could be delivered. Beyond surplus World War I material, there was very little America could immediately offer the

British Army, and Stimson spent "many a bitter hour with Allied leaders who could not believe that the American larder was bare." The United States did, however, possess two hundred old destroyers that were in storage. Numerous legal barriers stood in the way of making these ships available to the British Navy. In August, Roosevelt devised the idea of swapping fifty American destroyers for certain British bases in the Atlantic. Stimson fully supported the famous "Destroyers for Bases" deal as a means to strengthen both countries, demonstrate executive leadership, and highlight the plight of Britain and her need for American aid. He also served as liaison for the administration with the Republican Party to ensure that its presidential candidate, Wendell Willkie, would not oppose the action.

When "Destroyers for Bases" was announced on September 3, the measure itself and the president's handling of it greatly boosted the secretary of war's morale. He concluded that Roosevelt fully understood both international politics and the necessity of close relations with Great Britain and that he could provide the necessary wartime leadership for the nation. Moreover, Stimson believed that this arrangement marked "very possibly the turning point in the tide of the war, and that from now on we could hope for better things."[37] He knew full well that there were years of bloody trial still ahead; still, for the first time, he fully believed that the American people, through their overwhelming support of the deal, were willing to pay the necessary costs for victory and that the United States was finally beginning to provide leadership to the world.

Nevertheless, there was much to be done as the struggle to provide aid to Great Britain continued, and Stimson did not let himself pause long to ponder these thoughts. He worked to speed up production and find ways to transfer military supplies. As supplies started to become available in volume, two new problems arose. American laws restricted the ability of the administration to transfer weapons, and the British were running out of money. Stimson was frustrated by any restraints on the president. He believed the Congress was doing an "immense amount more harm than good and [members] restrict the power of the Commander in Chief in ways in which Congress cannot possibly wisely interfere. They don't know enough."[38] Roosevelt broke the logjam with his December 29 "Arsenal of Democracy" speech in which he pledged all-out aid to Great Britain through the proposed Lend-Lease Act. Lend-lease would allow the president "to sell, transfer title to, exchange, lease, lend, or otherwise dispose of" any defense article to any government deemed vital to the defense of the United States. Passed on March 11, 1941, the act provided the government with full legal authority over all military supplies and circumvented the British lack of funds. Furthermore, it avoided the whole issue of loans and war debts that caused so much difficulty after World War I.

To Stimson, it was one of the most important achievements of the war, because it represented a "declaration of economic war" against Germany. In five separate testimonies before Congress, Stimson argued that passage of the Lend-Lease Act was vital to the war effort to provide order to the current chaotic system of procuring weapons for the Allies, to permit the government to exercise centralized control over weapons, and to allow the president the full authority he needed in the time of national emergency. The War Department was well prepared for the bill's passage and shipped the first supplies out under the new law the same day it was approved.[39]

With the passage of lend-lease secured, Stimson turned his attention to the "policy of grand strategy" for U.S. involvement in the war. Stimson was the senior statesman in the administration and its most outspoken interventionist. No official had more consistently opposed isolationism and supported American international involvement than Stimson. He had never believed war could be avoided by rejecting political obligations abroad or through neutrality legislation, and he had always insisted that there were issues and principles more important than peace. Yet Stimson had never publicly called for American participation in the war, knowing that this would be rejected outright and that he would lose effective influence on the national debates thereby.

By the beginning of 1941, however, Stimson had concluded that the reality of war had to be faced and turned his efforts to persuading Roosevelt to take more energetic and active leadership in the defense of England and the preparation of the public for what he now saw as the inevitable American participation in the war. As early as December 1940 he had concluded that the nation would have to fight—"that this emergency could hardly be passed over without this country being drawn into the war eventually." It was, therefore, necessary to begin planning for that time. Europe, Stimson believed, had to be the primary concern. "The eventual big act," he noted, "will have to be to save the life line of Great Britain on the North Atlantic." Although he did not think young Americans, once they fully appreciated the issues at hand, would be willing to remain forever "toolmakers for other nations which fight," he acknowledged that conditions were not yet right for a public call to war. "That cannot yet be broached but it will come in time."[40]

By spring 1941, Stimson feared that Great Britain could not hold out much longer and that, unless the United States acted in a more dramatic and forthright manner toward the war, Germany would win. Specifically, he believed that for Great Britain to survive, the United States needed to commit its navy to battle in the Atlantic. It was the only means of ensuring the delivery of lend-lease supplies. Stimson had first raised the issue of American convoys during a cabinet discussion prior to Roosevelt's call for the United States to be the "arsenal of democracy." After noting the terrible amount of shipping being lost, over four million tons in 1940, Stimson argued that the United States should "forcibly stop the German submarines by our intervention." The president responded that "he hadn't quite reached that yet."[41] Beginning in April, he urged Roosevelt to get out in front on the issue and begin preparing public opinion for war. This was consistent with Stimson's whole conception of government and the need for the president to act as a leader and shaper of opinion. Stimson believed that convoys were necessary to protect supplies and to "give a lift to British morale"; only "naval action and vigorous action at that" would suffice.[42]

Roosevelt was unwilling to take this bold step. He was convinced "that it was too dangerous to ask the Congress for the power to convoy," and that such a measure would be defeated. Stimson noted his disagreement and believed the measure would pass provided the president "took the lead vigorously and showed the reasons for it." Instead, Roosevelt announced that the United States would patrol the western half of the Atlantic Ocean, thus freeing the British Navy to concentrate on the waters closer to home. He portrayed the actions as a defensive move to keep watch for any hostile actions close to American shores.[43]

The president's decision frustrated his secretary of war. Stimson believed that Roosevelt was not carrying out his obligation and duty to lead the nation and decided to raise the matter directly with him. On April 22, Stimson met with Roosevelt and warned him that he was going to "speak very frankly," and trusted that Roosevelt understood his "real loyalty and affection for him." Stimson argued that, since the passage of the Lend-Lease Act, there had been a "deterioration in the American political situation toward the war." He cautioned Roosevelt "on the necessity of taking the lead and that without a lead on his part it was useless to expect the people would voluntarily take the initiative in letting him know whether or not they would follow him." Few would have dared to speak so directly to the president, yet Stimson was not afraid to speak his mind and would, more than once during the course of the war, have sharp words with the president. Two days later, Stimson told FDR that the actions they were taking were clearly hostile acts toward Germany. Stimson was "prepared to take the responsibility of it," and he wanted the president to be forthright and not try to hide it. When Roosevelt noted the following day at a cabinet meeting that the patrols were "a step forward," Stimson immediately responded, "Well, I hope you keep on walking, Mr. President. Keep on walking."[44] The Colonel was convinced that the nation would support Roosevelt and see that force was necessary for dealing with Germany. Roosevelt was willing to wait on circumstances to bring about the conflict.

If the president was not willing to state the case for war directly to the American people, Stimson was. On May 6, he told a national radio audience that he was not one who believed "that the priceless freedom of our country can be saved without sacrifice." It was necessary to acknowledge that Germany was attempting to destroy the freedom of all nations. "Unless we on our side are ready to sacrifice," Stimson warned, "and, if need be, die for the conviction that the freedom of America must be saved, it will not be saved. Only by a readiness for the same sacrifice can that freedom be preserved."[45]

With the German invasion of the Soviet Union in June, Stimson made one last effort to persuade the president that the time for U.S. action was at hand. He saw this as "a great chance" for Roosevelt to begin full convoys for British ships on the Atlantic and to provide more aid to the Allies, including the Soviet Union. Moreover, he advised the president to make a dramatic personal statement in front of Congress concerning the inevitability of war. He wrote Roosevelt that, with this further evidence of "Nazi ambition and perfidy, the door is opened wide for you to lead directly towards the winning of the battle of the North Atlantic." Stimson proposed that the president tell Congress that he had done all he could to find a peaceful solution and to prevent the nation from getting drawn into the fighting, but that the "effort to avoid the use of force is proving ineffective." It was now clear, Stimson continued, that unless the United States did everything in its power to aid "those free nations who are still fighting for freedom in this world," the United States would find itself "fighting alone at an enormously greater danger than we should encounter today with their aid."[46]

Roosevelt once again rejected Stimson's recommendation for more direct and energetic action, and Stimson did not push the issue any further. It was clear to him that Roosevelt was "so far committed to his own more gradual course that nothing could change him."[47] Roosevelt was willing to take actions that were more and more hostile toward Germany, such as extending the American patrol sphere to Iceland and allowing American ships to shoot at German submarines. Still, the president was going to wait for the war to come to the United States. Roosevelt continued to exert his usual political acuity and was moving the nation as fast as he thought was possible. Stimson, not having to worry about political considerations, played a valuable role in keeping the big issues in front of the president and the public. He wished Roosevelt would move faster, but rarely found reasons to fault the president's ultimate judgments. Given the conviction of all the senior officials that the threat of Germany was much greater than that from Japan and that the decisive theater of the world crisis was Europe, it was somewhat ironic that, when war finally came for the United States, it came from the Pacific—not the Atlantic.

Pearl Harbor

Throughout 1940 and 1941, American efforts were concentrated primarily on Europe, a policy with which Stimson fully agreed. The survival of Great Britain was by no means certain, and if Germany should defeat the Soviet Union, its military and industry would be greatly strengthened thereby. Moreover, Stimson did not believe that Japan would be bold or foolish enough as to provoke the United States, much less attack it. It was clear to him that America was a much more powerful nation than Japan, and that Japan was so dependent on America for raw materials that Tokyo would see such a move as suicide. This did not mean that Japan was ignored: Stimson had been urging an economic boycott since Japan's invasion of China in 1937, and he continued to believe when he entered the Roosevelt administration that an embargo would serve as an adequate check to Japanese expansion.

Stimson supported the "moral embargo" that Roosevelt had established for munitions in 1938 and sought to extend and strengthen this policy throughout his first year in office. When Japan sought to take advantage of Germany's victory over France in 1940 by moving into northern Indo-China, Stimson fully backed the extension of the embargo to include scrap metal and iron as a sufficient response that would force Japan to alter its course. The Colonel believed that "when the United States indicates by clear language and bold actions that she intends to carry out a clear and affirmative policy in the Far East, Japan will yield to that policy even though it conflicts with her own Asiatic policy and conceived interests."[48] Stimson, therefore, consistently advocated a policy of firmness toward Japan while giving most of his time and energy to the crisis in Europe. He even went so far as to argue, in May 1941, for the removal of the American fleet from Hawaii to the Atlantic, given the primacy of the threat from Germany. Stimson could not envision Japan daring to strike against the United States or the British fleet in the Pacific, and he believed that time was an ally in East Asia.

The events of July 1941 completely changed Stimson's views. Japan's taking all of Indo-China indicated to him that there would be no stopping Tokyo's effort to establish its dominance throughout East Asia short of war. Stimson supported the imposing of a complete embargo against Japan that month, including blocking oil sales and freezing Japanese assets. Stimson's efforts now began to turn toward preparing for a Japanese attack. The most likely target was the Philippines, and Stimson was determined to provide all the aid and equipment he could to defend the archipelago. He was convinced by General Douglas MacArthur's optimistic reports and the development of the B-17 bomber that the islands could be held despite Japan's control of the surrounding area and seas. As negotiations between Secretary of State Cordell Hull and the Japanese broke down that fall, Stimson told Hull that "no promises of the Japs based on words would be worth anything," and that he needed three months to secure American defenses in the region. He, therefore, favored the "stringing out of negotiations if possible during that time." In mid-October, Stimson noted that, with war coming, it was important that American "diplomatic fencing" be done in such a way "so as to be sure that Japan was put into the wrong and made the first bad move—overt move."[49]

At the end of the month, Hull asked Stimson if he favored an immediate declaration of war against Japan. Stimson emphatically replied no. His purpose "was to take advantage of this wonderful opportunity of strengthening our position in the Philippines by air." Hull indicated that he still thought there was a chance that negotiations could succeed because he believed the Emperor was on his side and favored a peaceful settlement. Stimson indicated that the buildup of American forces in the Philippines could only strengthen his diplomatic efforts "in forcing the Japanese to keep away from Singapore and perhaps, if we are in good luck, to shake the Japanese out of the Axis." He said his policy could be summed up by quoting Theodore Roosevelt, "Speak softly and carry a big stick." What he needed was just a little more time to get the stick ready.[50]

By the end of November, it was clear that time was quickly running out. All American officials agreed that an attack was likely, and the question, Stimson noted, "was how we should maneuver them into the position of firing the first shot without allowing too much danger to ourselves."[51] It was believed that Japan would strike to the south in order to remove the American and British navies from the area and gain access to the riches of the region, in particular, the oil of the Dutch East Indies. Japan was not expected to attack American forces directly. The administration was united in its belief that an attack on the Philippines would bring national support for a declaration of war, and Stimson did what he could to prepare for the anticipated assault.

On December 6, Stimson canceled plans for a quick trip to Highhold as it was clear from all reports that war was imminent. Still, Stimson, along with most of the nation, was shocked when he learned from Roosevelt the next day that Japan had attacked Pearl Harbor. He had been monitoring reports of Japanese movements southward and in the Gulf of Siam where he anticipated the new fighting would begin. His initial reaction was one of "relief that the indecision was over and that a crisis had come in a way which would unite all our people." Japan had solved all his problems "by attacking us directly in Hawaii." Although the news coming in from the islands was very bad, Stimson was not discouraged. He fully believed that the nation, once united and in the war, had "practically nothing to fear." The only issue to be resolved was the question of a declaration of war. That night Roosevelt informed the first meeting of his advisors that the attack on Pearl Harbor was the most serious crisis for the nation since 1861. Stimson urged the president to seek a declaration of war against Germany as well as Japan, but received no support from the others.[52] The issue became moot three days later when Germany declared war on the United States.

While Stimson was relieved to have the issue of war finally resolved, he was troubled by the failure at Pearl Harbor. The charges of a conspiracy by the Roosevelt administration to set up an attack on Hawaii are preposterous, as any study of Stimson's actions makes clear. The secretary of war believed that the major responsibility for the surprise of the attack and the extensive damages rested with the local commanders who did not act fully on the alert sent out by Washington to all officers and bases in the Pacific. Still, Stimson realized that there were other significant factors, and he was willing to assume his share of the blame. He was genuinely surprised by the attack, had consistently misjudged Tokyo's intentions and goals, and had underestimated the capabilities of the Japanese military. These were serious shortcomings, but they were human errors that the Japanese successfully exploited in their daring move.

Stimson had little time to ponder these questions. He was now at the head of the American military fighting a world war. The immediate problem was the defense of the Philippines, a matter that Stimson thought was vital for both practical military reasons as well as from his own sense of responsibility for the islands. It quickly became apparent that air power alone could not defend the American colony. Stimson and Marshall, however, made the immediate decision that the American forces had to fight as best they could for as long as they could. Strategically, it was deemed important that the army prolong its resistance to delay Japanese advances in the region. The defense of the islands carried even more important political implications. The United States could not appear to be scuttling and thus create a defeatist attitude. The secretary of war and his chief of staff argued that the United States "could not give up the Philippines in that way," and that every effort had to be made to aid General MacArthur, "otherwise we would paralyze the activities of everybody in the Far East." Roosevelt endorsed this position over opposition from the navy. Stimson believed the navy attitude represented a defeatist philosophy and that it was important to do everything possible to prevent the Japanese from becoming "strongly ensconced in the southwestern Pacific." Furthermore, a withdrawal would lead to "the discouragement of China and in fact all of the four powers who are now fighting . . . [and] it would have a very bad effect on Russia."[53]

At the beginning of the new year, Stimson was pained to watch "the agonizing experience of seeing the doomed garrison gradually pulled down."[54] Yet the fighting was maintained for as long as possible. In February, Roosevelt, in a message drafted by Stimson, instructed MacArthur to "continue to keep our flag flying in the

Philippines so long as there remains any possibility of resistance."
It was imperative that the United States not "display weakness in
fact or spirit anywhere. It is mandatory that there be established
once and for all in the minds of all peoples complete evidence that
the American determination and indomitable will to win carries
on down to the last unit."[55] American and Filipino forces held on
through brutal conditions until early May, when they were finally
forced to surrender. This aggressive defense proved unsuccessful
in holding any areas other than Australia and a small piece of New
Guinea. Given the determination of the American people in the
wake of Pearl Harbor, it was also probably unnecessary for maintaining American resolve and demonstrating credibility. It would
be three long years before Americans would return there.

Although Stimson was mainly concerned with the war, he was
forced in the opening days of the fighting to confront two domestic
issues, which the secretary saw as distractions from his larger mission. In his dealing with the questions of blacks in the military and
Japanese Americans on the west coast, his lifelong prejudices and
pragmatic view of the war guided his decision making and led to
the greatest failing of his career, the internment of American citizens and immigrants of Japanese descent. Unfortunately, Stimson's
views and actions represented the majority opinion in the nation
and the government at the time.

Stimson viewed the issue of blacks in the military as insoluble
and believed that liberals within the administration only stirred
up trouble with the mistaken notion that they could use the crisis
of war for domestic reforms. The Colonel was not against blacks in
the military per se, but he worried about how they would be used.
He noted, in September 1940, that "colored troops do very well
under white officers but every time we try to lift them a little beyond where they can go, disaster and confusion follows." He
doubted African Americans could be successful flyers and believed
that "leadership is not imbeded [sic] in the negro race yet." He considered meetings with black leaders to be "harassing interruptions
with the main business with which the Secretary of War ought to
be engaged."[56]

Stimson perceived that duty to be preparing the nation's military for war. Demands for the equal treatment of African Americans, to his mind, created unnecessary divisions and brought
resistance from whites. In January 1942, he found that the "race
question is making trouble" for the department again. He recognized that the problem stemmed "from the persistent legacy of the

original crime of slavery." Because it was presidential policy, he was carrying through with the creation of black divisions and planned on using them in the fighting. Nonetheless, he thought the issue "was almost impossible of solution" and he could see "no theoretical or logical solution for it at war times like these." He held to his view that black troops could perform well only under white officers and that social equality was impossible. He was quite certain that the issue kept coming up due to "Mrs. Roosevelt's intrusive and impulsive folly" on this question.[57] Stimson was unable to overcome his long-held prejudices even as the successful performances of African Americans in the military contradicted his assessments of their abilities and potential.

On February 3, Stimson was brought what he termed the "very difficult problem on the west coast." General John DeWitt, the commander of the west coast, and other leaders were pressuring the administration to evacuate all the Japanese in the area. Stimson uncritically accepted the charges of general disloyalty among all Japanese Americans and the unsubstantiated claims of spying and sabotage. Without any real investigation, he concluded that, paradoxically, the younger generation who were citizens, the Nisei, were "probably a more dangerous element at the present time than their unnaturalized parents." He returned to this problem a week later in a discussion with Assistant Secretary McCloy. Stimson again argued that the Nisei posed the greatest danger and had to be removed. That could be done only, he noted, "as part of a total evacuation." He believed that "their racial characteristics are such that we cannot understand or trust even the citizen Japanese. This latter is a fact but I am afraid it will make a tremendous hole in our constitutional system to apply it." Pearl Harbor had taught him that the nation had "made an enormous mistake in underestimating the Japanese."[58] Stimson was not willing to make that mistake again and sided with what he saw as national security over civil liberties. Because of his and other officials' failures to estimate Japanese abilities and direction correctly, he now decided to heed any warnings, no matter how baseless, and to brand anyone related to the Japanese as untrustworthy.

After overcoming objections from the Department of Justice, Stimson obtained presidential approval for the evacuation of more than 110,000 Japanese Americans on February 19, 1942. Stimson saw Executive Order 9066 as "a long step forward towards a solution of a very dangerous and vexing problem," and he fully expected protests against the action. Stimson was well aware of the legal issues involved, but he defended his course by stating that, "in emergencies, where the safety of the Nation is involved, consideration of the rights of individuals must be subordinated to the common security."[59] The performance of Japanese Americans fighting in Europe demonstrated their loyalty beyond any doubt. Yet Stimson continued to support this injustice after the war as having been a necessary action to protect Japanese Americans from violence. Whatever his justifications, Stimson was wrong. There was no danger posed to the nation by the small Japanese community. Instead of providing leadership and a calming voice, he allowed the local hysteria and his own prejudice to overcome his knowledge that internment was a violation of the Japanese Americans' civil liberties.

Power

To those living after the Second World War, Stimson's views throughout the 1930s might not seem that notable or significant. They became standard American thinking during the war and shaped American foreign policy in the postwar period. Yet one needs to remember that, at the time, few others, particularly senior statesmen of Stimson's stature, were bold enough to make the case for active American opposition to German, Japanese, and Italian aggression so clearly and consistently. This was especially courageous, given that the most outspoken isolationists were fellow Republicans. It was, however, Stimson's commitment to internationalism, his integrity, and his forthright manner that had first gained him Roosevelt's respect and had led the president to name him secretary of war. Once in office, events proved that Stimson had been correct about the major issues from the start.

Stimson's first year and a half in office marked a series of achievements that extended throughout the war. He had secured the foundation for the buildup of the American military through the draft, organized the massive effort to produce weapons, munitions, airplanes, and everything else that went into equipping American forces, and played a central role in preparing the American people for the sacrifices and efforts that would bring victory over Germany and Japan and leave the United States in the position of the leading power in the world. To Stimson, the attack on Pearl Harbor "restored to America the freedom of action she had lost by many cunning bonds of her own citizens' contriving. The self-imprisoned giant was now free."[60] Throughout all the trials and tribulations that lay ahead, and many pessimistic estimates and setbacks, Stimson never lost faith in the correctness of what he was doing and America's war effort. This confidence rested upon the "belief that there is a Power in the universe that makes for righteousness and that Power cannot allow such a clear issue of right and wrong to go the wrong way." Still, the ultimate "decision rests upon the power and will of the American people."[61] It was now his job to marshal the nation's resources into an effective strategy for the Grand Alliance, while overseeing the largest single project of the war, the construction of the atomic bomb, to make sure that the power and will of the people were successful in achieving victory.

Notes

1. Stimson and Bundy, *On Active Service*, 672.
2. Ibid., 297–99.
3. Stimson Diary, 17 May 1934, HLSD.
4. Stimson to Roosevelt, 14 March 1933, 4 June 1935, President's Personal File (hereafter PPF), Box 20, Franklin D. Roosevelt Presidential Library, Hyde Park, N.Y. (hereafter FDRL).
5. Stimson and Bundy, *On Active Service*, 303–304; Stimson to Roosevelt, 4 June 1935, PPF, Box 20, FDRL; Stimson Diary, 7 April 1937, HLSD.
6. Stimson, *Democracy and Nationalism*.
7. Memorandum of Conversation Between Mr. Stimson and the President, 28 March 1933, HLSD.
8. Stimson, *Democracy and Nationalism*, 42, 86.
9. Stimson Diary, 14 March 1935, HLSD.
10. Stimson, "Neutrality and War Prevention," *International Conciliation* (September 1935), 347–57.
11. *New York Times*, 24 October 1935; Stimson and Bundy, *On Active Service*, 310–11.
12. Samuel Rosenman, ed., *The Public Papers and Addresses of Franklin D. Roosevelt*, 13 vols. (New York: Random House, 1938–50) 5:406–11.
13. Stimson to *New York Times*, 6 October 1937.
14. Ibid.
15. Stimson to Roosevelt, 15 November 1937, PPF, Box 20, FDRL.
16. Ibid., Roosevelt to Hull, 22 November 1937; Roosevelt to Stimson, 24 November 1937.
17. Stimson and Bundy, *On Active Service*, 314.
18. Stimson to *New York Times*, 24 January 1939.
19. Stimson and Bundy, *On Active Service*, 313.
20. Ibid., 314.
21. Stimson to *New York Times*, 6 March 1939.
22. Ibid.
23. Ibid.
24. *New York Times*, 6 April 1939.
25. Stimson to *New York Times*, 16 September 1939.
26. Stimson and Bundy, *On Active Service*, 317.
27. Stimson Diary, 23 October 1939, HLSD; Stimson, 10 January 1940, PPF, Box 20, FDRL.

28. Stimson and Bundy, *On Active Service*, 318–20.

29. Morison, *Turmoil and Tradition*, 395–99.

30. Stimson Diary, 25 June 1940, HLSD; Morison, *Turmoil and Tradition*, 398.

31. Harvey Bundy, Oral History, Columbia University Oral History Project.

32. Author's interview with McGeorge Bundy, 16 January 1996.

33. Stimson and Bundy, *On Active Service*, 341.

34. Harvey Bundy, Oral History, Columbia University Oral History Project.

35. Stimson, "Our Duty Is Clear," 31 July 1941, *Vital Speeches of the Day*, vol. 6, 647–48.

36. Stimson Diary, 26 August 1940, HLSD.

37. Ibid., 17 August 1940.

38. Ibid., 9 September 1940.

39. Stimson and Bundy, *On Active Service*, 361–62.

40. Stimson Diary, 16 December 1940, 29 December 1940, HLSD.

41. Ibid., 19 December 1940.

42. Ibid., 15 April 1940.

43. Ibid., 10 April 1940.

44. Ibid., 22 April 1941, 24 April 1941, 25 April 1941.

45. Stimson and Bundy, *On Active Service*, 370.

46. Stimson Diary, 22 June 1941, HLSD; Stimson to Roosevelt, 23 June 1941, HLSD; Stimson to Roosevelt, 3 July 1941, PPF, Box 20, FDRL.

47. Stimson and Bundy, *On Active Service*, 373.

48. Stimson Diary, 2 October 1940, HLSD.

49. Memorandum of Conference Between Secretary Hull and Secretary Stimson, 6 October 1941, HLSD; Stimson Diary, 16 October 1941, HLSD.

50. Stimson Diary, 28 October 1941, HLSD.

51. Ibid., 25 November 1941.

52. Ibid., 7 December 1941.

53. Ibid., 14 December 1941, 17 December 1941.

54. Ibid., 2 January 1942.

55. Stimson and Bundy, *On Active Service*, 400.

56. Stimson Diary, 27 September 1940, 18 June 1941, HLSD.

57. Ibid., 17 January 1942, 24 January 1942.

58. Ibid., 3 February 1942, 10 February 1942.

59. Ibid., 18 February 1942; Morison, *Turmoil and Tradition*, 454.

60. Stimson and Bundy, *On Active Service*, 394.

61. Stimson Diary, 27 July 1942, HLSD.

6

Architect of Victory

The bombing of Pearl Harbor allowed the United States to take the step Stimson had "looked forward to and prophesied for so long—that of an open declared war against the Axis minions of evil."[1] With the coming of the war, all the issues that Stimson had concerned himself with since July 1940 took on increasing urgency. The buildup of the military had to be accelerated, the mobilization of the economy increased, the strategy for winning the war devised, and new weapons systems developed. As the nation rallied to the flag, new recruits flooded enlistment offices, workers vowed not to strike, Congress extended the draft law to include all able-bodied males, and even former isolationists called for military victory. The year and a half Stimson had had to begin preparations was paying off. Industrial production was already approaching full capacity, new plants were being built to handle the greater demands, and munitions manufacturers were meeting the needs of the American military, while also producing for shipment of materials and weapons abroad.

These positive developments left Stimson free to concentrate on American wartime strategy and larger questions of policy. Three principles guided all of Stimson's thinking on these matters. Victory had to be won at the earliest possible moment, Europe must be the primary theater of the war, and the United States had to remain the arsenal of the Allies in order to defeat Germany. He was convinced that Japan could never match America's power. Germany, on the other hand, had the potential to withstand the Allies' attacks on the continent, particularly if it was successful in defeating the Soviet Union. Initial American energies, therefore, had to be concentrated on defending Great Britain. Moreover, for Stimson, the quickest route to victory was an attack at the center of German might. This required a cross-channel invasion of France at the earliest possible moment. Stimson was a consistent and dogged advocate of this policy from the beginning of the war until the actual D-Day landing in Normandy on June 6, 1944. This position led to a series of disagreements with President Franklin Roosevelt and British Prime Minister Winston Churchill. Although he was confident of victory, Stimson worried that the use of American forces in what he considered peripheral areas, such as the Mediterranean, the Balkans, or the Middle East, would serve to disillusion the American public, elicit pressure for the United States to concentrate its energies on Japan, and allow Germany time to defeat the Soviet Union.

Stimson had another reason for making Europe his primary concern—his knowledge of the Manhattan project, or "S-1," as he usually referred to it. The Colonel was an advocate of numerous new scientific advances in weapons throughout the war and an early proponent of the most notable of these achievements, the atomic bomb. He saw the Manhattan project as a race against Germany. Should the Nazis develop this new weapon first, an Allied victory would be thrown into doubt. Thus, an attack directly against German power was necessary to help relieve the pressure on the Russian Army and prevent its destruction, to shorten the war and minimize American losses, and to defeat Germany before it could turn out a weapon that could stop the Allied advance. By 1945, the development and possible use of an atomic weapon came to dominate Stimson's time and thinking, as he was the person primarily responsible for overseeing the Manhattan project.

The secretary of war also had had disagreements with President Roosevelt over postwar planning and policy. These centered on his opposition to Secretary of the Treasury Henry Morgenthau's plan to turn postwar Germany into a pastoral nation. Stimson believed that Germany would have to be rebuilt and democratized in order to ensure postwar prosperity and stability. He, therefore, opposed any punitive settlement that would embitter the German people and sow the seeds of future conflict. He was determined not to repeat the mistakes of the post–World War I period. Stimson ultimately persuaded Roosevelt to reverse his initial endorsement of Morgenthau's plan and convinced the president that any postwar settlement had to include a revived and strong industrial Germany.

After Roosevelt's death on April 12, 1945, Stimson continued in office until the end of the war under President Harry S. Truman. The secretary of war worked well with the new president after overcoming his initial negative views of Truman, formed when Truman was a senator from Missouri. Truman came to rely on Stimson for advice, particularly concerning the atomic bomb, and he earned Stimson's respect and trust. Stimson was an advocate of the use of the atomic bomb at the earliest possible moment, if that was necessary for victory, but he was willing to pursue a negotiated end to the war by providing the Japanese an assurance concerning the continuation of their emperorship. For Stimson, the most urgent issue was ending the war so that attention could be given to postwar stability and reconstruction. When that option was rejected, he fully supported the use of the bombs in August 1945, but he disagreed with Truman's secretary of state, James F. Byrnes, and others over their efforts to use the weapon as a means to force concessions from the Soviet Union. Although he would later become the leading public defender of the use of the bombs, Stimson was not comfortable with all the decisions made at the time nor in complete agreement with the use of the bomb as a diplomatic weapon. In the end, he concluded that providing the Japanese with some sort of guarantee of retaining the Emperor would have shortened the war and possibly made the use of the atomic bombs unnecessary.

Before leaving government for the last time on his seventy-eighth birthday, September 21, 1945, Stimson made a final effort to shape American postwar policy directly and head off the growing conflict with the Soviet Union. His too often overlooked arguments are important for understanding the question of atomic diplomacy and the development of the Cold War. There were different choices that American leaders could have made at this critical time. Although he failed to convert anyone that day to the particulars of his argument, Stimson's long service and legacy would influence American foreign policy during the period of the Cold War and throughout the next generation, albeit not always in a manner that he would have desired.

The Grand Alliance

Stimson was always at his best when his mind was clear to concentrate on one major issue at a time. As a lawyer, he was known for the thoroughness of his preparation and his briefs when he was working on one big case, and, as he got older, this cast of mind became more pronounced. The number of tasks, however, that demanded his attention during the early days of the war caused him constant distractions and annoyances. Fortunately, he was able to delegate many of these tasks to his senior staff. In addition, the groundwork laid during the prewar preparations proved to be a solid foundation on which to build up the military and ensure the adequate production of goods. By early 1942, Stimson was able to turn most of his attention to matters of strategy and victory.

In March 1942, the military was reorganized with the creation of a joint command of the chief of staff and senior officers of the army, the army air force, and the navy. In addition, the War Department was restructured with the creation of three commands under the chief of staff responsible for the ground forces, the air forces, and supply. This decentralization proved necessary to allow for the effective expansion of the military in 1942 and 1943. This system freed General Marshall and the General Staff to concentrate on military planning and supervision, with senior officers in direct charge of the day-to-day operations of the army. With the army alone growing from 1.4 million to 8.3 million soldiers in two years, an effective and flexible system of training, supply, and command was vital. Along with reorganization, the other major change that allowed the military to reach its full strength in numbers was reducing the draft age from twenty-one to eighteen. After the initial enthusiasm for enlistment had cooled down in 1942, it became evident that the military could not meet its target numbers without drawing older workers away from defense production. The solution was to lower the draft age to include men who were not yet in the workforce or deemed vital to certain industries.

Stimson wanted to take this matter one step further and supported the passage of a National Service Act that he believed would solve all problems related to the sufficiency of troops and workers for industry. It would extend the power of the government to compel civilians to take on certain work deemed vital to the war effort. This measure was stalled throughout 1942 and 1943 by lack of presidential support. Finally, in January 1944, Roosevelt endorsed the measure as the only fair and democratic method for organizing and recruiting American workers. Stimson worked hard to gain its passage, both because he thought it was necessary to victory at the earliest possible moment and because it reflected his view of every man's responsibility to serve. He argued in front of congressional committees that the measure was necessary to bring about maximum production and to prevent potential labor unrest that could create shortages of material for American soldiers. All men, he argued, had an equal obligation to the war effort. "The men in war production are not essentially different" from those serving in combat. National service was to prevent any disruptions in production and extend equally throughout the population the burden and duties of the American people to the war. Moreover, Stimson argued, "National service will be the means of hastening the end of *this* war. . . . Every month the war is prolonged will be measured in the lives of thousands of young men, in billions of dollars." Faced with intense opposition from organized labor and liberals, and Roosevelt's unwillingness to lobby for the bill, Congress refused to adopt this radical new principle, and it failed to be reported out of committee. A second effort in 1945 was defeated in the Senate.[2]

Stimson, however, actually found little to complain about in terms of war production. Labor mainly held to its no-strike pledge, industrial production increased from $1.5 billion to $37.5 billion in the first three years of the war, billions of dollars of lend-lease aid was shipped abroad, and the American military was the best equipped and most powerful that the world had ever seen. He was able to tell the press in April 1942 that, although the dictators had gotten the jump on the United States in the first stages of the war, America "could be counted on to show greater strength" and "would pull down its enemy by sheer endurance and unbreakable morale." In November, Stimson noted that the enormous expansion of munitions making was going well, with full production having been reached during the summer. "Great new factories have been built all over the country. Shortages of tools have been practically filled . . . and we have plenty of labor."[3] There were always areas of difficulties, shortages of some materials, and production lags, but these were specific problems best handled by those directly in charge. Given these conditions, the secretary left most of the work and worrying to Assistant Secretary of War Robert Patterson and only turned his attention to these issues sporadically, when decisions were necessary that only he could make or that impinged upon his main concerns of strategy and a quick and decisive military victory.

Throughout the first three years of the war, 1942 through 1944, the question of military strategy and the achievement of a quick victory over Germany commanded Stimson's time. Having prepared the nation for war, he now saw it as the area where he could make his greatest contribution to the war effort: Although the public might be clamoring for immediate action against Japan, Stimson saw Europe as the decisive area in the war. In his first wartime memorandum for the president, in December 1941, concerning the fundamental issues to be discussed with the British, Stimson made his views clear: "Our joint war plans," Stimson began, "have recognized the North Atlantic as our principal theatre of operations should America become involved in the war." In the aftermath of Pearl Harbor, the survival of Great Britain "should now be given primary consideration. . . . Its safety must underlie all our other efforts in the war." Roosevelt concurred, and he agreed that an American force should be sent immediately to Great Britain.[4]

With this and the decisions necessary to shore up American defenses and the fleet in the Pacific behind him, Stimson turned his attention in March to an overall plan for the war. He feared that the lack of a strategic commitment to use Great Britain as the base for offensive operations could lead to "a series of diversionary shipments of troops and supplies to other areas."[5] Stimson, therefore, sought to get Roosevelt to take the lead in formulating policy with the British and to make a cross-channel invasion the top priority. At a meeting of senior officials with the president on March 5, the secretary of war made his case. He argued that the war with Japan was mainly a naval affair, with only the opportunity for a limited offensive until the fleet could be strengthened. Direct aid to the Russians by sending forces through the Persian Gulf was infeasible, and action in the Mediterranean should not even be considered. The only acceptable strategy, Stimson concluded, was "sending an overwhelming force to the British Isles and threatening an attack on the Germans in France." It would sustain existing programs and raise British morale. Most important, "it would now have the effect of giving Hitler two fronts to fight on if it could be done in time while the Russians were still in." Both Chief of Staff Marshall and General Dwight D. Eisenhower agreed that the Pacific was "a secondary theatre." As Stimson put it: "If we win over Japan there, we might still not win the war; but if we lost there, we would surely lose the war." The key, Stimson recorded Eisenhower as saying the next day, "was to keep Russia in the war which was of primary importance for, if she went out of the war he could see nothing better than a stalemate for us." That dictated "a powerful attack through Great Britain into France."[6]

The British, however, favored a very different strategy. They sought an attack into North Africa that would begin the process of gaining control of the Mediterranean Sea and encircling Hitler's forces, while helping to secure contact with vital parts of their empire that were threatened by both the Germans and Japanese. The British strategic theory was that Germany could be defeated by a series of smaller engagements in Italy, Greece, and the Balkans. Hitting against the soft underbelly of German forces would better ensure a much-needed success in the first major engagement with the German Army and help to alleviate the pressure on the Russians. Stimson, recalling Churchill's opposition to the Western Front in 1915, was sure that the prime minister feared a repeat of the bloodletting of World War I, and that he did not want to risk another Dunkirk. Moreover, the prime minister was apparently willing to let the Russians do all the serious ground fighting. Thus, a right hook into the Mediterranean was Churchill's basic position for the next two years.

On March 25, Roosevelt again met with his top advisors, including Stimson, Knox, Marshall, and his special assistant Harry Hopkins, to discuss these ideas. Marshall forcefully made the presentation for a cross-channel invasion and warned the president against the dispersion of American forces into secondary areas. Roosevelt agreed to support the development of this plan, but it was clear he still was entertaining the Mediterranean option. Two days later, Stimson wrote Roosevelt a personal letter designed to gain his backing for his and Marshall's plan. He began by stating: "John Sherman said in 1877, 'The only way to resume specie payments is to resume.' Similarly, the only way to get the initiative in this war is to take it." When the plan for the attack on France was completed, Stimson advised Roosevelt to send his most trusted advocate to Churchill to press for its adoption. Once that was completed, every effort should be made to rearrange shipping allotments and ensure the "preparation of landing gear for the ultimate invasion," aiming for "a definite date of completion not later than September." The lack of landing barges was the only substantive British objection to the offensive. Stimson concluded by noting, "So long as we remain without our own plan of offensive, our forces will inevitably be dispersed and wasted."[7]

As this plan, code-named BOLERO, was developed, it called for a full-scale invasion of France in the spring of 1943. If the Russians were in danger of collapsing, it had a contingency for a smaller attack in the fall of 1942, SLEDGEHAMMER, to provide an immediate second front and relief to the beleaguered Soviet Army. Stimson, Marshall, and Eisenhower all realized that an attack in 1942 could fail, but noted that it was well worth the risk because of the need to keep Russia and its army in the war. Without an eastern front, it would be that much harder to dislodge Hitler from the rest of Europe. For these reasons, Stimson saw it as crucial that the United States commit itself to as early an assault on France as possible.

Roosevelt agreed to the plan on April 1 and took Stimson's advice by sending Hopkins and Marshall to London to meet with Churchill. After difficult negotiations, they gained Churchill's approval. Stimson could not have been more pleased. With the British agreement, he began to make preparations for moving the necessary troops and supplies to England. Stimson was, therefore, greatly shocked when, on June 17, Roosevelt, at the behest of Churchill, announced that the prime minister was coming to Washington for a new round of meetings to reopen the discussion of an operation in North Africa, code-named GYMNAST. With Marshall's full support, Stimson again wrote a personal letter to Roosevelt to state his case that the war could only be won by a cross-channel invasion.

The central point to be kept in mind, Stimson argued, was that "the only thing Hitler rightly dreaded was a second front. In establishing such a front lay the best hope of keeping the Russian Army in the War and thus ultimately defeating Hitler. To apply the rapidly developing manpower and industrial strength of America promptly to the opening of such a front was manifestly the only way it could be accomplished." The British Isles were the one safe spot to gather American forces and land supplies, and BOLERO, he reiterated, provided "the surest road, first to shaking Hitler's anti-Russian campaign of '42, and second, to the ultimate defeat of his armies and the victorious termination of the war. Geographically and historically," Stimson continued, it was the "easiest road to the center of our enemy's heart." Given this, Stimson opined that "an immense burden of proof rests upon any proposition which may impose the slightest risk of weakening Bolero."[8]

When Churchill arrived on June 21, he launched into an immediate attack on the American plan. Roosevelt, supported by Marshall, stood firm in support of BOLERO, going so far as to show Churchill Stimson's letter. A compromise was struck by which preparations for the attack on France would continue until September 1. At that point, there would be an evaluation of progress "to see if a real attack could be made without the danger of disaster."[9] By early July, the British were again challenging this agreement. Marshall informed Stimson that Churchill was reviving discussions of GYMNAST and seeking to reverse the decisions just reached in Washington. The chief of staff proposed that Stimson force a final showdown over the question. Stimson, greatly annoyed by London's efforts to renege on its promises, concluded that, if the "British won't go through with what they agreed to, we will turn our backs on them and take up the war with Japan."[10]

This was an idle threat that Stimson knew he would never act on. Roosevelt quickly dismissed the idea and assured Stimson that he fully supported the existing plans. The secretary of war was not so sure, fearing still that a Mediterranean action remained "the President's great secret baby." Even after the agreement of June 21, Roosevelt himself had brought the subject up with Churchill the next day. Stimson was furious, noting in his diary that he found the president's actions "irresponsible."[11] Stimson did his best to get Roosevelt to hold the line, arguing that the British action was the "result of a fatigued and defeatist government which had lost its initiative." He pointed out that Churchill was violating his agreement reached in June to go ahead with planning until September, and that planning had to continue to ensure a full-scale attack in 1943. Roosevelt expressed his disappointment in the British position, but noted that Marshall had informed him that the United States could not go ahead with SLEDGEHAMMER without British cooperation. In addition, the president believed he had to get American troops into action by the end of the year. Stimson, therefore, was not surprised when Roosevelt conceded later that month to British opposition and opted to attack North Africa that fall. The president was committed to some U.S. action in 1942, and with the British obstructing an attack on France and with no assurances that SLEDGEHAMMER would succeed, he found it necessary to accept Churchill's option, GYMNAST, now renamed Operation TORCH.[12]

Stimson sympathized with the president's position and understood his desire to get American forces into battle, but that did not convince him that the switchover was correct. Moreover, he rightly, if reluctantly, concluded that the postponement now would effectively "destroy Bolero even in 1943." The Colonel thought the decision marked the turning away from "the path of what I consider sound and correct strategy."[13] The president and Stimson shared the same objectives, to get American forces on the offensive in fighting the Germans and to provide some relief to the Russians. They disagreed over the best means to accomplish those ends.

It was at this time that Roosevelt's style of administration and decision making bothered the secretary of war most. Stimson, who liked clear lines of authority and standard procedures, found the multiple agencies Roosevelt would create with overlapping responsibilities and the easy access too many people had to the president's ear hindrances to planning. In this regard, he found Roosevelt the poorest administrator he ever worked under. More disturbing, however, was the president's constant shifting of positions. Stimson believed that Roosevelt's negotiations with Churchill were mishandled, and that his manner of talking about critical situations and plans was marked by the "frivolity and lack of responsibility of a child." Stimson "tired of these constant decisions which do not stay made" and the president's bending to British desires in lieu of the recommendations of his own staff, even after agreements had already been reached. The president, Stimson concluded, "has the happy capacity of fooling himself" to get out of contradictions and change direction without acknowledging that he has done so.[14] Nonetheless, Stimson recognized the enormous burdens of Roosevelt's office, and that he and the president still agreed on the major issues and goals of the war. Stimson, therefore, maintained his genuine respect for Roosevelt and considered him a great wartime leader even when he was frustrated by particular actions of the president.

Stimson pushed his arguments with the president as far as they could go, and then he and Marshall turned their attention to the matter of making the assault into North Africa a success. The fall and winter of 1942–1943 marked a great turning point in the war. First, the invasion of North Africa in November went as well as anyone could have hoped. Anglo-American forces successfully landed and engaged the Germans in November. Second, the Russians stopped the German advance at Stalingrad and began a counterattack that lessened fears that the Soviet Union would be defeated by Germany. The victory in North Africa raised the question of who would rule in areas liberated from the Nazis. This problem was compounded by the fact that the Vichy French government controlled much of the territory in which Allied troops were fighting. Stimson fully supported the American recognition of Admiral Jean Darlan's authority as a means of obtaining a cease-fire with Vichy forces and providing stability and a secure rear for American forces. He recognized that Darlan had been a collaborator with the Nazis, but argued that the accommodation was necessary due to the "hazardous nature of our operation in North Africa and the perilous condition in which our troops would have been in case there had been any delay caused by the obstruction of the French."[15]

Stimson believed that it was well worth the criticism he got for supporting Darlan to be able to cut the risks and increase the chances of military success against the German Army. He approvingly quoted Roosevelt as telling him about "a Balkan quotation which he had found which rather aptly fitted the present situation. It was somewhat to the effect that, if the devil offered to help you over a bridge, it was just as well to let him do so but not to continue to walk with him on the other side." Stimson's own analogy was "the story in the Bible of Joshua sending the spies to Jericho and their making a pact with Rahab the harlot which was ratified by Joshua." The president "roared with delight" when he heard it.[16]

Having lost the argument the first time, Stimson set out to make sure that a second front was opened in France in 1943. In preparation for the upcoming meeting between Roosevelt and Churchill at Casablanca, Morocco, Stimson met with Marshall in early 1943 to review the American position. They agreed that they were "adhering to their old line" that there should be an attack on the north coast of France that year. It was time to engage Germany's main forces and to begin to cripple their capacity to fight. As they feared, the British continued to resist this plan and argued for an attack against Italy instead; the underlying reality of the discussions, Marshall reported, was "the absolute refusal of the British to go on with Bolero."[17]

Roosevelt again agreed with the British, and there was little more Stimson could do to get a second front opened that year. For Stimson, this made Churchill's visit to Washington in May 1943 a critical meeting. He was determined that a cross-channel attack be agreed to for 1944. British obstruction of this plan had to be overcome once and for all. Stimson remained convinced that the British strategy was misguided and was only serving to prolong the war. Moreover, in the wake of the Anglo-American success in North Africa and the Russian victory at Stalingrad, Stimson could allow himself for the first time to begin thinking about the postwar world. This, too, influenced his arguments in favor of a real second front in 1944.

When Churchill and his advisors arrived, both sides renewed the arguments that they had made many times before, and a "very decided deadlock" emerged. The British were "holding back dead from going on with Bolero." Fortunately, Stimson noted, Roosevelt was refusing to compromise. The president told Stimson on May 17 that "he was coming to the conclusion that he would have to read the Riot Act to the other side and would have to be stiff." Stimson's reply indicated a new and growing concern: He replied that the British position reminded him of a story Lincoln told of "a pretty poor general who, although he couldn't skin the deer, could at least hold a leg. The British are trying to arrange this matter so that Britain and America hold the leg for Stalin to skin the deer." In addition to all his previous reasons for supporting a northern attack, Stimson now added his fear that any more delays "will be a dangerous business for us at the end of the war. Stalin won't have much of an opinion of people who have done that and we will not be able to share much of the post-war world with him."[18]

This time, Roosevelt held firm to the American position in his talks with Churchill, insisting that planning for an invasion of northern France, now named OVERLORD, was the top priority and that other matters could be discussed after that was set. Churchill finally yielded to the American plan on the condition that General Marshall accompany him on an inspection tour to North Africa. Stimson suspected that the prime minister hoped that he could persuade Marshall to change his views during the trip, but was not worried. "Marshall," he laconically recalled, "returned safe, and unconverted, to the Pentagon."[19]

Stimson traveled to England in July to visit American troops, inspect bases, and check on planning for the cross-channel attack. The invasion of Sicily had begun on July 10, and inevitably, Churchill brought up the subject of further operations in the Mediterranean. He noted that he continued to oppose Operation OVERLORD, which Stimson often still referred to as ROUNDHAMMER or BOLERO in his writing. Stimson told Churchill that, if the United States were to engage in any more operations on the periphery of Europe, it would appear that it was really fighting to preserve the British Empire and not to defeat Germany. The Italian campaign was no substitute for an attack on France. The American people, he told the prime minister, "did not hate the Italians but took them rather as a joke as fighters; that only by an intellectual effort had they been convinced that Germany was their most dangerous enemy and should be disposed [of] before Japan; that the enemy whom the American people really hated . . . was Japan which had dealt them a foul blow." If the United States "could not fulfill our purpose of Roundhammer in 1944, that situation would be a serious blow to the prestige of the President's war policy and therefore to the interests of the United States."[20]

Churchill returned to his criticism of OVERLORD in a subsequent conversation, "repeating assertions" depicting "the disastrous effect of having the Channel full of corpses of defeated allies." This pushed Stimson beyond his limit, and "for a few minutes we had at it hammer and tongs." The secretary told Churchill that such statements were "like hitting us in the eye," given the agreements already reached. Furthermore, he stated that "we could never win any battle by talking about corpses." Churchill backed down, admitting he did not favor OVERLORD, but that "he would go through with it loyally." Upon his departure, Stimson thought that if sufficiently pressured, Churchill would honor his commitment, "but that he was looking so constantly and vigorously for an easy way of ending the war without a trans-Channel assault that, if we expected to be ready for a Roundhammer which would be early enough in 1944 to avoid the dangers of bad weather, we must be constantly on the lookout against Mediterranean diversions."[21]

Knowing Churchill was again heading for North America, Stimson made sure that he returned home so that he could report to Roosevelt before the conference in Quebec. On August 10, Stimson had "one of the most satisfactory conferences I have ever had with the President." He warned Roosevelt that the British were only paying "lip service to the operation," and that "their hearts are not in it" because of the horrors of previous defeats. An American commander was, therefore, absolutely essential to the success of the plan. It was time, Stimson argued, for Roosevelt to "assume the responsibility for leadership in this great final movement of the European war. . . . We cannot afford to confer again and close with a lip tribute to Bolero." The British had twice before promised and then blocked this operation. The president now had to insist on it.[22]

Finally, Stimson pointed out the significance of these actions to the postwar period. He believed that the British view was "that the only heavy fighting which needs to be done will be done by the Russians." Given the difficult questions to be faced at the end of the war, Stimson found that attitude "terribly dangerous." The United States had pledged to Stalin that it would open "a real second front." The British policy broke that promise. "None of these methods of pinprick warfare can be counted on by us to fool Stalin into the belief that we have kept that pledge." The president agreed with every point, telling Stimson that he had "announced the conclusions which he had just come to himself" and gave his complete endorsement of the American policy. Roosevelt "was for setting up as rapidly as possible a larger force in Great Britain for the purpose of Roundhammer," and endorsed the appointment of an American commander.[23]

The cross-channel assault was finally Roosevelt's own policy, and he was prepared to fight for it in his meetings with Churchill. This proved unnecessary. Stimson had evidently convinced Churchill that there would be no turning back this time. At their meeting in Quebec, the prime minister informed Roosevelt of his continued support and voluntarily offered to accept Marshall as the commander of Allied troops. There was one final flare-up in October, when Churchill, at the meeting of foreign ministers in Moscow, again raised the question of an operation in the eastern Mediterranean. The American delegation assured Stalin that the cross-channel operation was going ahead as planned, but Stimson believed that this showed "how determined Churchill is with all his lip service to stick a knife in the back of Overlord."[24] The Colonel, therefore, made sure that he met with Roosevelt and Hopkins prior to the president's trip to Teheran and the first meeting of the Big Three in November 1943.

Since Stimson was not going to make the trip, he sought to ensure that Hopkins knew the full background and extent of the planning for OVERLORD and was provided with information "to hold the President in line if he could." Hopkins agreed that this plan "was the most important problem now before the world" and that he, too, was anxious "owing to the very doubtful attitude of the British Prime Minister."[25] At Teheran, Stalin sided completely with the American position. He made it clear that he thought OVERLORD the most important contribution that the Allied forces could make in providing assistance to the USSR and shortening the war. Each time Churchill raised the question of an operation in the eastern Mediterranean, it was rebuffed by the Soviet leader. "If we are here in order to discuss military questions," Stalin declared at one point, "we, the USSR, find OVERLORD the most important and decisive." All the other efforts were merely diversions.[26]

Stimson was greatly relieved that the plan survived this meeting. He wrote that he thanked "the Lord that Stalin was there. In my opinion, he saved the day." The Soviet leader "brushed away the diversionary attempts of the Prime Minister with a vigor which rejoiced my soul." It was now clear to everyone, Stimson believed, what was an actual supporting attack and what was merely a secondary operation. Churchill had no more Mediterranean avenues to pursue; the battle over strategy was finally won.[27] It was also decided that Eisenhower, and not Marshall, would be named supreme commander, and that the invasion would be launched before summer.

After two years of fighting, Stimson was finally assured that his idea for winning the war would be implemented. As Roosevelt told him when he returned from Teheran, "I have thus brought OVERLORD back to you safe and sound."[28] In looking back over the past three years and the accomplishments of the American military, Stimson concluded that 1941 was the year of our planning, 1942 the year of "defense and preparation," and 1943 the year "of our taking the initiative." But 1944 would be "the year of decision" when victory would finally come into view.[29]

For the next six months, the War Department worked furiously to prepare for the assault on Normandy. The waiting and the worrying were difficult for Stimson, but his confidence in his views and the army never flagged. On the eve of D-Day, Stimson took some time to reflect on its meaning and his role. He and his wife talked about the thousands of young men who were preparing for the assault and possibly facing death. It was, Stimson noted, "one of the great crises of the world, perhaps the greatest and sharpest crisis that the world has ever had, and it all . . . focused together on tonight." He recalled that he had been urging this action since December 1941 and had finally persuaded Roosevelt to take the lead and insist on this attack.[30] When the attack was finally launched, on June 6, 1944, and the first victories achieved, Stimson flew to England and then on to France to see the campaign in action for himself. He witnessed as reality that which he had fought so long and hard to achieve. The responsibility for the Allied success on D-Day and the battles that followed has to be shared by many, but certainly few deserved more credit than the Colonel as he walked once again on French soil during a world war.

Morgenthau Plan

In the wake of D-Day and the allied drive toward Germany, Stimson was able for the first time to turn his attention in a systematic manner to the questions of peace and the postwar world. Certain cardinal principles guided the secretary's thinking. First and foremost was the continuation of the alliance and friendship with Great Britain. Stimson had worked hard for years to develop the close relationship the two nations now had, and he believed that their interests were more closely aligned than those of any other two nations. For example, he told Secretary of State Cordell Hull in 1943 that his conviction was growing every day that all postwar plans must be designed "to continue after the war the same controls as have saved us during the war, namely close association between the English speaking countries." The American people must understand that greater American involvement in world affairs would be necessary, and that the United States would continue its close association with Great Britain, "because it saved us and because it is still necessary to keep us safe."[31] The disagreements over strategy had been serious, but they never led him to question this truth. They were, in fact, "trivial compared to his underlying conviction that the final interests of both the United States and Great Britain required the two nations to live together in constantly closer association."[32]

This relationship, of course, would not be enough in and of itself to maintain postwar peace. Stimson believed that the "essential basis of enduring peace must be economic."[33] He had learned the consequences of a settlement that hampered reconstruction and international trade, and thus weakened new governments that were economically dependent and built up resentments over their treatment. In brief, he wanted to avoid a repeat of the harsh Versailles settlement and its economically unfeasible demands. As he told Hull and Knox, the main mistakes of the Versailles Treaty were economic in that it failed to prevent "the rise of tariff barriers between the different states of Europe after the war." Germany would have to be punished and its leadership changed; "Germany had been so under the military clique, the militarist Prussians, that five times during a little over my lifetime she had been responsible for beginning an aggressive war in Europe." This "stamped her apart from the ordinary nation" and demanded the punishment of German leaders.[34]

To Stimson, the only solution was for the United States to seize this "second chance" for world leadership and structure a postwar system based upon liberal international trade, convertible currencies, and reconstruction of the defeated nations. The world, he believed, needed American leadership, ideals, and trade in order to have stability and peace. The treatment of Germany would determine whether or not America was successful in rebuilding a prosperous and peaceful world. That nation would have to be rebuilt and restored to the center of Europe's economy. For these reasons, Stimson supported war crimes trials for Nazi leaders, a denazification program to punish those responsible for the war, and creation of a democratic Germany. But he opposed a punitive settlement that would leave Germany at the mercy of the Allies and dependent on others for commerce and industry.

Upon his return to Washington from his trip to England and France, Stimson found himself at the center of a growing disagreement within the administration over the question of the treatment of Germany. In September 1944, Secretary of the Treasury Morgenthau proposed a policy that would effectively de-industrialize Germany and turn it into an agrarian nation as a means of punishment and of maintaining the peace. The Morgenthau Plan called for the German standard of living to be held down to subsistence levels, the Ruhr and the Saar to be transformed into nonindustrial areas devoted to farming, and Germany to be made so dependent on imports and exports for basic goods that it would have no capacity to convert its economy to war production.

Stimson deemed this proposal both preposterous and dangerous. In a memorandum to the president, Stimson argued that Germany was the most important nation for the materials, production, and commerce on which "the industrial and economic livelihood of Europe was based." Its production "could not be sealed up and obliterated . . . without manifestly causing a great dislocation to the trade upon which Europe has lived." He could not "treat as realistic the suggestion that such an area in the present economic condition of the world can be turned into a non-productive 'ghost territory' when it had become the center of one of the most industrialized continents." German productive capacity would be necessary to the recuperation of both Allied and enemy states after the war. Moreover, Morgenthau's program would "create tensions and resentments far outweighing any immediate advantage of security and would tend to obscure the guilt of the Nazis and the viciousness of their doctrines and their acts." Although punishment was necessary for many, and reeducation a requirement for the general population, "economic oppression" should not be added to this. "Such methods," Stimson concluded, ". . . do not prevent wars; they tend to breed war."[35]

The cabinet discussed these two competing views on September 6 and 9. At the first meeting, Roosevelt appeared to be backing Stimson, arguing that the Ruhr should not be dismantled, as "Great Britain was going to be in sore straits after the war" and the production from that region could be used to help its industries. For the second meeting, Morgenthau brought a new paper challenging the argument that a prosperous Europe needed a strong, revitalized Germany: Its production had been a competitor that hurt Great Britain and could be replaced by British industry. Morgenthau's arguments contained, Stimson believed, "a specious appeal to the President's expressed desire to help England" by arguing that shutting down the Ruhr would "give England a chance to jump into Germany's business of supplying Europe industrially."[36]

Roosevelt left for a meeting with Churchill in Quebec without reaching a decision. On September 13, Morgenthau was summoned to the meeting to present his ideas. Stimson tried to counter his influence by sending another memorandum that reiterated his earlier views. The treasury plan "would in the long run certainly defeat what we hope to attain by a complete military victory—that is, the peace of the world, and the assurance of social, economic and political stability in the world." Stimson noted that his difference of opinion with Morgenthau was over the means to the same objective of peace. But he could not believe that the "Carthaginian" treasury proposals would lead to a lasting peace. "In spirit and in emphasis they are punitive, not in my judgment, corrective or constructive. They will," Stimson concluded, "tend through bitterness and suffering to breed another war." This was the fundamental lesson of the past twenty-five years. "The question is not whether we want Germans to suffer for their sins. Many of us would like to see them suffer the tortures they have inflicted on others. The only question is whether over the years a group of seventy million educated, efficient and imaginative people can be kept within the bounds on such a low level of subsistence as the Treasury proposals contemplate. I do not believe that is humanly possible."[37]

On September 16, Roosevelt and Churchill signed off on the fundamentals of the Morgenthau Plan. They agreed that in order to punish Germany and to prevent its renewed military capacity, the "industries . . . in the Ruhr and in the Saar would . . . be necessarily put out of action and closed down." This program "for eliminating the war-making industries in the Ruhr and in the Saar is looking forward to converting Germany into a country primarily agricultural and pastoral in its character." Stimson was stunned and immediately prepared a third memorandum that set forth again his opposition and concerns. He asked Hopkins to deliver it immediately to the president who was resting at his home in Hyde Park. Stimson realized that another paper opposing the president's decision would "undoubtedly irritate him for he dislikes opposition when he had made up his mind." But both the serious consequences of the decision and Stimson's "self-respect" led him to present his views to Roosevelt.[38]

Roosevelt read Stimson's paper and let him know that he wanted to discuss the matter. Meanwhile, word of the adoption of the Morgenthau Plan was leaked to the press and met with immediate and widespread criticism. Roosevelt called Stimson at Highhold and indicated that he had changed his mind, that he had "made a false step and was trying to work out of it." The president informed Stimson that he did not intend to make Germany a solely agricultural nation, but that his main motive was to help England, which was broke. He was trying to find a means to give Great Britain more business by replacing some of Germany's industries. The two talked again the following week when they were both back in Washington. When Roosevelt repeated what he had said earlier, Stimson broke in, stating, "Mr. President, I do not like you to dissemble to me." He then read to him the relevant lines from the document he had initialed in Quebec. Roosevelt was "frankly staggered" and said he had "no idea how he could have initialed this," that he had "evidently done it without much thought."[39] Stimson and Roosevelt never spoke about the Morgenthau Plan again.

The secretary of war understood the president's position, that he had acted too soon in signing off on the Morgenthau Plan and was seeking a means to back off. A great politician and leader, to accomplish all that Roosevelt had, at times, needed to do that— and to be good at it. Stimson's sharp words to the president were meant to make sure that Roosevelt did not weaken again. With the Morgenthau Plan dropped as the basis of American policy, it was not yet clear which policy would replace it. The initial decision, known as J.C.S. 1067, ordered the American military commander to take no steps to strengthen or rehabilitate the German economy. Still, there were no orders for economic destruction, and Stimson thought it was "a fairly good paper" in contrast to Morgenthau's ideas.[40] Stimson consistently advocated a final policy that centered on denazification, demilitarization, and the economic rehabilitation of Germany, a policy that Roosevelt now fully supported but would not live long enough to implement.

Roosevelt's death on April 12, 1945, greatly saddened Stimson on many levels. The nation had lost a great leader, and there were many questions of postwar policy still left to be resolved. It was also a deep personal loss for the secretary of war. Roosevelt had provided him with the opportunity to serve the nation again, and for this Stimson was forever grateful. He noted at the time that, for "all his idiosyncrasies our Chief was a very kindly and friendly man." In particular, Stimson recalled his sense of humor during trying times and pleasantness to all who worked for him and "felt very keenly the loss of a real personal friend." Stimson never hid his belief that he "regarded his administrative procedure as disorderly, but his foreign policy was always founded on great foresight and keenness of vision, and coming at this period when the war is closing and will I feel sure be succeeded by a period of great confusion of ideas in this country, the loss of his leadership will be most serious." The situation was made all the more troubling because "no one knows what the new President's views are." Still, Stimson was confident about the future. He believed that Truman's advisors could set out "the pattern which had been followed hitherto."[41] It was important to keep in view Roosevelt's "vision over the broad reaches of events . . . guided by a very strong faith in the future of our country and of freedom, democracy and humanitarianism throughout the world." Stimson always found Roosevelt's policies and grand strategy to be sound. In this respect, Stimson concluded, he was "without exception the best war President the United States has ever had."[42]

Stimson's initial responses to Truman as president were positive. He impressed the secretary of war as "a man who is willing and anxious to learn and to do his best but who was necessarily laboring with the terrific handicap of coming into such an office where the threads of information were so multitudinous that only long previous familiarity could allow him to control them." Truman would have to trust his advisors while he learned the issues. He was further handicapped by following Roosevelt, who had "such immense prestige politically arising from his four successful campaigns for President that he carried a weight with the Congress and with general politicians of the country which Truman of course could not possibly have." Stimson concurred with Marshall in that they would not "know what he is really like until the pressure begins to be felt."[43] Stimson's role in providing advice to the new president was crucial during the transition to a new administration and the ending of the war, and his views would provide the outline for American postwar plans for Europe. Still, other advisors played a greater role in the new administration, and Truman would adopt policies concerning the final surrender of Japan and the use of the atomic bomb in America's postwar plans that Stimson did not endorse.

The Atomic Bomb and the Postwar World

Few events in Stimson's life or the nation's history were more important and have attracted more discussion and debate than the decision to drop two atomic bombs on Japan in August 1945. Stimson was intimately involved with the development of the atomic bomb after 1941, when President Roosevelt appointed him, along with Vice President Henry Wallace, General Marshall, Dr. Vannevar Bush, and Dr. James B. Conant, to a committee to oversee the development of the weapon and advise the president on questions of policy and use. On May 1, 1943, Roosevelt made Stimson directly responsible for the administration of the entire Manhattan project and his senior advisor on the military deployment of the atomic bomb. In addition, in 1943, Stimson was named chair of the Combined Policy Committee of American, British, and Canadian officials that cooperated in the building of the bomb. From 1941 to 1945, the Manhattan project occupied more and more of Stimson's time, and by April 1945, when he established the Interim Committee, composed of himself, Byrnes, Bush, Conant, George Harrison as Stimson's representative, William Clayton of the State Department, Ralph Bard of the Navy Department, and Dr. Karl Compton, it dominated his thinking about the war and the postwar period. The establishment of the Interim Committee was prompted by the imminent success of the development efforts and the need to make specific proposals for the bomb's use, including which cities to attack.

Concern over German efforts toward designing and manufacturing the weapon created a sense of immediate urgency in the development of the atomic bomb. Were Germany to win the race, the Allies would face the prospect of defeat. While this danger reinforced Stimson's arguments for an early cross-channel attack, it also made the Manhattan project an equally important strategy. Stimson fully endorsed Roosevelt's decision to spare no expense or effort in securing the weapon at the earliest possible moment and, when successful, to use it to shorten the war. Stimson was responsible for all aspects of the development of the new weapon, including securing the necessary funding from Congress while maintaining the secrecy of the project.

Stimson's views on the use of the atomic bomb were complex, and they have often been misinterpreted as either favoring atomic diplomacy or demonstrating inconsistency. The difficulty in deciphering Stimson's views was compounded by his postwar writings on the bomb, such as his famous February 1947 article in *Harper's Magazine*, "The Decision to Use the Atomic Bomb," in which he defended dropping the bombs on Japan as the "least abhorrent choice."[44] Although he supported the use of the bombs, he did not do so at the expense of other options to end the war, nor did he seek to use them as a means to intimidate the Soviet Union.

Stimson saw the bomb as a weapon of war and favored using it to end the war at the earliest possible time. He sought a rapid conclusion to the war in order to save lives, end the destruction and high costs of fighting, and facilitate postwar recovery, particularly in Europe. With these convictions, he never questioned whether the bomb should be used. He was, however, too sophisticated and intelligent a man not to realize the bomb's political implications. As one who had been engaged with questions of power both domestically and abroad for the past fifty years, Stimson fully understood the enormous impact of the bomb and how it would change international relations, particularly with the Soviet Union. Stimson sought to withhold detailed information on the bomb from the Soviets, not as a means of intimidating them or forcing concessions, but as part of broader negotiations to ensure postwar peace and recovery. His diary entries have been used to demonstrate that the bombs were dropped on Japan as a means of influencing postwar relations with the Soviet Union. That these writings reveal that this was central to much of American planning and actions during the summer of 1945, there can be little doubt. Yet that does not fully answer the question of Stimson's role and views. For Stimson, the objective was to end the war, not to use the bombs. He, however, recognized that there were others who sought to use the bomb as a lever against the Soviets and as the primary tool of American diplomacy, and he opposed this course of action. The actual use of the bombs and the reports Stimson read served to intensify these beliefs.

A close examination of his thoughts in 1945 and later shows that he was neither an advocate of atomic diplomacy nor a defender of the orthodoxy that is often attached to his name. Rather, he was a proponent of the simultaneous use of the bomb and negotiations. He can be criticized fairly for not thinking the issue fully through earlier or finding an effective means to act on his views. As the architect of the American military victory, he deserves much credit and blame for American policy, but he was not in complete command and he did not make the final decisions. The irony is that the person who articulated the traditional defense of the use of atomic bombs was also the first critic of atomic diplomacy.

From the outset of the war, Stimson was convinced that the success of the Manhattan project required absolute secrecy. Within a week of the bombing of Pearl Harbor, the War Department advised President Roosevelt that he should inform congressional leaders that the Truman Committee investigations of military spending should be ended. "It is in the public interest," Assistant Secretary of War Patterson wrote Roosevelt, "that the Committee should suspend for the time being. We are fighting a war and must throw all our vigor into its prosecution." It would hamper the military's ability to concentrate on the defeat of the enemy if its officers and civilian personnel were tied up in providing information to the committee. Furthermore, there was "the consideration that information useful to the enemy may unintentionally be revealed through the prosecution of the investigation at the present time." Patterson pointed to the Civil War and those congressional inquiries as "a classic example of how not to do it." There were leaks of information to the South, time wasted by military officers who should have been devoting their full energies to the defeat of the Confederacy, and junior officers encouraged to criticize their superiors, thus hampering the military effectiveness of the Northern forces.[45]

Congress disagreed with the executive branch, and the Truman Committee kept functioning during the war. The problems envisioned, however, never materialized. This was due mainly to Stimson's stature and probity. War Department requests for funds did not reveal the purpose of the spending on the Manhattan project, and Stimson was able to gain the appropriations based on his assurances that the funds were necessary and not being wasted. Stimson first met Truman in 1943, when then Senator Truman wanted to investigate the installation being constructed at Hanford, Washington. Stimson told Truman that he simply could not tell him what it was intended for, that it was "part of a very important secret development," and "that he would have to trust me implicitly" because he was one of only two or three people who knew. Truman replied that he understood, and that Stimson would not "have to say another word to me. Whenever you say that to me, that's all I want to hear."[46] This greatly impressed Stimson and was a point he would recall two years later when Truman became president.

By 1944, with annual requests topping $600 million, numerous secret installations, and questions being raised in Congress concerning such large expenditures for unspecified purposes, Stimson decided that he needed to inform congressional leaders in order to keep the situation under control and out of the public eye. On February 18, 1944, Stimson, accompanied by Bush and Marshall, went to the House of Representatives and met with Speaker Sam Rayburn, John McCormick, the Democratic leader, and Joe Martin, the Republican leader. They outlined the development of the Manhattan project, its military significance, and the "race with the enemy" for its completion. They also detailed their budget requirements and asked that secrecy be maintained. The congressmen agreed that the "matter should certainly be pursued at the utmost possible speed," and gave assurances of funding with no further questions.[47]

Before he could repeat this meeting with the leaders of the Senate, Stimson received a letter from Truman informing him that his committee was being pressed by other senators to investigate these large expenditures. Stimson replied sternly that he remembered their conversation from a year earlier and that he was not in any position to expand on his earlier statement or to take any additional people into his confidence as he was acting on "the express directions of the President of the United States." Privately, Stimson noted that he found Truman's letter annoying. He was "a nuisance," Stimson wrote in his diary, "and a pretty untrustworthy man. He talks smoothly but he acts meanly."[48] This was one opinion that Stimson later regretted, and he returned to the more favorable view that he had formed the previous year.

Stimson finally met with the Senate leaders in June to discuss the Manhattan project and the necessity to prevent "there being any public discussion of the item in regard to S-1 which was in the budget." He explained the development of the Manhattan project, Germany's head start, and that the atomic bomb could provide the "ultimate success of the war in case of a deadlock." The senators promised the project would receive the necessary funding and that they would maintain absolute secrecy as to the purpose of the money.[49]

In addition to congressional inquiries, Stimson blocked an effort by the Justice Department to bring an antitrust suit against the Du Pont Company and labor's efforts to organize workers at the University of California's Berkeley laboratory. Du Pont operated the two most important production plants in Washington and Tennessee for the Manhattan project. Stimson urged Roosevelt to curtail the attorney general's efforts because it would be "disastrous

... from the standpoint of our hurried manufacture to distract these key people who are handling our most secret and important project with the necessity of defending themselves in an antitrust suit."[50] Concerning the Berkeley laboratory, Stimson asked Roosevelt to speak with Philip Murray of the CIO to inform him that "this group simply cannot be unionized."[51] Roosevelt arranged for Stimson to speak with the labor leaders, and he was able to persuade them not to go any further in their efforts. There were few people, then or ever, who had spent as much time in the federal government as Stimson and whom other people from various backgrounds would automatically trust. Yet, that was Stimson's reputation. If he said something was so or necessary, then others tended to believe it was and yielded, throughout the war, to his requests.

At the end of 1944, Stimson met with Roosevelt to discuss the progress of the war, the Manhattan project, and the president's upcoming trip to Yalta to meet with Churchill and Stalin. After providing Roosevelt assurances that the German offensive, the Battle of the Bulge, had been blunted and that Allied forces would soon counterattack, the discussion turned to what Stimson termed the "troubles with Russia." Roosevelt informed Stimson that he believed Stalin was taking "Britain's desire to have a cordon sanitaire of friendly nations around it in past years as an excuse now for Russia's intention to have Czechoslovakia, Poland, and other nations whom it could control." Stimson responded that the timing was not good for any "easy concessions to Russia" and recommended that policy be based on "insisting upon a quid pro quo." This led Stimson to set out his "thoughts as to the future of S-1 in connection with Russia." Stimson told Roosevelt that he knew the Russians were spying on the project but "had not yet gotten any real knowledge of it and that, while I was troubled about the possible effect of keeping from them even now that work, I believed that it was essential not to take them into our confidence until we were sure to get a real quid pro quo from our frankness." Stimson had "no illusions as to the possibility of keeping permanently such a secret," but he and the president concurred that the time was not yet right to share it with the Soviets.[52] Stimson's thinking and actions throughout 1945 would remain consistent with this view that difficulties with the Soviets could be settled through negotiations and that the atomic bomb would play a large role in that process. For Stimson, the highest priorities were winning the war as quickly as possible and then turning to the task of postwar reconstruction and peace. Within this framework, he saw cooperation with the

Soviet Union, not as a choice, but as an essential component of post-war American foreign policy.

Two factors dominated Stimson's thinking about relations with the Soviet Union. First, he was greatly impressed with Soviet power and its achievement in helping to defeat Nazi Germany. Second, he believed that the only basis for a permanent peace was through the continuation of the Grand Alliance and postwar cooperation among the United States, Great Britain, and the Soviet Union. The secretary of war was well aware of the enormous destruction inflicted on the Soviet Union by the German armies, and he understood the Russian desire that there be no anti-Soviet states along the Soviet border. The only aspect of relations with the Soviet Union that gave him any concern was the lack of individual political freedom inside Russia, and he saw this as the major stumbling block to an effective postwar settlement and cooperation. He told Bush, in February 1945, that he still did not want to begin sharing information with the Soviets "until we had gotten all we could in Russia in the way of liberalization in exchange for S-1." This is what he meant by a quid pro quo.[53] Nonetheless, Stimson fully supported Roosevelt's policies toward the Soviet Union and efforts to construct peace on the basis of Big Three cooperation and agreement. Policy should never, Stimson believed, lean too heavily upon the atomic bomb. As he noted in April, although all predictions up to that time had been fulfilled, and "success is 99% assured, yet only by the first actual war trial of the weapon can any certainty be fixed."[54]

Stimson soon found himself out of step with the impatience and critical attitude toward the Soviet Union that took shape in the early days of the Truman administration. As tensions grew over Soviet policy in Poland, Stimson opposed the recommendation that Truman lodge a vigorous protest and take a strong stance in opposition to the government established there by Stalin. Stimson told Secretary of State Edward Stettinius that "we simply cannot allow a rift to come between the two nations without endangerous [sic] the peace of the world." In military matters, the Soviet Union "kept her word and carried out her engagements. We must remember that she has not learned the amenities of diplomatic intercourse and we must expect bad language from her." He concluded that it was "time for me to use all the restraint I can on these people who have been apparently getting a little more irritated." Relations had to be approached in a calm and thoughtful manner. If the United States set out its position with "perfectly cold-blooded firmness," issues could be resolved.[55]

Stimson told the new president on April 23, 1945, that he was greatly troubled by this new approach and feared "that we were rushing into a situation where we would find ourselves breaking our relations with Russia." He believed the United States "ought to be very careful and see whether we couldn't get ironed out on the situation without getting into a headon [*sic*] collision." Stimson noted that he "believed in firmness on the minor matters where we had been yielding in the past and have said so frequently," but he stated that the Polish problem "was too big a question to take chances on." He thought Truman was in a difficult position and sympathized with him, "because he is so new on his job and he has been brought into a situation which ought not to have been allowed to come in this way." It was clear to Stimson that, although the Russians had agreed at Yalta to restructure the Polish government on a more representative basis, they did not share the American view that this should be done by a free election and they would not yield on a question that was so central to their concerns for postwar security.[56]

Stimson told the cabinet meeting that day that he thought "it was important to find out what the Soviets were driving at." He noted, and General Marshall concurred, that "in the big military matters the Soviet Government had kept their word and that the military authorities of the United States had come to count on it." It was important "to find out what motives they had in mind in regard to these border countries and that their ideas of independence and democracy in areas that they regarded as vital to the Soviet Union" were different from those held by the United States. Moreover, it was necessary to remember "how seriously the Russians took this Polish question," and that the United States was "heading into very dangerous waters." He concluded that, on Poland, "the Russians perhaps were being more realistic than we in regard to their own security," and that he believed that "the Russians would not yield on the Polish question."[57]

Given this discussion, Stimson concluded that he could not wait any longer to provide Truman a complete report on the Manhattan project. The secretary of war had briefly noted to the new president right after he took office that he had a matter of some urgency to speak to him about, but he realized how busy Truman was in the first days after Roosevelt's death, given the myriad new issues he had to learn about and confront. With work still progressing, he decided to wait until Truman had had a chance to settle into his office before raising this crucial issue. The cabinet discussion surprised and greatly bothered Stimson, and he was upset that he "could not give the considered and careful answer to the President" that he wanted. He immediately set an appointment with Truman for April 25 to discuss the atomic bomb.

The briefing had a dual purpose. On the one hand, Stimson wanted to inform the president about the project and provide him with the latest update on the manufacturing operation. For this purpose, he brought General Leslie Groves with him to explain the process and answer any questions. On the other hand, Stimson wanted to open up the discussion with Truman about the military and political implications of the weapon and to reassert his view that caution and cooperation rather than confrontation should guide American policy toward the Soviet Union. After Stimson set out the basic parameters of the project, Truman recalled how Stimson had refused to let him as a senator investigate this project, and stated "that he understood now perfectly well why it was inadvisable" for Stimson "to have taken any other course." Stimson explained to Truman that, within four months, the United States would most likely "have completed the most terrible weapon ever known in human history, one bomb of which could destroy a whole city." Whether or not the weapon should be used was never discussed or questioned. Rather, the focus was on what to do with the knowledge of the bomb. Up to this point, Stimson noted, the development of the weapon was only being shared with the United Kingdom. As a practical matter that situation could not last. Once the process was demonstrated, the Soviet Union could begin production within a few years' time. Given this, the key question became: Upon what terms should this knowledge be shared with other nations? American "leadership in the war and in the development of this weapon," Stimson argued, "has placed a certain moral responsibility upon us which we cannot shirk without very serious responsibility for any disaster to civilization which it would further." Thus, the key was "the proper use of this weapon." If it could be found, "we would have the opportunity to bring the world into a pattern in which the peace of the world and our civilization can be saved."[58] In order to provide careful consideration of these questions, Stimson proposed, and Truman agreed to, the establishment of the Interim Committee. It was "charged with the function of advising the President on the various questions raised by our apparently imminent success in developing an atomic weapon."[59]

At this time, central to Stimson's thinking about the Soviet Union, the atomic bomb, and the ending of the war with Japan was the need for stability and the rapid economic reconstruction of Germany and Western Europe. In May, he prepared a lengthy memorandum for the president that set out his views. Stimson's main point was that a settlement that punished Germany economically for the war would be "a grave mistake." Stimson supported trying Germany's "war criminals in full measure" and abolishing Germany's weapons and general staff. "But do not," Stimson urged Truman, "deprive her of the means of building up ultimately a contented Germany interested in following non-militaristic methods of civilization." Moreover, some industry was necessary because Germany's future stability would determine the political balance of the continent. "A solution must be found," Stimson concluded, for Germany's "future peaceful existence," and it was in America's and the world's interest that it "should not be driven by stress of hardship into a non-democratic and necessarily predatory habit of life."[60]

With the final defeat of Germany, Stimson turned his full attention to the related problems of the defeat of Japan, the atomic bomb, and relations with the Soviet Union. On May 10, he met with Ambassador to the Soviet Union Averell Harriman to gain a better understanding "on the situation in Russia and the chances of getting a Russia we could work with." Harriman presented a rather "gloomy report." He found little "chance of getting the seeds of liberalism into Russia." There was, however, a basis for hope. Harriman made it clear that the Soviets wanted continued good relations with the United States and that "Russia is really afraid of our power or at least respects it and, although she is going to ride roughshod over her neighbors in Europe, he thought that she really was afraid of us." Stimson concluded from this that his idea for a quid pro quo on a liberalization of Soviet rule in return for information on the bomb remained viable. He also met that day with Marshall to discuss "rather deep matters" related to the atomic bomb. He wanted to know if any invasion of Japan could be held off "until after we had tried out S-1." Marshall believed that was the probable timing, that there could be a "trial before the locking of arms came and much bloodshed."[61]

Given these circumstances, Stimson sought to allow time to pass and for the pressure on the Soviet Union to build. He told Marshall on May 14 that the "method now to deal with Russia was to keep our mouths shut and let our actions speak for words. The Russians will understand them better than anything else." The United States needed to use its aid and power more wisely. This, Stimson said, "was a place where we really held all the cards. I called it a royal straight flush and we mustn't be a fool about the way we play it. They can't get along without our help and industries and we have coming into action a weapon which will be unique." It was important to avoid "any unnecessary quarrels" or "to indicate any weakness by talking too much; let our actions speak for themselves." The next day, he learned that Truman was scheduled to meet with Stalin and Churchill at the beginning of July. He worried that key decision would have to be made without full knowledge about the atomic bomb. It was, Stimson noted, "a terrible thing to gamble with such big stakes in diplomacy without having your master card in your hand."[62]

Stimson met with Truman on May 16 to discuss the war with Japan and postwar reconstruction. His principal contention was that there was no immediate advantage to pushing for a final engagement of American and Japanese troops, and that American troops should never be used to attack the main Japanese Army in China. The United States should continue its current strategy of moving closer to the main islands and relying on air power to attack Japan. This would increase the pressure on Japan without any loss of momentum while waiting for the testing of the atomic bomb. Of much greater concern was the situation in Europe. A rapid end to the war with Japan was necessary so that the nation could turn its full attention to postwar recovery. "All agree," Stimson informed Truman, "as to the probability of pestilence and famine in central Europe next winter. This is likely to be followed by political revolution and Communist infiltration." The only defense was to keep the countries of Belgium, Denmark, France, Holland, Italy, Luxembourg, and Norway afloat through aid to prevent them from being driven to "revolution or Communism by famine."

This demanded a coordinated effort by the United States to provide short-term relief and long-term planning and necessitated policies that would aid the economic recovery of Europe, including Germany. "The eighty million Germans and Austrians in central Europe today necessarily swing the balance of that continent." Stimson recounted for Truman his understanding of Roosevelt's policy that Nazi war criminals should be punished, and Germany should lose its capacity to wage war, but that a "contented Germany" had to be created that was "interested in following non-militaristic methods of civilization," which included industrialization and economic recovery. This was "a tough problem," Stimson concluded, and one that required coordination and cooperation with the Soviet Union. "Russia will occupy most of the good food lands of central Europe while we have the industrial portions. We must find some way of persuading Russia to play ball."[63]

The Colonel returned to these themes a few days later in discussions with his staff. He thought that the nation had to continue to follow Roosevelt's position of mediating disputes in Europe and reaching negotiated settlements with the Soviet Union rather than following the hard line advocated by Churchill. It was "perfectly possible," Stimson noted, for the United States and the Soviet Union "to get along without fighting; that as long as she did not threaten any of our vital interests . . . we need never fight the Soviets." American "position and strength justified and made advisable an . . . attitude toward Russia" independent from that of Great Britain.[64]

Stimson was, therefore, open to the idea of hastening the ending of the war in the Pacific by modifying the stance on unconditional surrender and giving Japan some assurance concerning retention of Emperor Hirohito. He met with Joseph Grew, the former longtime ambassador to Japan and leading State Department proponent of the idea that the war could be ended through such a guarantee, at the end of May. He informed Grew that he "was inclined to agree with giving the Japanese a modification of the unconditional surrender formula and some hope to induce them to practically make an unconditional surrender without the use of those words." He believed, however, that the timing was not yet right. Apparently, he was waiting for the fall of Okinawa and for the full force of American air power to reach the home islands before proposing a change in American policy.[65]

This last point relates directly to the meetings of the Interim Committee in May and its June 1 recommendation to the president that the bomb should be used against Japan without warning and as soon as it was available in order to prompt a Japanese surrender. As Stimson noted, the committee's function was "entirely advisory," and the "ultimate responsibility for the recommendation to the President rested upon me." He had reached this conclusion independent of the committee and prior to its meetings. The key was to carry out American actions so as to "extract a genuine surrender from the Emperor."[66] This, Stimson thought, should be done at the earliest possible time with or without the use of the bomb.

Stimson informed the Interim Committee on May 31 that he did not regard the atomic bomb "as a new weapon merely but as a revolutionary change in the relations of man to the universe." The project "might even mean the doom of civilization or it might mean the perfection of civilization; that it might be a Frankenstein which would eat us up or it might be a project 'by which the peace of the world would be helped in becoming secure.' " Stimson believed that he had convinced the scientists that he and Marshall were looking at the question of using the bomb "like statesmen and not . . . merely soldiers anxious to win the war at any cost." For Stimson, it was one part of a developing situation and strategy and not the sole weapon or means to peace.[67]

Stimson met with Truman on June 6 to inform him of the Interim Committee's decisions. First, they argued that there should be "no revelation to Russia or anyone else of our work on S-1 until the first bomb had been successfully laid on Japan." The greatest complication was what might happen at the upcoming meeting of the Big Three at Potsdam. Truman interrupted at that juncture to inform Stimson that he had postponed the meeting until July 15 to give them more time to conduct the test prior to the meeting. While Stimson was pleased with this news, he noted that there might be delays and that, if the Soviets brought the matter up, it would be best just to tell them that the United States was not quite ready to discuss it. The discussion turned to what conditions would be necessary for the sharing of the information on the atomic bomb, and what quid pro quos the United States should expect. Truman suggested that he was thinking of the necessity for a "settlement of the Polish, Rumanian, Yugoslavian, and Manchurian problems."[68]

One final decision had been reached that Stimson did not tell the president. He had taken Kyoto off the list of possible target cities due to its historical and cultural significance to the Japanese. For Stimson, who had visited the city when he was governor general of the Philippines, the preservation of Kyoto was necessary for a stable and friendly postwar Japan. He was not going to be responsible for the destruction of the greatest religious center in Japan. As he struck Kyoto from the list he told Groves, "This is one time I'm going to be the final deciding authority. Nobody's going to tell me what to do on this. On this matter I am the kingpin."[69]

With these decisions behind him, Stimson returned to the question of the terms of Japan's surrender and the problems of postwar Europe. He raised these issues on June 19 in his regular meetings with the heads of the State and Navy Departments. All agreed "that it would be deplorable if we have to go through the military program with all its stubborn fighting to the finish." Although plans had to be developed for that contingency, all three departments agreed "that some way should be found of inducing Japan to yield without a fight to the finish." The State Department had already proposed to Truman that "a new warning be issued as soon as Okinawa has fallen," but the president did not want to take any action until he met with Stalin and Churchill. Stimson did not think there was any pressing deadline other than the actual landing of ground forces in Japan, and that would not take place until November. Thus, he thought that current plans "provide for enough time to bring in the sanctions to our warning in the shape of heavy ordinary bombing attack and an attack of S-1." Marshall added that an additional dimension to the warning would come "in the shape of an entry by the Russians into the war" that was planned for mid-August. "That," Stimson concluded, "would certainly coordinate all the threats possible to Japan." He noted later in the month that he felt "very strongly" that it was necessary to find some means to have Japan surrender "by giving her a warning," and that "the country will not be satisfied unless every effort is made to shorten the war." To these ends, he began preparing a memorandum to Truman making the case for a modification of unconditional surrender and the issuing of a warning to Japan.[70]

After two weeks of study and consultation, Stimson completed his memorandum for the president and met with him on July 2 to discuss his ideas regarding plans for Japan and the occupation and treatment of Germany. "I regard these two subjects," Stimson wrote, "the effort to shorten the Japanese war by a surrender and the proper handling of Germany so as not to create such harshness in seeking vengeance as to make it impossible to lay the foundations of a new Germany which will be a proper member of the family of nations, as two of the largest and most important problems" that he had dealt with as secretary of war. They first took up the question of "whether it was worthwhile to try to warn Japan into surrender." Truman read Stimson's six-page memorandum on the question before they proceeded. In it Stimson outlined the current status of the war and the desperate situation Japan found itself in with no allies, practically no navy, no effective means to prevent air attacks upon the home islands, and the ever-increasing power of the United States. In brief, Japan had been defeated and should be able to recognize that fact. The problem was how to "translate these advantages into prompt and economical achievement of our objectives." Was there an effective alternative that would "secure for us the equivalent of an unconditional surrender . . . and a permanent destruction of her power to again strike an aggressive blow

at the 'peace of the Pacific'?" The best means, Stimson argued, was
to offer Japan surrender terms that would undercut the position of
the "fanatical military group" that seized power in 1931 but still
uphold the appearance of unconditional surrender.[71]

Stimson believed it was possible to shorten the war through a
warning that made clear the extent of damage and destruction Japan could expect if it continued to pursue its hopeless cause, combined with a promise that the Emperor could be retained. Stimson
wrote that he thought "Japan *is* susceptible to reason in such a crisis to a much greater extent" than most people believed. "Japan,"
he continued, "is not a nation composed wholly of mad fanatics of
an entirely different mentality from ours. On the contrary, she has
within the past century shown herself to possess extremely intelligent people, capable in an unprecedently [*sic*] short time of adopt-
ing not only the complicated technique of Occidental civilization
but to a substantial extent their culture and their political and social ideas." This move from the "isolated feudalism of centuries
into the position of one of the six or seven great powers of the
world" indicated to Stimson that "the Japanese nation has the mental intelligence and versatile capacity in such a crisis to recognize
the folly of a fight to the finish and to accept the proffer of what
will amount to an unconditional surrender." On the other hand, an
invasion would bring about "a fusion of race solidity [*sic*] and
antipathy" that would lead to a "fanatical resistance to repel" the
attack.[72]

Stimson recommended a "carefully timed warning . . . calling
upon Japan to surrender and permit the occupation of her country
in order to insure its complete demilitarization for the sake of future peace." The warning needed to include a clear statement of
the overwhelming force about to be launched against the home islands, the inevitability of defeat, and the completeness of the destruction that further resistance would bring. It should demonstrate
the determination of the Allies to remove those from power who
were responsible for the war and to make sure Japan was powerless to wage war again, and include a statement of the intention of
the Allies not to destroy Japan, but rather to "permit the Japanese
to maintain such industries . . . which can produce a sustaining
economy, and provide a reasonable standard of living." Moreover,
it should be made clear that Allied forces would be withdrawn "as
soon as there has been established a peacefully inclined government, of a character representative of the masses of the Japanese
people." Stimson also believed that "we should add that we do not

exclude a constitutional monarchy under her present dynasty," and that this last point "would substantially add to the chances of acceptance."[73] Stimson had already formulated the basis of the Potsdam Declaration calling for the surrender of Japan. All but his last point concerning the Emperor would be used.

Truman approved Stimson's arguments, which he found "very powerful." As Truman had other meetings scheduled, he asked Stimson to return the next day to continue the discussion. Before leaving, Stimson raised the question of his attendance at the Potsdam meeting. He inquired whether the president had not asked him to go along to spare him possible overexertion. Truman replied that was just it, and he agreed with Stimson that it would be good to have his advice at the meeting. The next day the two men discussed the questions of Germany and the atomic bomb and whether to discuss the latter with Russia at Potsdam. They decided that Truman should tell Stalin that the United States was working on a new weapon and intended to use it against Japan. If all went according to plan, they would discuss it with the Soviets afterward, "with the purpose of having it make the world peaceful and safe rather than to destroy civilization." If pressed for details, they agreed to stay with the previous plan and respond that they were not yet prepared to discuss the matter.[74]

Concerning Germany, Stimson again argued that the solution of the German question was "vital to the success" of all America's postwar plans for economic recovery. It was essential that the president resist all efforts for a vindictive peace to ensure German cooperation and inclusion in a peaceful postwar order. The Nazi leaders should be punished, and "the rest of the country should be rehabilitated." Truman agreed and gave the War Department the authority to run the American occupation zone on this basis. Stimson found that the president "seemed to side entirely with the view of the War Department as to how Germany should be treated." The meeting concluded with Truman assuring Stimson that he wanted to have him at Potsdam for his counsel.[75] As he would not attend the actual meetings of the Big Three, Stimson's role was to provide Truman with updates on the Manhattan project and the course of the war against Japan and give his advice and analysis concerning the ongoing negotiations.

Once in Europe for the conference, Stimson was overwhelmed by the extent of the devastation he saw. He was even more adamant then that the rebuilding of Germany was a matter of the very survival of Europe and demanded as quick an end to the war with

Japan as could be managed. He, therefore, reiterated his reasons for a warning to Japan "designed to bring about her capitulation as quickly as possible. While that war is going on, it will be most difficult politically and economically to make substantial contributions to the reestablishment of stable conditions abroad." The German situation demanded more than rehabilitation; it required, Stimson believed, the United States to take responsibility for the reconstruction of Europe. Beyond immediate stability, the United States had to act to preserve the "concepts of individual liberty, free thought, and free speech," and prevent famine and conditions of distress from turning people away from these main tenets of Western society. If action was not taken, "all the opposite concepts [would] flourish." Germany must "be given an opportunity to live and work" with a minimum of restraints from the occupying powers, and the "economic groupings of Germany should be disturbed only where considerations make it inescapable." Moreover, trade had to be reestablished, along with transportation systems and a stable currency. This would require a "completely coordinated plan . . . for the economic rehabilitation of Europe as a whole." A single agency, headed by the United States, would be necessary to coordinate and implement these activities. A revitalized Germany, Stimson believed, would alleviate the need for long-term American aid to Europe, protect American interests, "achieve stability in Europe with the promptitude and in the degree necessary to preserve democratic governments," and provide the only sure road to future peace.[76] Relations with the Soviet Union and the approaching deployment of the atomic bomb complicated these efforts at postwar planning and reconstruction.

On Wednesday, July 18, the first news of the atomic test at Los Alamos, New Mexico, arrived. Truman was "highly delighted" and filled with a new optimism. He "asserted that he was confident of sustaining the Open Door policy," and "greatly reenforced" by the intelligence from home. Stimson cautioned him concerning the "importance of going over the matter detail by detail so as to be sure that there would be no misunderstanding" over how to relate the news to the Soviets and to use this new weapon.[77] Worried about the president's reaction and the plan of Jimmy Byrnes, now the secretary of state, to use the bomb to force concessions from the Soviets, Stimson sought to ensure that the final success of the bomb did not create a situation in which differences with the Soviet Union could lead to a permanent break in the Grand Alliance. He, therefore, sat down the next day and dictated a memorandum to the president, entitled "Reflections on the Basic Problems Which Confront Us."

It was now clear, Stimson wrote, that with the end of the war "the great basic problem of the future is the stability of the relations of the Western democracies with Russia." The problem, Stimson believed, "arises out of the fundamental differences between a nation of free thought, free speech, free elections, in fact, a really free people, with a nation which is not basically free but which is systematically controlled from above by Secret Police and in which free speech is not permitted." This made it difficult to conduct ongoing relations. The question, then, was "how to deal with this basic difference which exists as a flaw in our desired accord." Stimson's answer was that it was not necessary to "accept the present situation as permanent for the result will then almost inevitably be a new war and the destruction of our civilization." Rather, the United States had to find a means and time through diplomacy to address these concerns and work toward the liberalization of the Soviet system. This was best accomplished, he continued, by encouraging open dialogue between the two nations concerning their differences and by making clear the conditions under which the United States would make concessions on territory, loans, and other matters.[78]

It was precisely on this point, Stimson believed, that the atomic bomb became critical in Soviet–American relations. The "revolutionary discovery" of the atomic bomb played a crucial role, Stimson wrote, because "upon the successful control of that energy depends the future successful development or destruction of the modern civilized world." The Interim Committee had already determined that this meant placing the scientific knowledge on the bomb under the control of an international organization. This was the crux of the problem. While sharing the knowledge was vital to future peace, it was not clear that this could be done "safely under any system of control until Russia puts into effective action" greater political freedoms. "If this is a necessary condition," Stimson concluded, then the United States should use this opportunity to explore the question of how "the Russian desire to participate can be used to bring us nearer to the removal of the basic difficulties which I have emphasized."[79] In essence, Stimson was arguing that the United States needed to continue good relations with the Soviets for its own interests, and that, by granting concessions to the Soviets in exchange for liberalization and participation in an international atomic agency, the Grand Alliance could be continued. Thus, for Stimson, the atomic bomb was a means of pursuing negotiations and cooperation with the Soviet Union. This was a very different view from that being developed and practiced by Byrnes and, eventually, by Truman.

On July 21, a complete report on the atomic test arrived from General Groves. It was clear, Stimson observed, that it was a "tremendous success" and "revealed far greater destructive power than we expected in S-1." The secretary brought the report over to the "Little White House" that afternoon, where he went over it with the president and secretary of state. "They were immensely pleased," Stimson recalled, and "the President was tremendously pepped up" by the news. Truman said "it gave him an entirely new feeling of confidence." With this news, the president went to his scheduled meeting with Stalin and Churchill. Stimson met again the next morning with Truman to discuss further the use of the atomic bomb and his "Reflections" on relations with Russia, which he had left with the president the previous day. The time had arrived, Stimson believed, when some crucial decisions had to be made. The Colonel told Truman that his paper "represented an analysis which I thought was correct and a program of what I hoped might sometime be done." Truman read the paper and told his secretary of war that he "agreed with it," but nothing more was said.[80]

Stimson also informed the president that he had received two important messages from Washington the previous evening. The first indicated that the actual deployment of a bomb would be possible earlier than previously thought; the second asked for permission to reverse Stimson's earlier order to strike Kyoto from the list of acceptable target cities. Truman was greatly pleased to learn of the accelerated timetable and supported Stimson's refusal to change his position regarding Kyoto.[81]

From his meeting with Truman, Stimson went to see Churchill to inform him of the results of the test. The prime minister told him that "he had noticed at the meeting of the Three yesterday that Truman was evidently much fortified by something that had happened and that he stood up to the Russians in a most emphatic and decisive manner, telling them as to certain demands that they absolutely could not have and the United States was entirely against them." He continued: "Now I know what happened to Truman yesterday. . . . He told the Russians just where they got on and off and generally bossed the whole meeting." Stimson had this interpretation confirmed the next day in his meeting with Truman, when the president informed him that the Soviets were making a new

series of demands, but "that the United States was standing firm."
The president, Stimson noted, "was apparently relying greatly upon
the information as to S-1."[82]

Truman also asked Stimson if he and Marshall now thought it
was necessary to have the Soviets enter into the war against Japan
"or whether we could get along without them." Stimson met with
Marshall, and they agreed that the original reason for seeking a
Soviet entry into the war, to tie down the main Japanese Army in
China, was now accomplished by the Soviet redeployment of troops
to the east. In the end, the two agreed that "with our new weapon
we would not need the assistance of the Russians to conquer Japan." The conclusion that Japan was on the verge of defeat made
the issuing of a warning and terms of surrender the crucial question left to be decided. The following day, Stimson reported his
and Marshall's discussion to Truman together with the news that a
firm beginning date for the use of atomic weapons against Japan
was set for early August.[83]

This information, Truman told Stimson, was his cue for sending Japan the so-called Potsdam Declaration for surrender. The final ultimatum, sent on July 26, closely followed Stimson's
recommendation of July 2. It warned Japan that if it continued the
war "the full application of our military power, backed by our resolve, will mean the inevitable and complete destruction of the Japanese armed forces and just as inevitably the utter destruction of
the Japanese homeland." But it included no mention of the Japanese Emperor. Stimson was alarmed by this omission, particularly
given that the United States had agreed to retain the monarchy after the surrender. He knew that Byrnes opposed him, and that he
was in fact alone among senior officials in advocating this course
of action. Nonetheless, he remained convinced that it was the only
issue preventing an immediate end to the fighting. Stimson, therefore, urged Truman one last time to reconsider this point. He noted
that it was important to provide a "reassurance [to] the Japanese
on the continuance of their dynasty," and that the "insertion of that
in the formal warning was important and might be just the thing"
that would ensure their acceptance. Realizing no change would be
made, Stimson "hoped that the President would watch carefully so
that the Japanese might be reassured verbally through diplomatic
channels if it was found that they were hanging fire on that one
point."[84]

Stimson again raised the question of keeping Kyoto off the target list. Truman reiterated his support for Stimson's decision, and

agreed that "the bitterness which would be caused by such a wanton act might make it impossible during the long post-war period to reconcile the Japanese to us . . . rather than to the Russians. It might thus . . . be the means of preventing what our policy demanded, namely a sympathetic Japan to the United States in case there should be any aggression by Russia in Manchuria."[85] When Japan responded on July 28 by announcing it would take no notice of the Potsdam Declaration, it was clear the bombs would be used as soon as they were ready.

On July 25, Stimson met Stalin for the only time in his life. Stimson began by thanking Stalin for the opportunity to meet, and for the position he had taken earlier in the war regarding the second front. He told Stalin he "distinctly remembered the Generalissimo's language—it was terse and clear—that he distinguished between a supporting action and an action which was a mere diversion." Stalin's support, Stimson said, had greatly contributed to the Anglo-American success in France and Germany. The secretary of war then shifted the conversation to postwar relations. He told Stalin that he "was familiar with history and that I had taken great satisfaction in knowing that the two countries—Russia and the United States—had had no issues or differences during the time of the existence of my government." Stalin chose to ignore the American intervention during the Russian Revolution and the years of nonrecognition and concurred with Stimson. The Colonel continued that there were "no reasons for dispute, and that our natural objectives were the same." Stalin responded that, unlike Russia's relations with the British or the French, "the Russians and the Americans easily understood each other" and had common goals. Stimson replied that he hoped that was the case and that he intended to "do everything in my power to follow that line. I stated that I had noticed . . . that our soldiers encountered no difficulty in working together. I therefore thought that it was important that our commanders should make every effort to live together like our soldiers." Stalin, Stimson noted afterward, "appeared to be entirely in agreement with this view."[86]

Stimson had done all he could at Potsdam to try to shape policy and prevent a break in relations with the Soviet Union. He left Germany the next day and returned to his Highhold estate in Huntington to rest from the trip. He received word of the successful atomic attack on Hiroshima on August 6 by phone from Marshall and spent most of that day talking to his staff and Marshall about the impact of the bombing and how to coordinate the release of information to the press. He returned to Washington the next day to prepare for a meeting with Truman on the eighth to discuss how to secure the Japanese surrender. The meeting began with a review of the damage to Hiroshima. Stimson then raised the question of how the United States should "proceed with Japan in a way which would produce as quickly as possible her surrender." Achieving that would largely depend on how the United States acted in the wake of the atomic bomb. It was important, Stimson believed, to show "kindness or tact in handling this matter." He told the president that continued punishment would not win the support of the Japanese for America's postwar policies and that the United States needed to establish good terms with them. The matter was left without resolution pending statements from the Japanese government.[87] It was clear to Stimson that the bomb, and the promised Soviet entry into the war that day, would "certainly have an effect on hastening the victory. But just how much that effect is on how long . . . to accomplish that victory, it is impossible yet to determine." Stimson was still seeking the quickest route to ending the war and continued to advocate with the president and Byrnes an intelligent and "sympathetic handling of the Japanese in negotiating a surrender."[88]

That morning, Stimson had what he called "a rather sharp little attack" at five a.m. After concluding their discussion on surrender, Stimson informed the president of his condition: His doctors had informed him that he needed complete rest and "that meant leaving the Department finally in a short time." Truman told him that he wanted him to stay and asked that he take a month off to rest and then come back to work for him. This, too, was left without a final decision.[89]

The next day, word arrived of another successful atomic attack, this time on Nagasaki. These were two quick and heavy blows to Japan. Yet Stimson knew that there would be "quite a little space" before another bomb could be prepared and used. "During that time," he wrote on the ninth, "I hope something may be done in negotiating a surrender. I have done the best I could to promote that in my talks with the President and with Byrnes and I think they are both in full sympathy with the aim." Stimson made his first public comments on the bomb that day, telling the press that "great events have happened." The bombs were being used to "save the lives of American soldiers and bring more quickly to an end the horror of this war." Yet, although the two atomic bombings were momentous achievements for the nation, "Any satisfaction we may feel must be overshadowed by deeper emotions." Stimson set out briefly his view of what was necessary. The nation needed to realize that the "world is changed and it is time for sober thought." The results of the bomb were "so terrific that the responsibility of its possession and its use must weigh heavily on our minds and on our hearts." Americans could not contemplate the impact of these new weapons "without a determination that after this war is over this great force shall be used for the welfare and not the destruction of mankind."[90]

Word arrived on August 10 that the Japanese were willing to surrender on the terms of the Potsdam Declaration with only a reservation concerning the sovereignty of the Emperor. The end of the war was within grasp. Still, Japan sought an assurance, even after the two atomic bombs, that this would not "comprise any demand which prejudices the prerogatives of His Majesty as a Sovereign Ruler." Truman met with his senior advisors that morning to discuss the offer. Some still wanted to hold out for an unconditional surrender and were willing to keep fighting until that was achieved. Stimson had not changed his mind on the advisability of providing such an assurance to the Japanese. It was the only way to bring the war to a full and immediate end. Indeed, he told Truman that "if the question hadn't been raised by the Japanese we would have to continue the Emperor ourselves in order to get into surrender the many scattered armies of the Japanese who would own no other authority and that something like this use of the Emperor must be made in order to save us from a score of bloody Iwo Jimas and Okinawas all over China and the New Netherlands. He was the only source of authority in Japan under the Japanese theory of the State."[91]

The White House meeting was adjourned with the decision that a reply would technically hold to unconditional surrender while providing the Japanese the assurance they sought. This had been Stimson's position since June. Byrnes drafted the initial reply to which Stimson gave his full approval. Truman endorsed the draft later that day. As Stimson commented later, "While the Allied reply made no promises other than those already given, it implicitly recognized the Emperor's position by prescribing that his power must be subject to the orders of the Allied supreme commander."[92] The Japanese accepted these terms on August 14, and the Second World War came to an end. Stimson's great objective of the defeat of the Axis powers had finally been achieved.

Still, Stimson was to wonder if that objective could not have been accomplished earlier if a different diplomatic and military policy had been followed. He notes in his memoirs that "interviews after the war indicated clearly that a large element of the Japanese Cabinet was ready in the spring to accept substantially the same terms as those finally agreed on." Moreover, he wrote, "It is possible, in the light of the final surrender, that a clearer and earlier exposition of American willingness to retain the Emperor would have produced an earlier ending to the war." He had advocated just such a policy, but it was rejected by Truman and Byrnes, who sought an unconditional surrender. Stimson concluded, in 1948, "that history might find that the United States, by its delay in stating its position, had prolonged the war."[93]

Coda

These last meetings drained Stimson's remaining energy and his doctors ordered immediate rest. This, along with the exhaustion from more than five years in office, convinced him it was time to retire. Stimson went up to the Ausable Club in the Adirondack Mountains of New York for three weeks. He arrived on August 12, and got the news of Japan's final surrender there on August 14. It showed, Stimson noted, "the complete success of the program which I had urged. The Emperor at once sent his orders out to his various armies, and the armies in general obeyed them quickly and with very little dissent, thereby saving tremendous loss of life over what would have happened if we had gone on with an attack." Stimson also addressed what he saw as the great question confronting the nation: "the treatment of Russia in respect to the atomic bomb." On this issue, he believed, hinged the prospect of peace, and he began to draft a report to Truman outlining his worries, thoughts, and proposals. McCloy came up twice with reports and worked with Stimson on his paper for the president. Stimson was greatly concerned about the attitude, represented by Secretary of State Byrnes, that the United States could force concessions from the Soviets by negotiating with "the implied threat of the bomb in his pocket." It was clear that Byrnes was "radically opposed to any approach to Stalin whatever." As Stimson noted at a victory dinner celebration at Ausable, "In this war, we have been compelled to invent and unleash forces of terrific destructiveness." It was now imperative that new means be found to conduct international life.

The bomb was not just another weapon, but a categorical change in the relationship of humans to the world. If a method was not found to make "war impossible, we will with another war end our civilization."[94]

Stimson returned to Washington on September 4 prepared to retire. He presented his letter of resignation to Truman that day at lunch. The Colonel, however, was also determined to try to shape policy concerning the bomb and the Soviet Union one last time before leaving office. Meeting with Byrnes that day, Stimson discovered that the secretary of state was very much set "against any attempt to cooperate." In preparing for upcoming negotiations, it was clear that Byrnes saw "having the presence of the bomb in his pocket, so to speak, as a great weapon" to get what he wants. This view, and a general hostility toward the Soviet Union, seemed to Stimson a dangerous stance that would ruin any chances for postwar cooperation and peace.

Stimson met the next day with Truman to explain his differences with Byrnes. As he had only fifteen minutes, all he could do was outline his thoughts and inform the president that he would soon be giving him a memorandum with a detailed analysis of the question regarding the atomic bomb and the Soviet Union and his proposals. He did assert that he thought there was "less danger" in his method, and that Byrnes's approach was the "wrong path . . . and would be tending to revert to power politics."[95]

Stimson completed his remarkable document on September 11 along with a cover letter for the president. He still recognized the difficulty of the issue that they had discussed at Potsdam concerning whether it was safe to share atomic secrets with the Soviet Union while it was still a police state. Yet he concluded that it was not "possible to use our possession of the atomic bomb as a direct lever to produce" a change in the Soviet attitude toward the individual, and that this issue should not delay an approach to Moscow on this critical question.[96] Stimson systematically worked through the question of the impact of the atomic bomb on international relations and how it "affected political considerations in all sections of the globe."[97]

Avoiding any specific mention of Byrnes, and thereby any direct criticism of Truman's close friend, Stimson noted that the central issue was that "in many quarters [the atomic bomb] has been interpreted as a substantial offset to the growth of Russian influence on the continent." It was certain that the "Soviet government has sensed this tendency," and will work to acquire the new weapon in the shortest time possible. "Accordingly, unless the Soviets are voluntarily invited into the partnership upon a basis of cooperation and trust," the United States would have to "maintain the Anglo-Saxon bloc against the Soviets in the possession of this weapon." That would spur feverish activity on their part and would begin "a secret arms race of a rather desperate character." When the Soviets would obtain the weapon, within four years or twenty years, was not nearly so important as how they would come to have it. "The problem of our satisfactory relations with Russia," Stimson declared, was not "merely connected with but . . . virtually dominated by the problem of the atomic bomb." In ordinary times, the establishment of mutual confidence between the United States and the Soviet Union "could afford to await the slow progress of time." But the emergence of the atomic bomb made this question urgent. "Those relations," he told the president, "may be perhaps irretrievably embittered by the way in which we approach the solution of the bomb with Russia."[98]

If the United States continued to approach negotiations on all issues, "having this weapon rather ostentatiously on our hip," Soviet "suspicions and their distrust of our purposes and motives will increase." Stimson then turned to the heart of his message. "The chief lesson I have learned in a long life is that the only way you can make a man trustworthy is to trust him; and the surest way to make him untrustworthy is to distrust him and show your distrust." If the bomb were just another, albeit more devastating, weapon, that would be one thing. Then the United States could follow "the old custom of secrecy and nationalistic military superiority." But it was not merely another weapon: It was "too revolutionary and dangerous to fit into the old concepts" of international relations. The United States, therefore, should prepare a direct proposal to the Soviet Union "to control and limit the use of the atomic bomb as an instrument of war and so far as possible direct and encourage the development of atomic power for peaceful and humanitarian purposes," and gain an agreement that under no circumstances would a bomb be used in war unless the United States, Great Britain, and the Soviet Union all agreed.[99]

It had previously been arranged that Stimson would retire on September 21, 1945, his seventy-eighth birthday. The cabinet meeting that day would be his final chance to influence postwar policy directly and shape the question of the atomic bomb and relations with Russia. Stimson repeated the views he had set forth in his memorandum to Truman on September 11. His central purpose was to redirect American policy "back to the great principle of direct negotiation on basic issues which had been so long pursued by Franklin Roosevelt."[100] He emphasized his central concern that the United States could not use the new weapon as a means to intimidate the Soviet Union. That policy and approach was bound to fail. Rather, the United States had to "approach Russia at once with an opportunity to share on a proper quid pro quo the bomb." He reiterated his view that the only way to make the Soviets trustworthy was to trust them, and that this was a matter of urgency. Even if the chance for success was small, any effort, he believed, was justified by the greatness of the objective at stake. As he recalled after the meeting, Byrnes was away in Europe and had told him before his departure that he "proposed to keep the bomb, so to speak, in his hip pocket," with no suggestion of sharing it with Russia.[101] Stimson was unable to convince anyone of the validity of his views, and his opinions were ignored. Moreover, he did not have the strength to press his views further as he prepared for his final retirement. Still, he thought the basic difficulties of relations with the Soviet Union could be worked out, and that good relations were not "an idle dream."[102]

After the cabinet meeting ended, Stimson said his final farewell to Truman who earlier that day had awarded him the Distinguished Service Medal. He was met at Washington Airport by both his civilian staff and all the general officers in Washington who had lined up to say their good-byes. A nineteen-gun salute was given to Stimson and his wife as they reached the two lines of generals waiting by the stairs to the plane that was to take Stimson home from government service for the last time. A military band played "Happy Birthday" and "Auld Lang Syne," while Stimson shook hands with everyone assembled, gave a general salute to the crowd, then shook hands with his top commanders and General Marshall, and finally with his civilian staff. With one last wave, he and Mabel boarded the plane for home at Highhold.

Stimson had accomplished his main goal of organizing and overseeing the American triumph at war. Indeed, he was the architect of victory. His managerial skill and ability to recruit key, talented subordinates provided the planning and supervision for the massive buildup of American forces and military production that made victory possible. U.S. troops were the best equipped the world had ever seen, as the War Department turned the productive capacity of the American economy into military power while simultaneously providing over $50 billion in lend-lease aid to the Allies.

In addition, Stimson's leadership of the Manhattan project was essential for its successful completion and for bringing an end to the war in the Pacific.

Stimson also represented the bipartisan support that allowed the nation to meet the trials of and make the necessary sacrifices associated with four years of global war. The Colonel and most of his senior civilian staff were Republicans who opposed many of

President Harry S. Truman awards Stimson the Distinguished Service Medal. Mabel Stimson is between the two men. *Henry Lewis Stimson Papers, Manuscripts and Archives, Yale University Library*

the Democrats' New Deal programs. But as internationalists, they supported Roosevelt's war policies and strove for a consensus on foreign policy that took international affairs out of the realm of politics and left them in the hands of the president and his senior advisors.

In the areas of strategy and postwar planning, Stimson's acuity and influence were also decisive. He saw clearly from the outset of the war what the priorities of the United States must be to ensure victory. The Colonel advocated the Europe-first position from the beginning and was the driving force behind the Normandy landing and the victorious campaigns against Nazi Germany. Moreover, both in his opposition to the Morgenthau Plan and his own proposals concerning postwar Germany, Stimson set out the fundamental positions for postwar planning and reconstruction in Europe.

Given the different histories, ideologies, and concerns of the United States and the Soviet Union, Stimson was aware that there would be some areas of tension and conflict between the two nations in the postwar period. Still, he sought means to continue the cooperation that marked the Grand Alliance and urged others to take Soviet concerns and needs seriously. Only through negotiation, trust, and compromise among the great powers could peace, particularly in an atomic age, be guaranteed. He did not, however, see how his own conception of the U.S. role in the world—as leader and hegemon—could contribute to the growing confrontation with the Soviet Union that he sought to avoid. Stimson's influence would continue after he left office, in terms of his bipartisanship, commitment to the reconstruction of Germany and Japan, and vision of America's role. But these would no longer be the Colonel's daily concerns. He would have to trust those he trained and inspired to carry forward his ideas and implement American postwar policy now that the nation had taken on the role of world leader that Stimson had worked so long and hard to secure.

Notes

1. Stimson to Muirhead, 15 December 1941, Stimson Papers, reel 105.
2. Stimson and Bundy, *On Active Service*, 483–84 (emphasis in the original).
3. Stimson, "Statement at Press Conference," 17 April 1942, HLSD; Stimson Diary, 25 November 1942, HLSD.
4. Stimson to Roosevelt, 20 December 1941, HLSD; Memorandum of Decision at White House, 21 December 1941, HLSD.
5. Stimson and Bundy, *On Active Service*, 415–16.
6. Stimson Diary, 5 March 1942, 6 March 1942, HLSD.
7. Stimson to Roosevelt, 27 March 1942, President's Secretary File, Box 84, FDRL.
8. Stimson to Roosevelt, 19 June 1942, HLSD.
9. Stimson Diary, 21 June 1942, HLSD.
10. Ibid., 10 July 1942.
11. Ibid., 21 June 1942.
12. Ibid., 21 June 1942, 22 June 1942.
13. Ibid., 23 July 1942, 24 July 1942, 25 July 1942.
14. Ibid., 22 June 1942, 10 July 1942, 7 August 1942.
15. Ibid., 16 November 1942.
16. Ibid., 16 November 1942, 11 December 1942.

17. Ibid., 7 January 1943, 30 January 1943.

18. Ibid., 17 May 1943.

19. Stimson and Bundy, *On Active Service*, 428.

20. "Brief Report of Certain Features of Overseas Trip," 4 August 1943, HLSD.

21. Ibid.

22. Stimson Diary, 10 August 1943, HLSD; Stimson to Roosevelt, 10 August 1943, HLSD.

23. Ibid.

24. Stimson Diary, 28 October 1943, HLSD.

25. Stimson Diary, 9 November 1943, HLSD; Stimson to Hopkins, 10 November 1943, HLSD.

26. McCloy to Stimson, 2 December 1943, Stimson Papers, reel 108.

27. Stimson Diary, 5 December 1943, HLSD.

28. Ibid., 18 December 1943.

29. Ibid., 31 December 1943.

30. Ibid., 5 June 1944.

31. "Memorandum of Conference Between the Secretary of State, the Secretary of War, and the Secretary of Navy," 11 May 1943, Stimson Papers, reel 127.

32. Stimson and Bundy, *On Active Service*, 448.

33. Ibid., 567.

34. Stimson Diary, 4 April 1944, HLSD.

35. Ibid., Memorandum, 5 September 1944.

36. Ibid., Stimson Diary, 6 September 1944, 9 September 1944.

37. Ibid., Memorandum For the President, 15 September 1944.

38. Stimson and Bundy, *On Active Service*, 576–77; Stimson Diary, 17 September 1944, HLSD.

39. Stimson Diary, 27 September 1944, 3 October 1944, HLSD; Morison, *Turmoil and Tradition*, 505.

40. Stimson Diary, 29 March 1945, HLSD.

41. Ibid., 12 April 1945.

42. Ibid., 15 April 1945.

43. Ibid., 13 April 1945.

44. Stimson, "The Decision to Use the Atomic Bomb," *Harper's Magazine* (February 1947).

45. Patterson to Roosevelt, 13 December 1941, Official File 25, Box 6, FDRL.

46. Stimson Diary, 17 June 1943, HLSD; Morison, *Turmoil and Tradition*, 511.

47. Bush to Bundy, 24 February 1944, Stimson Papers, reel 109.

48. Stimson to Truman, 13 March 1944, HLSD; Stimson Diary, 13 March 1944, HLSD.

49. Stimson Diary, 10 June 1944, HLSD.

50. Ibid., 22 May 1944.

51. Ibid., 9 September 1943.

52. "Memorandum of Conference with the President," 31 December 1944, Stimson Papers, reel 128.

53. Stimson Diary, 13 February 1945, 15 February 1945, HLSD.

54. Ibid., 6–11 April 1945.

55. Ibid., 2 April 1945, 3 April 1945.

56. Ibid., 23 April 1945.

57. Quoted in *Major Problems in American History since 1945*, ed. Robert Griffith (Lexington, MA: D. C. Heath, 1992), 101–102.

58. Stimson Diary, 25 April 1945; "Memorandum Discussed with the President," 25 April 1945, HLSD.

59. Stimson and Bundy, *On Active Service*, 616.

60. Stimson to Truman, 16 May 1945, HLSD.

61. Ibid., 10 May 1945.

62. Ibid., 14 and 15 May 1945.

63. Ibid., Stimson to Truman, 16 May 1945.

64. McCloy, "Memorandum of Telephone Conversation with the Secretary of War," 19 May 1945, Stimson Papers, reel 128.

65. Stimson Diary, 29 May 1945, HLSD.

66. Stimson and Bundy, *On Active Service*, 617.

67. Stimson Diary, 31 May 1945, HLSD.

68. Stimson, "Memorandum of Conversation with the President," 6 June 1945, Stimson Papers, reel 128.

69. Quoted in Martin Sherwin, *A World Destroyed*, 230.

70. Stimson Diary, 19 June 1945, 26–30 June 1945, HLSD.

71. Ibid., 2 July 1945; Stimson, "Memorandum for the President," 2 July 1945.

72. Stimson, "Memorandum for the President," 2 July 1945, HLSD (emphasis in the original).

73. Ibid.

74. Stimson Diary, 2 July 1945, 3 July 1945, HLSD.

75. Stimson, "Notes for Talk with the President," 3 July 1945, Stimson Papers, reel 128; Stimson Diary, 3 July 1945, HLSD.

76. Stimson, Memorandum for the President, "The Conduct of the War with Japan," 16 July 1945; Stimson to Truman, "The Rehabilitation of Europe as a Whole," 22 July 1945, HLSP, reel 113.

77. Stimson Diary, 18 July 1945, HLSD.

78. Stimson, "Reflections on the Basic Problems Which Confront Us," 19 July 1945, HLSD.

79. Ibid.

80. Stimson Diary, 21 July 1945, 22 July 1945, HLSD.

81. Ibid.

82. Ibid., 22 July 1945, 23 July 1945.

83. Ibid., 23 July 1945, 24 July 1945.

84. Ibid., 24 July 1945.

85. Ibid.

86. "Conference with Generalissimo Stalin, 25 July 1945," HLSD.

87. "Memorandum of Conference with the President," 8 August 1945, HLSD.

88. Stimson Diary, 9 August 1945, HLSD.

89. Ibid., 8 August 1945.

90. Ibid., 9 August 1945; "Memorandum for the Press," 9 August 1945, HLSD.

91. Stimson Diary, 10 August 1945, HLSD.

92. Stimson and Bundy, *On Active Service*, 627.

93. Ibid., 628–29.

94. Stimson Diary, 12 August–3 September 1945; "H.L.S. Statement at the Ausable Club," 18 August 1945, HLSD.

95. Stimson Diary, 4 September 1945, 5 September 1945, HLSD.

96. Stimson to Truman, 11 September 1945, HLSD.

97. "Proposed Action for Control of Atomic Bombs," 11 September 1945, HLSD.

98. Ibid.

99. Ibid.

100. Stimson and Bundy, *On Active Service,* 648.

101. Stimson Diary, 21 September 1945, HLSD.

102. Morison, *Turmoil and Tradition,* 531.

Conclusion

Elder Statesman

Upon his return to Highhold, Stimson was confined to his bed as he attempted to recuperate from the strains of more than five years in office. At first, the rest appeared to be working, but in late October he suffered a massive coronary occlusion. Recovery was slow and it was not until Christmas that Stimson was able to leave his room. Along with his heart ailment, Stimson suffered from severe arthritis that had forced him to give up horseback riding. His outdoor activities were restricted to some skeet shooting and fishing from a wheelchair. But his mind remained clear, and Stimson sought to ensure through a series of writings that his ideas and the lessons he had learned were available to the nation.

In spring 1946, Stimson began to work on his memoirs. He was assisted in this effort by McGeorge Bundy, son of his old friend and colleague Harvey Bundy and a junior fellow in the Society of Fellows at Harvard University. Bundy moved into the caretaker's house at Highhold, and for the next eighteen months the two men met almost daily to discuss Stimson's career, review records, and revise Bundy's manuscript. Although written in the third person, *On Active Service in Peace and War* represented Stimson's views and opinions of his public life and service. The Colonel added an introduction on his family and personal history and a brief afterword to Bundy's text. Published in 1948, the book chronicled Stimson's long career by weaving together lengthy excerpts from Stimson's papers and diaries with his recollections of events and their meaning.

In his "summing up" in the Afterword, Stimson remained optimistic about the progress of the world and the United States. "Since 1906," he observed, "the problems of our national life have expanded in scope and difficulties beyond anything we ever dreamed of in those early times." Yet he did not "wish that the clock could be turned back." It was true that many terrible mistakes had been made, and he was sad that more than half the book was concerned with the problems of warmaking. "Yet even so," he opined, "it is well also to reflect how much worse the state of mankind would be if the victorious peoples in each of the two world wars had not been willing to undergo the sacrifices which were the price of victory." This was, for Stimson, the main lesson the nation had to learn. Those who now bore the responsibility of governing should learn from both his generation's achievements and its mistakes, but they could not afford to "turn aside from what they have to do, nor think that criticism excuses inaction."[1]

Stimson took time, as well, to address some of the most pressing matters facing the nation after World War II. In January 1947, he published a defense of the Nuremberg Trials in the journal *Foreign Affairs*. Some had criticized the procedures as ex post facto law in naming aggressive war as a punishable crime. Stimson countered that the legal justification lay in the Kellogg-Briand Pact of 1928 that had outlawed war. The fact that nations did not have the courage prior to 1939 to enforce the pact did not void its standing. Moreover, "the defendants at Nuremberg were leaders of the most highly organized and extensive wickedness in history. It was not a trick of law that brought them to the bar; it was the 'massed angered forces of common humanity.' " Stimson concluded that "the law made effective by the trial at Nuremberg is righteous law long overdue. It is in just such cases as this one that the law becomes more nearly what Mr. Justice [Oliver Wendell] Holmes called it: 'the witness and external deposit of our moral life.' "[2] Stimson deemed this the great accomplishment of Nuremberg.

The next month, Stimson's "The Decision to Use the Atomic Bomb" appeared in *Harper's Magazine*. This article stemmed from a request by James Conant, president of Harvard University and a member of Stimson's Interim Committee, that Stimson write an article on "the decision to use the bomb." Conant was irritated by the "spreading accusation that it was entirely unnecessary to use the atomic bomb at all" and believed a definitive account was required to silence the critics.[3] Conant's concerns stemmed from a number of sources, most notably the U.S. Strategic Bombing Survey Report released in July 1946, which concluded that the Japanese would have surrendered before the end of 1945, even if the atomic bombs had not been dropped and even without the threat of an American invasion. Commentary in leading opinion sources, such as the *New York Times* and the *Saturday Review of Literature*, that questioned the morality of the atomic attacks was also troubling. Stimson agreed to use of his name on the article as long as Bundy did the actual writing.

Placing the decision to use the bomb solely in the context of the Pacific War, the *Harper's* article argued that the bombs were used "in order to end the war in the shortest possible time and to avoid the enormous loss of human life which otherwise confronted us." The bombs effectively served their intended purpose: to compel the Japanese Emperor to use his influence for peace. Given the available alternatives, "No man, in our position and subject to our responsibilities, holding in his hand a weapon of such possibilities for accomplishing this purpose and saving those lives, could have failed to use it and afterwards looked his countrymen in the face." Certainly the decision to use the bombs led to the deaths of over one hundred thousand Japanese. "No explanation," Stimson concluded, "could change that fact. . . . But this deliberate, premeditated destruction was our least abhorrent choice. The destruction of Hiroshima and Nagasaki put an end to the Japanese war. It stopped the fire raids, and the strangling blockade; it ended the ghastly specter of a clash of great land armies."[4]

The article avoided a detailed discussion of the debate over the modification of the unconditional surrender terms. For Stimson, this was a difficult dilemma. On the one hand, he did not want to aid the critics because he feared a return to isolationism, particularly in the Republican Party, and an unwillingness to assume the duties of a great power; and he therefore found himself compelled to defend the policies of the Truman administration. On the other hand, as his comments in his memoirs would reveal, he knew the critics had some valid points concerning whether or not the bombs were necessary for ending the war. In *On Active Service*, Stimson acknowledged that the Japanese Cabinet was prepared as early as the spring of 1945 "to accept substantially the same terms [of surrender] as those finally agreed on," and that, on the question of providing assurances concerning the Emperor, "history might find that the United States, by its delay in stating its position, had prolonged the war."[5]

Stimson's concern about the direction of American foreign policy and support for Truman's Cold War policies led to his last significant essay on American foreign policy. Published in *Foreign Affairs* on his eightieth birthday, in September 1947, "The Challenge to Americans" marked Stimson's summation of America's role in the world and his outline of how foreign policy should be

Secretary of the Army Kenneth Royall and Stimson at Stimson's 80th birthday at Highhold. *Collection of the Huntington Historical Society, Long Island, New York*

conducted. He called for a middle-course policy between the ones advocated by those who ignored the Soviet threat and by those who argued that only force would stop Communism. Stimson saw anyone who still believed the United States could "make common cause with present-day communism" as "living in a world that does not exist." Yet, it was equally wrong-headed to think that the Soviets could be forced to capitulate through intimidation or to advocate preventive war. This was, to Stimson, "worse than nonsense; it results from a hopeless misunderstanding of the geographic and military situation, and a cynical incomprehension of what the people of the world will tolerate from *any* nation." Rather, the goal of American policy should be to contain Soviet expansion while leaving open the door to negotiations. "We must make it wholly evident that a nonaggressive Russia will have nothing to fear from us. We must make it clear, too," Stimson continued, "that the Western noncommunist world is going to survive in growing economic and political stability. If we can do this, then slowly—perhaps less slowly than we now believe—the Russian leaders may either change their minds or lose their jobs."[6]

The specific policies were not, however, Stimson's main concern. His central point was to instruct the American people on their obligations and to challenge them to meet the demands of world leadership. The key question was "one of will and understanding." Stimson believed that the events of the past two decades should have convinced the American people beyond any doubt that their nation's welfare was interrelated with world developments and that the United States could never prosper or have peace if it tried to act as an island unto itself. "Our stake in the peace and freedom of the world is not a limited liability. Time after time in other years we have tried to solve our problems with halfway measures, acting under the illusion that we could be partly in the world and partly irresponsible." These measures had all failed. Stimson exhorted his readers to take up the burden of postwar reconstruction and the direction of world affairs. The necessity for this acceptance existed independent of the actions of the Soviet Union. "The essential question," Stimson explained, "is one which we should have to answer if there were not a Communist alive. Can we make freedom and prosperity real in the present world?" The most pressing immediate concern was the reconstruction of Western Europe. This was "a task from which Americans can decide to stand apart only if they wish to desert every principle by which they claim to live. And, as a decision of policy, it would be the most tragic mistake in our history." Only by rebuilding Europe and Japan could the United States sustain peacetime production and maintain domestic prosperity.[7]

Stimson concluded by noting that this task would be neither easy nor readily achievable. "The construction of a stable peace is a longer, more complex, and greater task than the relatively simple work of warmaking. But the nature of the challenge is the same. The issue before us today is at least as significant as the one which we finally faced in 1941." If the United States would act now, "with vigor and understanding, with steadiness and without fear, we can peacefully safeguard our freedom. It is only when we turn our backs, in mistaken complacency or mistrusting timidity, that war may again become inevitable." How soon the nation would "fully understand the size and nature of its present mission" Stimson could not say. But he was certain "that in a very large degree the future of mankind depends on the answer to this question," and he was "confident that if the issues are clearly presented, the American people will give the right answer." Surely, this was "a fair and tempting challenge to all Americans, and especially to the nation's leaders, in and out of office."[8] In conjunction with the publication of his memoirs, Stimson's article set out the parameters of and the case for an activist foreign policy conducted in a bipartisan spirit in pursuit of American hegemony. These postwar writings stand as a testament to what became establishment thinking and made Stimson the paragon of an American statesman.

Stimson's last public comment came in defense of Truman and Secretary of State Dean Acheson and their foreign policy. At stake was the effective implementation of American policy then under attack by Senator Joseph McCarthy and those Stimson called "these little men" with their wild accusations of disloyalty and treason by high officials. If McCarthy were interested in the question of loyalty, there were established methods for investigation and weighing of charges that he could employ. "The fact," Stimson wrote to the *New York Times* on March 27, 1950, "that the accuser has wholly ignored this well-established method indicates that his interest is of a different character." The real motive was to discredit Dean Acheson. But the significance went beyond the attacks on one individual whose "extraordinary record" put him beyond the reach of a McCarthy. "The man who seeks to gain political advantage from personal attacks on a Secretary of State is a man who seeks political advantage from damage to his country." The Truman administration was providing wise leadership in a time of tumult and change. This was, therefore, "no time to let the noisy antics of a few upset the steady purpose of our country or distract our leaders from their proper tasks. This is rather a time for stern rebuke of such antics and outspoken support of the distinguished public servants against whom they are directed."[9]

Too few others, particularly in his own party, were willing to stand up with Stimson and challenge McCarthy in 1950, and he was too old and frail to sustain the fight. His health continued to deteriorate throughout the year. On October 20, 1950, Stimson and his wife started out on a drive to enjoy the fall colors on Long Island when Stimson began to feel distress. Their driver turned around, returned to Highhold, and with the nurse carried Stimson up to his room. He died soon afterward with his wife at his side.

In all, Stimson's was a remarkable career, spanning over four decades. He maintained his ideals and beliefs through numerous disappointments and crises, convinced that he would prevail and that the nation would heed his advice and take up its proper role as world leader. Stimson provided the link between the foreign policy of late-nineteenth-century imperialism and the internationalism of the Cold War era. His was a life shaped by a sense of duty and service to the nation and a belief that the United States was destined to become a world power.

Stimson and the United States experienced failures along the way. The Colonel's stemmed from his limited worldview that held to American superiority and the inferiority of nonwhites and blinded him to the negative consequences of American interventions abroad. He thought that American institutions and values were universally applicable and did not need to be modified or take account of local traditions, history, and culture. Other peoples just needed exposure to Americans, knowledge of what they had to offer, and tutelage by the United States. He fully supported American possession of the Philippines and set the course for American support of military dictatorships in Nicaragua and El Salvador in the name of defending freedom. Moreover, his views on the benevolent nature of American imperialism and intervention would be echoed later, albeit in modified form, to justify U.S. involvement in Vietnam. Still, as evidenced by his rejection of the Roosevelt Corollary and withdrawal of American forces from Nicaragua, Stimson believed there were limits to American power and that intervention should focus on political and economic solutions. Nonetheless, his support for intervention became a central component of American foreign policy in various regions of the world with, at times, tragic results.

Yet his achievements were considerable. He successfully modernized the military under President Taft in 1911 while ensuring continued civilian control over the armed forces. This allowed the nation to mobilize successfully for both World Wars. As secretary of state, he worked to bring the United States to the center of the world by setting out the ideas that would become the cornerstones of American foreign policy after World War II. The Stimson Doctrine marked the beginning of a decade-long effort to oppose international aggression and promote collective security in the face of the challenges posed by Japan and Germany. His most notable accomplishments came as secretary of war during World War II. He oversaw the American military buildup and victory, guided the development of the atomic bomb, and set out the bases for the postwar reconstruction of Europe and Japan.

Stimson's effort and example moved the nation beyond traditional imperialism and isolationism to internationalism and taking up its role of world leader. Moreover, he became the exemplar of the bipartisan, centrist policy that he had advocated for so long. In doing so, he set the standard for service to the nation that many were to follow in the postwar years, and he provided the rationale for American global commitments and quest for hegemony. The nation was at a crossroads when Stimson left office in 1945, and he would not be there to oversee the implementation of his views as policy. As Vannevar Bush noted in 1945, "Stimson is a very wise man, I only wish he had more of the vigor of youth."[10] But the first wise man could only watch. It was up to those like-minded men he gathered around him, such as John McCloy, Robert Lovett, Dean Acheson, Robert Patterson, and later McGeorge Bundy, who went on to conduct the nation's foreign policy, to use properly the power and influence that Stimson had worked so long and hard to obtain for the United States.

After Franklin Roosevelt, Woodrow Wilson, and Theodore Roosevelt, Stimson ranks as the most important American policymaker of the first forty-five years of the twentieth century. His multiple roles, his consistent advocacy of internationalism, and his lasting influence on those who served him shaped the nation's emergence as a great power and the belief that the United States should be the leader of the world. In doing so, Stimson's life forces us to confront the continuity, rather than the breaks, in American thinking on foreign affairs and involvement in the world. The United States did not just suddenly emerge as a world leader after 1945; the process had been under way since the turn of the twentieth century, and Stimson's service and ideas had paved that national path.

Notes

1. Stimson and Bundy, *On Active Service*, 671–72.

2. Stimson, "The Nuremberg Trial: Landmark in Law," *Foreign Affairs* (January 1947), 179–89.

3. Conant to Stimson, 22 January 1947, Stimson Papers, reel 116.

4. Stimson, "The Decision to Use the Atomic Bomb," *Harper's Magazine* (February 1947), 97–107.

5. Stimson and Bundy, *On Active Service*, 628–29.

6. Stimson, "The Challenge to Americans," *Foreign Affairs* (October 1947), 5–14 (emphasis in the original).

7. Ibid.

8. Ibid.

9. *New York Times*, 27 March 1950.

10. Quoted in Hodgson, *The Colonel*, 310.

Bibliographic Essay

The essential starting place for any study of Henry L. Stimson is his papers and diaries, in the Sterling Library, Manuscripts and Archives, Yale University, New Haven, Connecticut. The papers, covering Stimson's life from 1891 to 1950, are voluminous. They consist of 284 boxes of letters, memoranda, speeches, special subjects, personal papers, documents produced while serving in various positions and on trips, printed materials and notes related to Stimson's books and articles, newspaper clippings, business records, photographs, and miscellaneous items. The first 248 boxes, which include everything except the printed materials, newspaper clippings, personal business, and photographs, are available on 169 reels of microfilm. A hundred-page guide to the microfilmed collection is available from Yale. The diaries that Stimson began in 1906 consist of 52 volumes that average 180 pages each. The entries from 1906 to 1930, though extensive, are episodic and, for the most part, were written as remembrances of events. For the period of 1930 to 1933 and again for 1940 through 1945, there are entries for almost every day that record Stimson's actions and thoughts in great detail and are often accompanied by memoranda or other supporting materials. These daily entries were usually dictated early the next morning after each day covered. From 1933 through 1939, the entries are less regular. The complete set is on 9 reels of microfilm that include detailed name and subject indexes and a tenth reel that contains only the 9 indexes. The Huntington Historical Society, Huntington, New York, has a small collection, mostly newspaper clippings and photographs, on Stimson and Highhold. It also has a copy of Stimson's *My Vacations* (privately printed, 1949) that discusses many aspects of his private life, travels, and home.

In addition to his papers and diaries, Stimson's books and articles on his career and American foreign policy are invaluable. *American Policy in Nicaragua* (New York: Scribner's, 1927); *Democracy and Nationalism* (Princeton: Princeton University Press, 1934); *The Far Eastern Crisis: Recollections and Observations* (New York:

Harper & Brothers, 1936); and his memoirs, written with McGeorge Bundy, *On Active Service in Peace and War* (New York: Harper & Brothers, 1948), cover various aspects of Stimson's career. See also "Future Philippine Policy Under the Jones Act," *Foreign Affairs* (April 1927), 459–71; "The United States and the Other American Republics," 6 February 1931 (Washington, D.C.: Government Printing Office, 1931); "Bases of American Policy During the Past Four Years," *Foreign Affairs* (April 1933), 383–96; "The Nuremberg Trial: Landmark in Law," *Foreign Affairs* (January 1947), 179–89; "The Decision to Use the Atomic Bomb," *Harper's Magazine* (February 1947), 99–107; "The Challenge to Americans," *Foreign Affairs* (October 1947), 5–14; and Stimson's frequent letters to the *New York Times.*

Manuscript collections that contain significant amounts of material on Stimson are the Herbert Hoover Presidential Library, West Branch, Iowa, for his term as secretary of state, and the Franklin D. Roosevelt Presidential Library, Hyde Park, New York, and the Harry S. Truman Presidential Library, Independence, Missouri, for Stimson's second term as secretary of war. Columbia University Library's Oral History of Harvey Bundy is a must for understanding Stimson's thinking and policies and his relationship with his staff. Essential also for Stimson's tenure as secretary of state are the State Department Records, Record Group 59, National Archives, College Park, Maryland. In addition, see the relevant volumes of the Department of State's *Foreign Relations of the United States* (Washington, D.C.: Government Printing Office) for Stimson's years as secretary of state; *Foreign Relations of the United States: The Conference of Berlin (Potsdam)* (Washington, D.C.: Government Printing Office, 1960); and *The United States and Nicaragua: A Survey of the Relations from 1909 to 1932* (Washington, D.C.: Government Printing Office, 1932).

On Stimson, Godfrey Hodgson, *The Colonel: The Life and Wars of Henry Stimson, 1867–1950* (New York: Knopf, 1990) is insightful but not definitive. Elting E. Morison, *Turmoil and Tradition: A Study of the Life and Times of Henry L. Stimson* (Boston: Houghton Mifflin, 1960), which was commissioned by the Stimson Estate, has much useful material that cannot be found elsewhere but was written before the opening of many records. Robert H. Ferrell, *American Secretaries of State and Their Diplomacy: Frank B. Kellogg and Henry L. Stimson* (New York: Cooper Square Publishers, 1963), and Armin Rappaport, *Henry L. Stimson and Japan, 1931–33* (Chicago: University of Chicago Press, 1963), are both useful but dated, while Richard N. Current's *Secretary Stimson: A Study in Statecraft* (New Brunswick: Rutgers University Press, 1954), is unreliable. Paul H. Boeker, ed., *Henry L. Stimson's American Policy in Nicaragua: The Lasting Legacy* (New York: Markus Wiener, 1991), provides a reprint of Stimson's book on Nicaragua, essays, and documents.

For an understanding of Elihu Root, Richard Leopold's *Elihu Root and the Conservative Tradition* (Boston: Little, Brown, 1954), remains essential. On Theodore Roosevelt, see H. W. Brands, *TR: The Last Romantic* (New York: Basic Books, 1997); John Morton Blum, *The Republican Roosevelt*, 2d ed. (Cambridge: Harvard University Press, 1977); and Richard H. Collin, *Theodore Roosevelt's Caribbean: The Panama Canal, the Monroe Doctrine, and the Latin American Context* (Baton Rouge: Louisiana State University Press, 1990). Useful memoirs include Dean Acheson, *Present at the Creation: My Years in the State Department* (New York: Norton, 1969); Herbert Hoover, *Memoirs: The Cabinet and the Presidency* (New York: Macmillan, 1952); Cordell Hull, *The Memoirs of Cordell Hull*, 2 vols. (New York: Macmillan, 1948); and Harry S. Truman, *Year of Decisions* (Garden City, NY: Doubleday, 1955).

For broader studies of the early period of Stimson's life, see Robert Wiebe, *The Search for Order, 1877–1920* (New York: Hill & Wang, 1967), and Nell Irvin Painter, *Standing at Armageddon: The United States, 1877–1919* (New York: Norton, 1987). On foreign policy, see Walter LaFeber, *The New Empire: An Interpretation of American Expansion, 1860–1898* (Ithaca: Cornell University Press, 1963), idem, *Inevitable Revolutions: The United States in Central America*, 2d ed. (New York: Norton, 1993); Robert Beisner, *From the Old Diplomacy to the New, 1865–1900*, 2d ed. (Arlington Heights, IL: Harlan Davidson, 1986); Emily S. Rosenberg, *Spreading the American Dream: American Economic and Cultural Expansion, 1890–1945* (New York: Hill & Wang, 1982); and Michael Hunt, *Ideology and U.S. Foreign Policy* (New Haven: Yale University Press, 1987). For American policy toward Cuba, see Louis A. Perez, Jr., *Cuba Between Empires, 1878–1902* (Pittsburgh: University of Pittsburgh Press, 1983); idem, *The War of 1898* (Chapel Hill: University of North Carolina Press,1998); on the Philippines, go to Richard Welch, *Response to Imperialism: The United States and the Philippine-American War, 1899–1902* (Chapel Hill: University of North Carolina Press, 1979); Glen A. May, *Social Engineering in the Philippines: The Aims, Execution, and Impact of American Colonial Policy, 1900–1913* (Westport, CT: Greenwood Press, 1980); Stuart Creighton Miller, *"Benevolent Assimilation": The American Conquest of the Philippines, 1899–1903*

(New Haven: Yale University Press, 1982); and H. W. Brands, *Bound to Empire: The United States and the Philippines* (New York: Oxford University Press, 1992).

Concerning the influence of race on American foreign policy, see Hunt, *Ideology and U.S. Foreign Policy*; Walter L. Williams, "United States Indian Policy and Debate Over Philippine Annexation: Implications for the Origins of American Imperialism," *Journal of American History* 66 (March 1980), 810–31; Reginald Horsman, *Race and Manifest Destiny: The Origins of American Racial Anglo-Saxonism* (Cambridge, MA: Harvard University Press, 1981); Ruben F. Weston, *Racism in U.S. Imperialism: The Influence of Racial Assumptions on U.S. Foreign Policy, 1893–1946* (Columbia: University of South Carolina Press, 1982); and Joseph A. Fry, "Phases of Empire: Late Nineteenth-Century U.S. Foreign Relations," in Charles W. Calhoun, ed., *The Gilded Age: Essays on the Origins of Modern America* (Wilmington, DE: Scholarly Resources, 1996), 261–88.

The essential works on Woodrow Wilson's diplomacy, the Versailles Conference, and the battle over the League of Nations are Arno N. Mayer, *Politics and Diplomacy of Peacemaking: Containment and Counterrevolution at Versailles, 1918–1919* (New York: Knopf, 1967); N. Gordon Levin, *Woodrow Wilson and World Politics: America's Response to War and Revolution* (New York: Oxford University Press, 1968); Lloyd Gardner, *Safe for Democracy: The Anglo-American Response to Revolution, 1913–1923* (New York: Oxford University Press, 1984); William C. Widenor, *Henry Cabot Lodge and the Search for an American Foreign Policy* (Berkeley: University of California Press, 1980); and Thomas J. Knock, *To End All Wars: Woodrow Wilson and the Quest for a New World Order* (New York: Oxford, 1992). On the economic impact of Versailles on Europe, see Klaus Schwabe, *Woodrow Wilson, Revolutionary Germany, and Peacemaking, 1918–1919: Missionary Diplomacy and the Realities of Power*, trans. Rita and Robert Kimber (Chapel Hill: University of North Carolina Press, 1985); and Stephen Schuker, *The End of French Predominance in Europe: The Financial Crisis and the Adoption of the Dawes Plan* (Chapel Hill: University of North Carolina Press, 1976).

A brief but excellent introduction to American foreign policy during the 1920s is found in Warren I. Cohen, *Empire Without Tears: American Foreign Policy, 1921–1933* (New York: Knopf, 1987). For American policy toward Europe, see Melvyn P. Leffler, *The Elusive Quest: America's Pursuit of European Stability and French Security, 1919–1933* (Chapel Hill: University of North Carolina Press, 1979); and Frank Costigliola, *Awkward Dominion: American Political, Eco-*

nomic, and Cultural Relations with Europe, 1919–1933 (Ithaca: Cornell University Press, 1984). On Latin America, Lester D. Langley, *The United States and the Caribbean in the Twentieth Century*, rev. ed. (Athens: University of Georgia Press, 1985); and Bryce Wood, *The Making of the Good Neighbor Policy* (New York: Columbia University Press, 1961), are good places to start, along with Michael Krenn, *U.S. Policy Toward Economic Nationalism in Latin America, 1917–1929* (Wilmington: Scholarly Resources, 1990); and James J. Horn, "U.S. Diplomacy and 'The Specter of Bolshevism' in Mexico," *Americas* 32 (July 1975), 31–45. Richard Millett, *Guardians of the Dynasty* (Maryknoll, NY: Orbis Books, 1977) and William Kammen, *A Search for Stability: U.S. Diplomacy Toward Nicaragua, 1925–1933* (Notre Dame: University of Notre Dame Press, 1968), are must-reads on Nicaragua, as are Thomas P. Anderson, *Matanza: El Salvador's Communist Revolt of 1932* (Lincoln: University of Nebraska Press, 1971); Kenneth J. Grieb, "The United States and the Rise of General Maximiliano Hernández Martínez," *Journal of Latin American Studies* 3 (November 1971), 151–72; and Raymond Bonner, *Weakness and Deceit: U.S. Policy and El Salvador* (New York: Times Books, 1984), for El Salvador. The Manchurian crisis has attracted a great deal of attention from historians. In addition to the works on Stimson noted above, see Sara Smith, *The Manchurian Crisis, 1931–1933: A Tragedy in International Relations* (New York: Columbia University Press, 1948); and Justus Doenecke, *When the Wicked Rise: American Opinion-Makers and the Manchurian Crisis of 1931–1933* (London: Associated University Presses, 1984), for critical examinations of Stimson's actions; and Christopher Thorne, *The Limits of Foreign Policy: The West, the League, and the Far Eastern Crisis of 1931–1933* (New York: Putnam's, 1972), for the most thorough study of the event.

The literature on World War II is vast. Start with Warren F. Kimball, *The Juggler: Franklin Roosevelt as Wartime Statesman* (Princeton: Princeton University Press, 1991), idem, ed., *Churchill & Roosevelt: The Complete Correspondence*, 3 vols. (Princeton: Princeton University Press, 1984); Lloyd Gardner, *Spheres of Influence: The Great Powers Partition Europe, from Munich to Yalta* (Chicago: Ivan R. Dee, 1993); Robert Dallek, *Franklin D. Roosevelt and American Foreign Policy* (New York: Oxford University Press, 1979); Kent Roberts Greenfield, *American Strategy in World War II: A Reconsideration* (Baltimore: Johns Hopkins University Press, 1963); and Christopher Thorne, *Allies of a Kind* (New York: Oxford University Press, 1978). For more specific works, go to Forrest C. Pogue, *George C. Marshall: Organizer of Victory* (New York: Viking, 1973); Stephen E. Ambrose, *Eisenhower:*

Soldier, General of the Army, President-Elect, 1890–1952 (New York: Simon & Schuster, 1983); and Eric Larrabee, *Commander in Chief: Franklin D. Roosevelt, His Lieutenants and Their War* (New York: Harper & Row, 1987). On the Morgenthau Plan, see Warren F. Kimball, *Swords or Ploughshares? The Morgenthau Plan for Defeated Nazi Germany* (Philadelphia: Lippincott, 1976).

The excellent essays in Michael J. Hogan, ed., *Hiroshima in History and Memory* (New York: Cambridge University Press, 1996), are the best introduction to the issues and controversies surrounding the dropping of the atomic bombs. See as well Barton J. Bernstein, "The Atomic Bombings Reconsidered," *Foreign Affairs* (January–February 1995), 135–52; Martin J. Sherwin, *A World Destroyed: Hiroshima and the Origins of the Arms Race* (New York: Vintage, 1987); Richard Rhodes, *The Making of the Atomic Bomb* (New York: Simon & Schuster, 1986); Gar Alperovitz, *The Decision to Use the Atomic Bomb and the Architecture of an American Myth* (New York: Knopf, 1995); and J. Samuel Walker, *Prompt & Utter Destruction: Truman and the Use of Atomic Bombs Against Japan* (Chapel Hill: University of North Carolina Press, 1997). For examinations of the *Enola Gay* exhibit at the Smithsonian Institution, see "History and the Public: What Can We Handle? A Round Table About History and the *Enola Gay* Controversy," *Journal of American History* (December 1995), 1029–1144; and Kai Bird and Lawrence Lifschultz, eds., *Hiroshima's Shadow: Writings on the Denial of History and the Smithsonian Controversy* (Stony Creek, CT: Pamphleteer's Press, 1998).

Index

Acheson, Dean, 208, 210
Ainsworth, Fred C., 24, 25, 26–27
American Sugar Refining Corpo-
ration, 15
Araujo, Arturo, 93, 95, 96, 97
Ausable Club, 193
Austria, 74, 82, 120

Baker, Newton, 41
Bard, Ralph, 171
Belgium, 180
Bolivia, 92
Bolshevik Revolution, 48
Boone & Crockett Club, 1–2, 3
Borah, William E., 53, 110, 130
Bruening, Heinrich, 87; and
danger of Bolshevism, 87–88
Bryan, William Jennings, 12–13
Bundy, Harvey, 80, 107, 134, 135,
203
Bundy, McGeorge, 114, 202, 205,
210
Bush, Vannevar, 171, 174, 176, 210
Byrnes, James F., 153, 171, 186;
and atomic diplomacy, 189, 191,
192, 193, 194, 196

Caffery, Jefferson, 97–98
Calles, Plutarco Elías, 51
Castle, William, 80, 107, 114
Central American treaties, 50, 52
Chamorro, Emiliano, 51, 52
Chile, 54
China: threatened by Japan, 59,
78, 105, 106, 108, 109, 110, 111,
125, 126, 127; and Open Door
policy, 74, 77, 78, 102, 103, 104,
106, 108
Churchill, Winston, 152, 157, 158,
175, 180, 181, 183, 188; and
second front, 160, 161–64, 168

Clark, Grenville, 132
Clark, J. Reuben, 92
Clark Memorandum, 92, 97
Clayton, William, 171
Cleveland, Grover, 12
Cold War, 153, 193–96
Compton, Karl, 171
Conant, James B., 171, 204
Coolidge, Calvin, 44, 48, 51, 52,
54, 56, 58, 65
Cotton, Joseph, 80
Crowder, Enoch, 26, 40
Cuba, 11, 23, 30, 31, 92, 113
Czechoslovakia, 120

D-Day, 165
Darlan, Jean, 160–61
Dawes, Charles, 77
Dawes Plan, 77, 83
Debt moratorium, 83, 84, 87, 88
Denmark, 180
"Destroyers for Bases" deal, 138
DeWitt, John, 147
Díaz, Adolfo, 52, 54, 55, 56
Dominican Republic, 23, 30, 31,
47, 101

Eberhardt, Charles, 57
Eisenhower, Dwight D., 156, 157,
165
Elkins Act (1903), 13
El Salvador, 92–101, 209; and
"Communist" revolt in, 93, 98,
99, 100; and *matanza*, 93, 98,
100, 101
Ethiopia, 120, 124

Feis, Herbert, 80
France, 39, 128, 143, 190; admired
by Stimson, 38; war debts and
reparations, 76, 77, 84, 87, 89,